WINDOWSCAPING

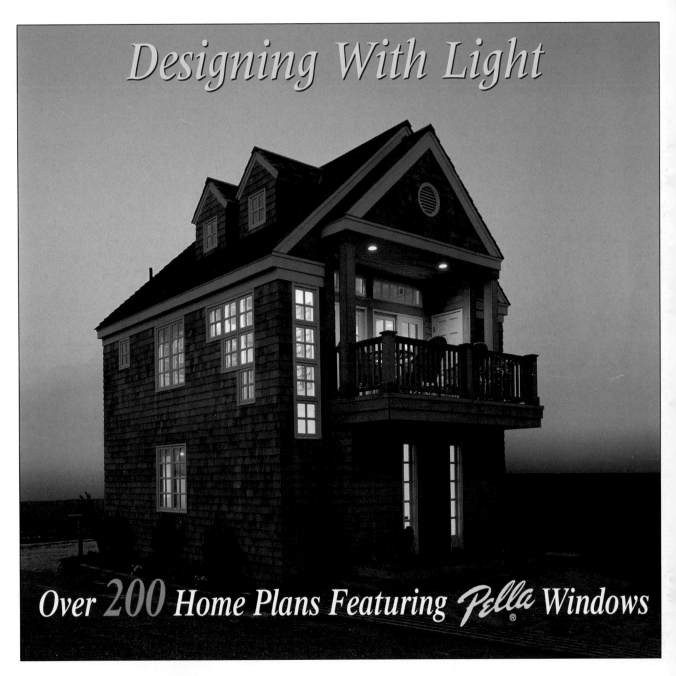

Designing With Light

Over *200* Home Plans Featuring *Pella* Windows

 VIEWED TO BE THE BEST™

 HOME PLANNERS

Published for Pella Corporation by Home Planners, LLC
Wholly owned by Hanley-Wood, Inc.
Editorial and Corporate Offices:
3275 West Ina Road, Suite 110
Tucson, Arizona 85741

Distribution Center:
29333 Lorie Lane
Wixom, MI 48393

Rickard D. Bailey/CEO and Publisher
Stephen Williams/Director of Sales & Marketing
Cindy Coatsworth Lewis/Director of Publications
Jan Prideaux/Senior Editor
Paulette Mulvin/Special Projects and Acquisitions Editor
Sara Lisa Rappaport/Manufacturing Coordinator
Paul Fitzgerald/Senior Graphic Designer
Kay Sanders/Copywriting

Photo Credits
Front Cover: Design 4559, page 43. Photo courtesy of Pella Corporation
Back Cover: Design G207, page 38. Photo by Elizabeth Brauer/Brauer Photography

First Printing January 1999
10 9 8 7 6 5 4 3 2 1

WINDOWSCAPING®

Design 6652, see page 81

Table Of Contents

WINDOWSCAPING®

Whether you are building a new home, or remodeling an existing home, windows can capture the very essence of fine design and quality craftsmanship.

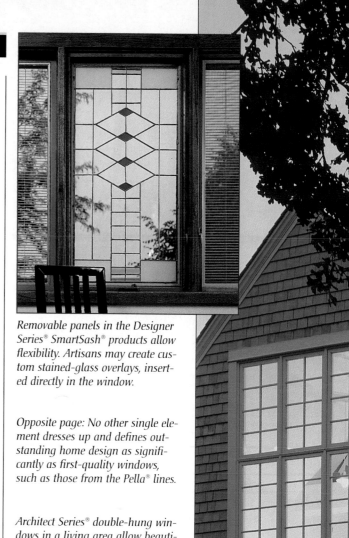

A s you begin planning your remodeling or building project, you will likely have many questions about windows. Windows are indeed an important component to consider. Besides providing a barrier to the elements and a view to the outside, they can make the difference between a home that's stunning and a home that's standard.

To help you get the most design impact from your window budget, Pella Corporation, one of the world's most popular and trusted window manufacturers, and Home Planners, a leading supplier of remodeling and building plans, have teamed together to supply Windowscaping® ideas to help you make informed purchase decisions. Home Planners is known for quality, comprehensive and creative plans for new homes and remodeling projects, all designed by highly qualified architects. Pella is known for products of unsurpassed beauty, performance and innovation. This trusted Iowa manufacturer has brought to market such innovative products as between-the-glass window shades and blinds, Rolscreen® retractable window screens, and self-closing screen doors.

The selection of windows and doors is a decision that you will live with for years. It's a decision so significant that you may want to make it yourself, rather than leave it to someone else. After all, quality windows contribute to the livability and durability of your home—to year-round comfort, to energy efficiency, and to minimal maintenance. Quality wood windows also contribute to the eye appeal of your home, both inside and out. Wood windows add richness and warmth to the interior of your home, and can be painted or stained to match your decor. Thanks

Removable panels in the Designer Series® SmartSash® products allow flexibility. Artisans may create custom stained-glass overlays, inserted directly in the window.

Opposite page: No other single element dresses up and defines outstanding home design as significantly as first-quality windows, such as those from the Pella® lines.

Architect Series® double-hung windows in a living area allow beautiful light and views, and open to permit fresh air to circulate throughout the room.

to advancements in window engineering and glazing technology, now you can indulge in a stunning window wall or two without sacrificing energy efficiency or the comfort of stable indoor temperature.

We recommend that you take the time to educate yourself about the unique features and benefits of various window products. The more you know, the more confident you'll feel when it's time to make this important purchase decision. Consider this a short course in selecting quality windows.

ELEMENTS OF DESIGN

More than any other structural element, windows can give character, charisma and a sense of personal style to a house. Think about the houses in your neighborhood or town that literally stop traffic. Chances are that an impressive arrangement of windows contributes to that curb appeal.

Just as windows spark personality in the exterior of a house, they can transform a room from ordinary to extraordinary. Visualize the most stunning, most impressive room you've ever walked into. Isn't it true that windows give that room its impact?

The Magic of Glass

It may sound dramatic, but it's true, that windows create interior magic. Windows annex a view. If you have a lovely scene outside your home—a lake, a colorful garden, a stand of evergreen trees—capture and frame that view. A window that showcases the bounty of nature is more impressive than the most elegant wall hanging.

Windows stretch space. They let you look through a wall, opening the room to the outdoors. Using windows is a favorite strategy of designers who want to make a cramped space feel grand.

Windows cheer a room with a healthy dose of light. They enliven a room with the dance of sunbeams and shadows. They freshen a room with sprightly breezes.

Imagination Enhances Design

When you're thinking about windows for your building project, let your imagination soar. Whether you're building or remodeling, creative use of windows will distin-

Imagine how dull this room would feel without the light-giving properties of Pella® casement windows. Circleheads above the casements set them off and add even more height and interest.

Adding skylights to a room—especially one that has a soaring cathedral ceiling—provides architectural interest and brightness, without compromising privacy.

guish your home from the neighbors' and make your home look and live like your dreams.

Don't be stopped by the old rule that large expanses of glass are not energy-efficient. That rule has been thrown out the window by new glazing technologies and superior weatherstripping materials and techniques.

All too often, new house plans position windows in typical places. You can break that mold. Don't be limited to one or two windows per wall. You can garner a custom look without paying custom prices by combining standard window shapes and sizes in non-standard configurations.

Install a trio of casement windows side by side, then top each with an awning window. Flank a hinged French door with double-hung windows. Accent a narrow wall with a stack of awning windows, then top the stack with a circlehead.

Here are some more idea-starters for using windows in ingenious ways.

- A single window above the sink has long been the kitchen standard. Venture beyond the standard! Bump out the sink wall (or any exterior wall) with a bow or bay window. Or stretch your horizontal view with two or three double-hung or casement windows.

- For something different in the kitchen, install a series of awning windows in the backsplash to illuminate your countertops. Install another series above wall-hung cabinets. If some or all of the awning windows are vented, you'll generate a natural cycle of ventilation. The lower windows pull in fresh air from outdoors; the top windows expel the warmer interior air.

- Most bathrooms have no window or one tiny window. Protect your privacy and capture the sun (and the moon and stars) with a skylight. You may want to adopt the opposite strategy and build a sumptuous bath with a wall of windows. (Choose Pella® Designer Series® windows and opt for between-the-glass blinds or shades for privacy.)

- Dramatize a boring entryway. Flank the door with tall, narrow windows (sidelights), then top all three units with a circlehead.

- Gain some privacy and quiet in a home office without isolating the room by replacing the solid door with an elegant French door.

- Build a breathtaking window wall in the dining room or family room by stacking windows floor-to-ceiling.

The Pella Outlook

There are as many visions for a home as there are homeowners. Some homeowners want to recreate a period look, complete with the handcrafted details of bygone eras. Others take a more casual approach, adapting and mixing favorite components from various periods and styles. Still others express themselves with exuberant, contemporary architectural lines.

Language of Windows

Fixed Window: A window that doesn't open and close.
Vent Window: An operable window; one that does open and close.

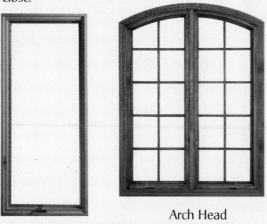

Casement

Arch Head

Sliding Patio Door

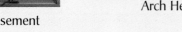

Double-Hung

Circlehead

Awning

Pella® Bow Window

A Bow or a Bay? What's the Difference?

The captivating beauty of bow and bay windows makes them popular with remodelers and home builders. Even with limited wall space, a bow or bay window allows you to have more windows and more view. It also can make a relatively small room appear much larger and much more elegant.

A bow window is a combination of four or more casement windows, shaped into a gentle curve. Any number of the windows can be operable. A bay typically consists of three windows. The center window usually is fixed; the side windows (casement or double-hung units) usually are operable.

Pella® Bay Window

What's A Circlehead?

The Pella® Circlehead is available as a full-circle, a half-circle, and a quarter-circle in a wide assortment of sizes, so you can use it alone or to top any configuration of windows and doors.

Pella® Circlehead Window

Pella® casement windows with fixed transoms above create a dramatic use of space and grace it with sophisticated elegance.

echo or complement another graphic element in the room. Pella can do it. Windows and doors in the Architect Series line also are available without muntins or with removable wood muntins that snap onto the interior side of the window.

Customize the exterior look, too. Select the traditional look of painted wood, or aluminum cladding with Pella's EnduraClad™ coating, available in a full array of colors, including custom colors.

Designer Series®

Do you love to redecorate, to rejuvenate your home periodically with a new look, a new mood? If so, Pella's Designer Series® windows and doors suit your style perfectly...no matter how often your style changes.

The Designer Series line offers unmatched versatility. It lets you put Slimshade® blinds or pleated shades between the interior and exterior panes of glass. Choose Pella® blinds or shades in a color that coordinates with your decor. When it's time to change the color scheme

Pella produces the three distinctive product lines described below to meet all design expectations, be they classic or contemporary, sophisticated or simple. These three product lines make Pella quality available to every homeowner, regardless of budget.

Architect Series®

This line of products offers superb energy efficiency with versatile design options that are ideal for any traditionally styled home, from Mission-style to French Provincial. The best of the best, Pella's Architect Series® products marry the energy efficiency of contemporary technology with a traditional divided-light appearance in a patented process called Integral Light Technology™.

The superbly crafted windows and doors in the Architect Series line can be customized to meet the most exacting design standards. Pella will put arch tops on doors as well as casement and double-hung windows. Further, the company will create custom shapes, such as triangles and trapezoids.

This series offers three elegant muntin patterns as standard—traditional style, prairie style, and 9-lite prairie style. If those styles don't meet your needs, Pella professionals will work with you to design a muntin pattern that does. Perhaps you want your window muntins to

Designer Series® casement windows with transoms and a hinged door with sidelights work well in a high-traffic family room and bring the outdoors into casual areas.

The Pella® In-Swing French door fits in well with fixed windows in almost any setting.

or the decor, you can change these between-glass accessories, too. The interior panel of window glass is removable, so you can switch blinds and shades or change their color.

Another option is to have wood muntins between the interior and exterior panes of glass. When your mood calls for a traditional look, install the muntins. When you want a wide-open, casual, contemporary look, remove the muntins. It's that easy. The removable panel of glass lets you customize your windows even further by adding stained glass overlays.

Homeowners who hate dusting love the idea of Pella's between-glass shades, blinds and muntins. Their position between panes of glass keeps them free of household dust and also protects them from damage.

Products in this line are protected from extreme

Language of Windows

Muntins: Small decorative bars that divide a windowpane into segments.
Light: A windowpane.
Divided Light: A pane segmented physically or visually by muntins.

---

weather conditions by aluminum cladding on the exterior. The aluminum cladding is coated with Pella's durable EnduraClad™ finish, available in a full palette of colors.

ProLine®

ProLine® windows and doors incorporate the quality characteristics for which Pella is renowned, at a price that's amenable to almost every budget. A simplified product offering of standard sizes, colors, and glazings makes ProLine products a great value.

ProLine windows and doors feature all-wood construction, energy-efficient glazing options, superior weatherstripping, and aluminum-clad exteriors with Pella's EnduraClad finish. ProLine products also include optional wood muntin bars that attach to the interior of the window for a classic look.

ELEMENTS OF FUNCTION

Knowledge is power. That old adage is especially appropriate when it comes to shopping. The more you know, the more likely you are to make sound purchasing decisions. Here's the information you need to be a smart window-shopper.

Anatomy of a Window

Talk the talk. When you're discussing windows with your builder or remodeler and sales personnel, be clear about the parts of a window.

1. **Head:** The top of the frame.
2. **Jamb:** The side of the frame.
3. **Sill:** The bottom of the frame.
4. **Frame:** The combination of the head, two jambs and sill that form a precise opening in which a window sash fits.
5. **Sash:** An assembly of stiles (sides) and rails (top and bottom) made into a movable frame (except on fixed windows). The sash holds the glass and fits into the frame.
6. **Glazing:** Sheet of glass.
7. **Pane:** A framed sheet of glass within a window.
8. **Muntin bar, grille, windowpane divider:** Any small bar that divides a window's glass into sections.

Energy Efficiency is Cost-Effective

Are windows that significant in the overall design of an energy-efficient home? As you shop for windows, you'll become aware that energy-efficient windows bear higher price tags than their lower-quality counterparts. Is the quality difference worth the extra cost?

You know the answer if you've ever experienced windows with inferior efficiency. Have you ever sat in front of a window in winter and gotten so chilled that you had to put on a sweater or crank up the furnace? Does your air conditioner run non-stop on a blistering summer day? Do you dread the arrival of your energy bill every month? Answer yes to these questions and chances are you've paid the price of poor quality windows.

Now is the time to end the hassle of poor windows. Whether you're building a new home or remodeling your current one, the installation of energy-efficient windows is an investment that will pay dividends for years—in the comfort of your home and in the cost effective-

By combining Architect Series® casement windows with transoms, a pleasing melange of fenestration emerges to make even a square box of a house come alive.

Bring the beach right inside with the right windows on your vacation or second home. Quality windows, such as those by Pella, will pay off in the long-run and allow you to enjoy your time away with comfort and energy-efficiency.

ness of your heating/cooling system. Quality windows help to keep the outside air outside and to prevent leakage of the interior air that you pay to heat or cool.

There are several ways to ensure that you're buying energy-efficient windows. The window industry has established rating systems (see box below) so consumers have a way to compare window brands before making a purchase decision.

Compare the Numbers

Insulation Value– The window industry has developed a standard system for rating the energy efficiency of window and door products. Many window and door products now feature the National Fenestration Rating Council (NFRC) label. The NFRC rating system allows consumers to compare the insulating qualities (measured by "u-value") of window and door products. The lower the u-value, the better the window or door will insulate against heat and cold. Products with lower u-values will keep out summer heat and winter cold better than windows with higher u-values, increasing your comfort and saving you money on heating and cooling bills.

Air Infiltration– Most window manufacturers publish air infiltration ratings for their products. A lower number means that less air will leak through the closed window, increasing comfort and energy savings. When comparing air infiltration numbers, it's important to know how the manufacturer determines its published values. At the present time, there is no standardized way for manufacturers to report this number. Pella chooses

to publish the maximum air leakage for its products. In addition, only Pella tests most venting windows for air infiltration before they leave the factory. If they don't pass, they don't go out the door. Many manufacturers publish an average based on random tests. Some products will perform better than the average and some worse, but they have no way of knowing how an individual product actually performs.

Fade Protection– Many window and door manufacturers talk about how much of the sun's ultraviolet (UV) rays their products block, and, they claim, that predicts how well a window or door will protect interior furnishings from fading. They aren't telling the entire story. Other types of solar radiation also contribute to fading. In addition to the UV blocking figure, Pella publishes LBL (Lawrence Berkeley Laboratory) fade protection ratings for its products. This rating takes into account the fading potential of the entire spectrum of solar radiation, and is a better measure of the ability of a glazing system to protect furnishings from fading than a measure of UV reduction alone.

ELEMENTS OF QUALITY

Quality Reaps Dividends…
In Comfort
In Energy Efficiency
In Ease of Maintenance
In Beauty

It's true. We know that a quality product is a wise investment that pays for itself over time. When you're building or remodeling a home, think long-term, especially when it comes to the basic structural elements, including windows and doors. When you think long-term, you buy quality—for all the reasons above, and because quality products don't require frequent replacement.

What constitutes quality in a window? Because Pella is considered a leader in the industry, we're using Pella products here as a benchmark for quality. When shopping for windows and doors, look for these features.

All-Wood Construction

Like fine furniture, wood windows are a certain sign of quality. Wood is energy-efficient. Wood is pleasing to the eye. Wood is durable. To buy the best, inspect the craftsmanship of construction. How the corners are joined is a telltale clue to durability and sturdiness. Pella sash corners are joined in three ways: interlocking wood joints, glue and metal fasteners.

The wood construction of a Pella® hinged door means that it is not only beautiful to look at, but will provide enduring service and energy efficiency. These doors also feature Pella's between-the-glass Slimshade® blinds.

Exterior Protection

The exterior of a wood window needs to be protected from moisture and harsh weather conditions. For exterior protection of the wood and to ensure minimal maintenance requirements, Pella offers aluminum cladding, which in turn is protected by a seven-step baked-on coating process. This EnduraClad™ exterior finish won't crack and it resists chalking, fading and corrosion. Pella offers a full spectrum of EnduraClad colors including custom colors to match or accent the siding on the house.

Interior Finish

The beauty of all-wood construction in a window is…the beauty of wood. Wood is warm and mellow and elegant. Wood is versatile. It can be stained or painted to coordinate with your interior decor. If you change your decor, you can change the look of wood.

Between-the-Glass Options

Without doubt, one of the most tedious household chores is dusting the blinds. To minimize that task and other hassles of blinds and pleated shades, Pella invented a way to put these window coverings between the interior and exterior panes of glass. This option is available on Designer Series® windows and patio doors. Another option is to place wood muntins between the panes of glass.

Glazing Choices to Suit the Climate

Not all glazing technologies are appropriate for all climates. Homeowners in cold climates, for example, may not want to completely block the sun's rays. They prefer to capture the solar heat. A good window manufacturer

Pella's tilt double-hung windows can't be beat for easy cleaning and solid performance. Shown here, a ProLine® double-hung window.

provides a selection of glazing choices, appropriate for different environments. Pella offers glazing technologies in a variety of combinations. The four most popular are described below.

Argon-filled InsulShield® Insulating Glass: This system combines low-E coatings and argon gas. Two panes of glass are treated with low-E coatings to block heat gain from the sun; argon gas in the air space between the panes decreases heat transfer. The system can reduce energy bills by up to 24 percent compared to single-pane wood windows.*

Standard Insulating Glass: There's no low-E coating. There are two panes of glass with an air space between them. This system is economical and allows some solar gain. The technology may reduce heating/cooling bills by up to 10 percent compared to single-pane wood windows.*

SmartSash® II: This system uses Pella's SmartEdge® technology to position two panes of glass so there's enough space between them to install wood muntin bars and blinds or pleated shades. (Not all glazing and between-the-glass options are available on all products.) As an option, the interior pane may be low-E coated. This glazing system can reduce energy bills by up to 17

percent compared to single-pane wood windows.* The addition of blinds or shades increases energy savings.

SmartSash® III: Again using the SmartEdge technology, this system adds a third panel of glass. The two interior panels can be low-E coated. This system may reduce energy bills by up to 28 percent compared to single-pane wood windows.* With SmartSash III, you can choose one between-the-glass option: muntins, blinds, or shades.

SmartSash II and III are available in Pella's Designer Series® windows and doors.

Convenient Cleaning

One of the most ingenious and most appreciated features of Pella® windows is the easy-does-it approach to cleaning. You can clean the outside glass of venting windows from the inside of your home. On double-hung windows, the top and bottom sashes pivot. On casement and awning windows, the sash moves toward the center of the frame.

* Computer simulation average compared to single-pane wood windows. Actual savings may vary.

and brass. Choose the finish that coordinates best with your interior decor.

■ An optional folding handle on casement and awning windows eliminates the hang-up for window coverings.

■ Multi-point locks on both sliding and hinged patio doors have earned the industry's highest security rating.

■ Cam-action locks on double-hung windows increase leverage on the closed window, creating a superior, weather-resistant seal.

■ Larger casement windows are equipped with top and bottom locks that pull the sash tight against the weatherstripping. Both

The convenience and appeal of Pella's Designer Series® products with Slimshade® blinds are evident, particularly in a sliding patio door.

Details Count

Windows and doors are important factors in any building or remodeling project, providing function and aesthetics. Consider the attention to detail evident in these Pella® features.

■ Interior hardware on windows and sliding doors is available in three finishes—white, champagne,

A Guarantee of Quality

A warranty indicates the manufacturer's confidence in its product. Pella's solid warranty protects your investment. Simply put, the glass in Pella® windows is guaranteed for 20 years; the other components of the window are guaranteed for 10 years. Further details may be found in the manufacturer's written warranty.

New windows in a remodeling project bring new life to the finished project.

The Retractable Window Screen Stops Insects

Pella's Rolscreen® retractable window screen rolls up and down like a window shade. When not in use the screen is hidden behind an attractive housing at the head of the window. This convenient product eliminates the hassle of removing and storing the screen and allows homeowners the enjoyment of a clear and unobstructed view. Screens are constructed of unobtrusive black fiberglass that will not rust and are designed to fit all standard Pella® Architect Series® and Designer Series® rectangular casement windows.

Turn the Corner

It's distinctive. It's stunning. A window that wraps a corner in light, with a view that draws all eyes. The Pella® CornerView® window is distinctive because it has virtually none of the distortion that's inherent with bent-glass products. Instead of bending the glass, Pella miters two pieces and bonds them together to form a nearly invisible seam.

locks are operated simultaneously by one latch at the bottom of the window.

■ There's a self-closing screen (optional) on Designer Series® sliding patio doors. This feature gently closes and latches the screen after it has been opened wide enough for someone to pass through.

■ As a further bonus, Pella's glazing systems help insulate your home from outdoor noise.

Warning: Use caution when children are around open windows and doors. Insect screens are not designed to retain children. For safety's sake, always keep children away from open windows.

Home Plans Follow

Now, turn the page to review our collection of over 200 home plans, all designed by architects. There are plans for new homes and plans for remodeling projects. There are plans to satisfy almost every style preference, size

requirement and budget; one of them is bound to be a springboard to creating your ideal house.

Every new house and remodeling plan in this book is blessed with a full complement of windows and doors, arranged for balance and gracefulness and to capture maximum light, views and ventilation. Nevertheless, you may want to make alterations. Do you have a breathtaking view? By all means, highlight the beauty of your site and enhance the drama of your home by installing more windows—maybe a bow, a bay or floor-to-ceiling windows. Are you a family that loves to be outdoors? Then, provide more access to your patio, deck or garden by installing additional patio doors, perhaps in the master bedroom or kitchen. Whatever your window and door requirements, Pella can help you turn your dream home into a reality.

GREAT ADAPTATIONS:
Remodeling plans with a bright future

CONCRETE PATIO

STONE WALL

COMPUTER

VAULTED CEILING

FAX MACHINE

FILES

STONE HEARTH

DESK

CONFRENCE TABLE

KITCHEN

PLANT SHELF ABOVE

WOOD BEAMS

GARAGE

COVERED PORCH

Remodeled Floor Plan

TERRACE

RAISED HEARTH

BATH

MASTER BED RM.
12⁶ x 11⁰

LIVING RM.
18⁴ x 16⁸

DINING RM
13⁰ x 10⁴

BATH

HALL

EATING

KITCHEN
13-9⁹ x 12⁸

BED RM.
9⁸ x 10⁴

BED RM-STUDY
9⁹ x 10⁴

ENTRY

STORAGE

PORCH

OVENS

RANGE

CURB

GARAGE
21⁴ x 21⁸

Original Floor Plan

Remodeled Rendering

DESIGN R117

PROBLEM

◆ Kitchen boxed in by garage is too dark.
◆ There is no casual living space.

SOLUTION

◆ Adding several windows and opening the kitchen onto the family room creates an appealing, sun-filled living area.
◆ Doors now open onto a sheltered porch, allowing easy access.

Complete Pella Window Specfications Provided With Every Home Plan

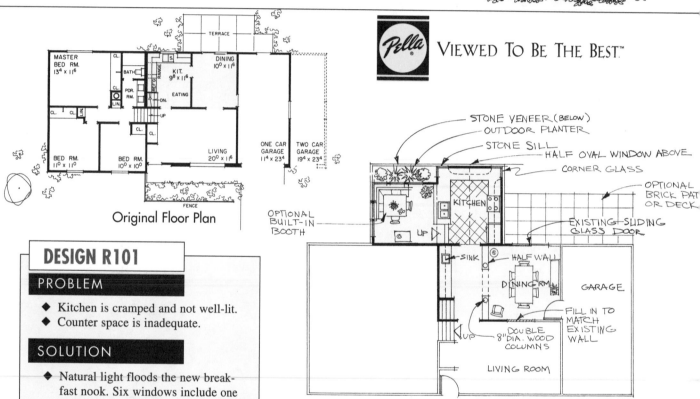

Original Floor Plan

VIEWED TO BE THE BEST™

STONE VENEER (BELOW)
OUTDOOR PLANTER
STONE SILL
HALF OVAL WINDOW ABOVE
CORNER GLASS
OPTIONAL BRICK PAT OR DECK
EXISTING SLIDING GLASS DOOR
FILL IN TO MATCH EXISTING WALL
OPTIONAL BUILT-IN BOOTH
KITCHEN
SINK
HALF WALL
DINING RM.
GARAGE
LIVING ROOM
DOUBLE 8"DIA. WOOD COLUMNS

Remodeled Floor Plan

DESIGN R101

PROBLEM

◆ Kitchen is cramped and not well-lit.
◆ Counter space is inadequate.

SOLUTION

◆ Natural light floods the new break-fast nook. Six windows include one that wraps at the corner.
◆ New windows and rooflines accent the rear elevation.

Complete Pella Window Specfications Provided With Every Home Plan

Remodeled Rendering

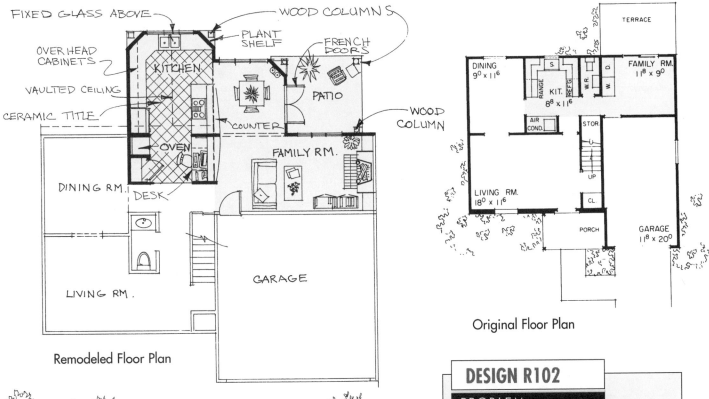

FIXED GLASS ABOVE

WOOD COLUMNS

OVERHEAD CABINETS

PLANT SHELF

FRENCH DOORS

VAULTED CEILING

KITCHEN

CERAMIC TITLE

PATIO

COUNTER

WOOD COLUMN

OVEN

FAMILY RM.

DINING RM.

DESK

LIVING RM.

GARAGE

Remodeled Floor Plan

TERRACE

DINING 9⁰ x 11⁶

S.

FAMILY RM. 11⁸ x 9⁰

RANGE

KIT. 8⁸ x 11⁶

REFG.

W.R.

D.

W.

AIR COND.

STOR.

UP

LIVING RM. 18⁰ x 11⁶

CL.

PORCH

GARAGE 11⁸ x 20⁰

Original Floor Plan

Remodeled Rendering

DESIGN R102

PROBLEM

◆ Small windows make kitchen and family room drab.
◆ Existing second story limits addition's height.

SOLUTION

◆ Family room, kitchen and breakfast nook now feature wide windows that enhance backyard views.
◆ French doors open onto the patio for extended outdoor dining.

Complete Pella Window Specfications Provided With Every Home Plan

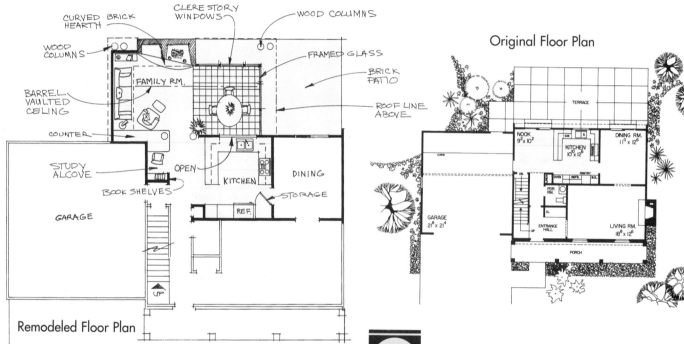

CURVED BRICK HEARTH

CLERE STORY WINDOWS

WOOD COLUMNS

WOOD COLUMNS

FRAMED GLASS

BRICK PATIO

BARREL VAULTED CEILING

FAMILY RM.

ROOF LINE ABOVE

COUNTER

STUDY ALCOVE

OPEN

BOOK SHELVES

KITCHEN

DINING

STORAGE

GARAGE

REF.

UP

Remodeled Floor Plan

Original Floor Plan

TERRACE

NOOK 9² x 10²

KITCHEN 10' x 12⁶

DINING RM. 11⁰ x 12⁶

CURB

OVEN

REF

PDR. RM.

ENTRANCE HALL

LIVING RM. 18⁸ x 12⁶

GARAGE 21⁸ x 21⁴

PORCH

Pella
VIEWED TO BE THE BEST.™

DESIGN R113

PROBLEM

◆ The rear elevation lacks light as well as design interest.
◆ There is no informal living space.

SOLUTION

◆ The glass-filled arch at the end of the vault draws attention to its shape.
◆ A large breakfast nook lined with windows leads to a covered patio.

Remodeled Rendering

Complete Pella Window Specfications Provided With Every Home Plan

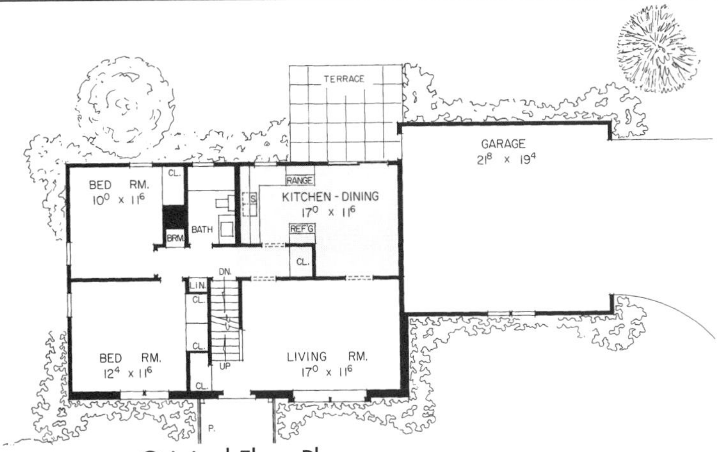

Original Floor Plan

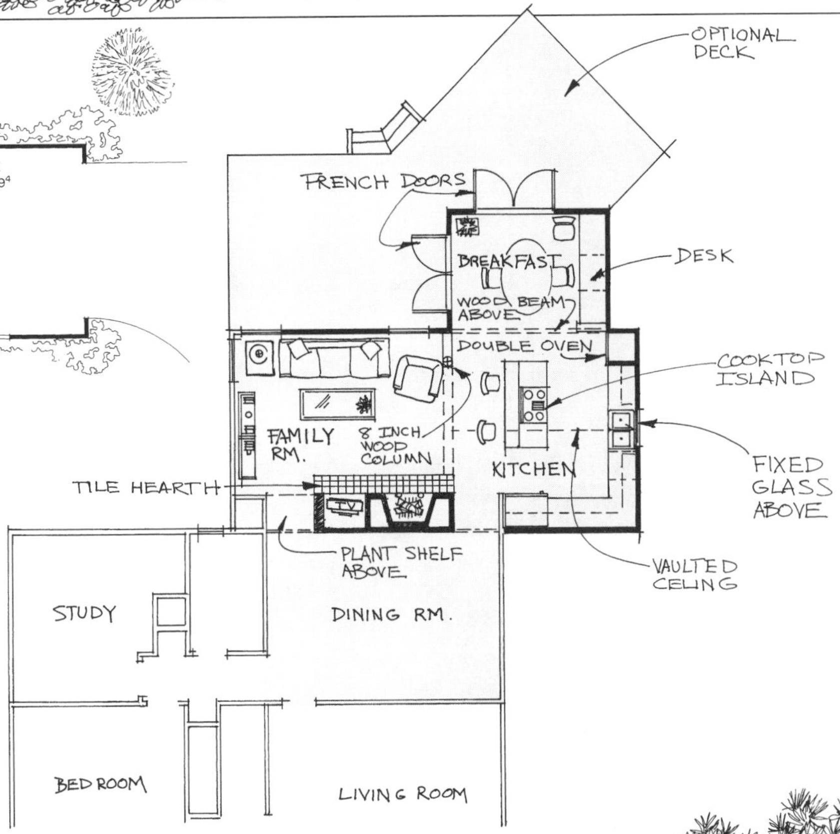

DESIGN R116

PROBLEM

◆ Kitchen/dining room is small and dark.
◆ Patio access is limited.

SOLUTION

◆ The new 13-foot-high family room uses a double tier of windows to bring in light.
◆ Two sets of French doors fill the breakfast room with light and provide dual access to the deck.

Remodeled Floor Plan

Remodeled Rendering

Complete Pella Window Specfications Provided With Every Home Plan

Original Floor Plan

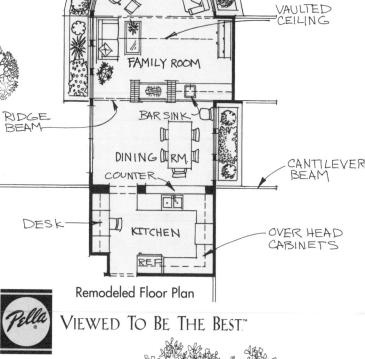

EXTERIOR PLANTER

VAULTED CEILING

FAMILY ROOM

RIDGE BEAM

BAR SINK

DINING RM.

COUNTER

CANTILEVER BEAM

DESK

KITCHEN

OVER HEAD CABINETS

REF.

Remodeled Floor Plan

DESIGN R115

PROBLEM

◆ Cramped dining room shares space with a small kitchen that lacks natural light.
◆ Existing traffic pattern cuts the living room in two.

SOLUTION

◆ The sweep of windows in the family room and the 8-foot-high windows in the dining room flood the new space with light.
◆ Windows that follow the roofline and the semi-circular wall of windows add sophistication.

Pella®

VIEWED TO BE THE BEST™

Remodeled Rendering

Complete Pella Window Specfications Provided With Every Home Plan

WINDOWSCAPING®
Design by Home Planners

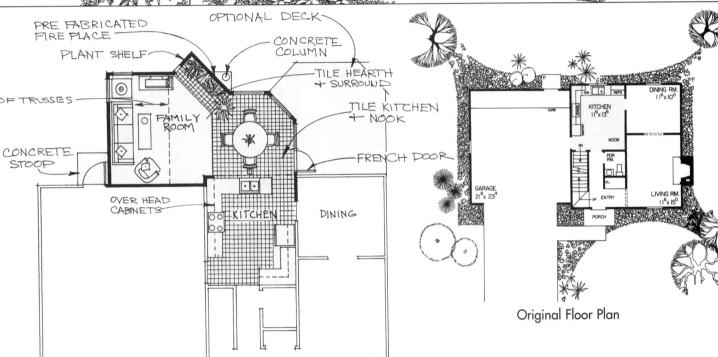

Remodeled Floor Plan

Original Floor Plan

Remodeled Rendering

Complete Pella Window Specfications Provided With Every Home Plan

DESIGN R114

PROBLEM

◆ Existing dining nook has no windows and kitchen is dark.
◆ Addition must not obscure second-floor windows.

SOLUTION

◆ From the sun-filled nook, one sees the quarter-circle clerestory windows and tile hearth in the new family room.
◆ New dining nook features two sides of windows and a pair of French doors that lead to the deck.

Original Floor Plan

Pella VIEWED TO BE THE BEST™

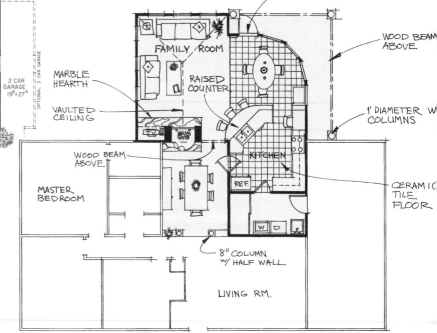

Remodeled Floor Plan

DESIGN R100

PROBLEM

◆ Spaces are cramped, dark and small.
◆ Flow from room to room is poor.

SOLUTION

◆ The family room is now surrounded by windows, allowing full enjoyment of every season by bringing in the gifts of nature.
◆ The new design provides a pleasant porch which frames the quarter-circle of windows that frame the breakfast bay.

Remodeled Rendering

Complete Pella Window Specfications Provided With Every Home Plan

SKYLIGHTS ABOVE

LIVING AREA

STEP UP

BRICK PIERS

WOOD COLUMNS

BRICK PLANTER

CONCRETE WALK

RVICE TRANCE

HANDRAIL

UP

KYLIGHTS

VER HEAD ABINETS

SEAT

KITCHEN

CLOSET

BEDROOM

DINING ROOM

BATH

REF.

STONE SILL

EXISTING DRIVEWAY

Remodeled Floor Plan

Original Floor Plan

TERRACE

NOOK 8' x 13'

FAMILY RM. 19'⁸ x 13'⁶

KITCHEN 9'⁵ x 13'⁵

WASH RM.

SERVICE ENTRANCE

GARAGE 20'⁵ x 23'⁵

LIVING RM. 19'⁸ x 13'⁶

ENTRY

DINING RM. 11'² x 13'⁶

PORCH

DESIGN R118

PROBLEM

◆ Additional space for a light and airy guest house is needed.
◆ Space must be private as well as filled with natural light.

SOLUTION

◆ An abundance of windows provide plenty of light to both the bedroom and the living area.
◆ Skylights over the kitchen and living room enhance the natural lighting for this addition.

Remodeled Rendering

Complete Pella Window Specfications Provided With Every Home Plan

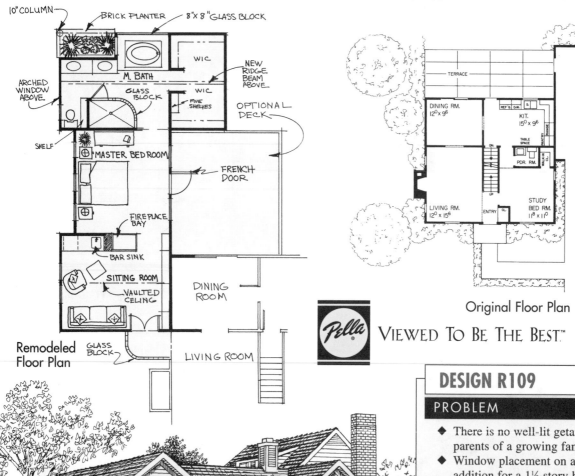

10" COLUMN

BRICK PLANTER

8"X 8" GLASS BLOCK

WIC

NEW RIDGE BEAM ABOVE

ARCHED WINDOW ABOVE

M. BATH

GLASS BLOCK

WIC

FIVE SHELVES

OPTIONAL DECK

SHELF

MASTER BEDROOM

FRENCH DOOR

FIREPLACE BAY

BAR SINK

SITTING ROOM

VAULTED CEILING

DINING ROOM

Remodeled Floor Plan

GLASS BLOCK

LIVING ROOM

TERRACE

GARAGE 11⁸ x 23⁴

DINING RM. 12⁰ x 9⁶

REF'G. D.W.

KIT. 15⁰ x 9⁶

TABLE SPACE

PDR. RM.

LIVING RM. 12⁰ x 15⁶

ENTRY

STUDY BED RM. 11⁸ x 11⁰

Original Floor Plan

Pella VIEWED TO BE THE BEST™

DESIGN R109

PROBLEM

- There is no well-lit getaway space for parents of a growing family.
- Window placement on a one-story addition for a 1½-story home presents a design challenge.

SOLUTION

- Clerestory windows protect privacy in the bedroom. French doors on the side yard lead to a patio or deck.
- From the living room, a glass-block wall leads to a pair of French doors that open onto the private sitting room.

Remodeled Rendering

Complete Pella Window Specfications Provided With Every Home Plan

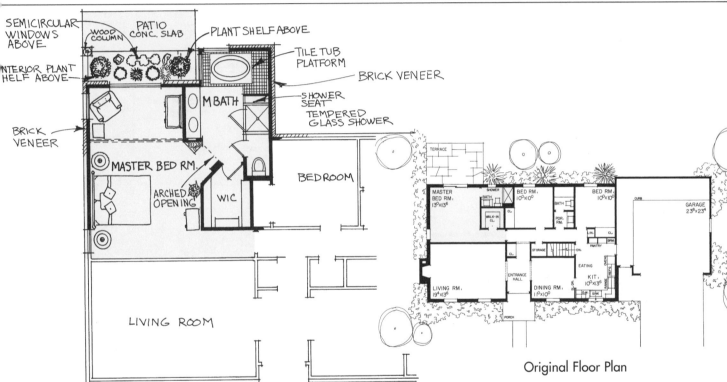

SEMICIRCULAR
WINDOWS
ABOVE.

WOOD
COLUMN

PATIO
CONC. SLAB

PLANT SHELF ABOVE

TILE TUB
PLATFORM

INTERIOR PLANT
SHELF ABOVE

BRICK VENEER

M BATH

SHOWER
SEAT

TEMPERED
GLASS SHOWER

BRICK
VENEER

MASTER BED RM.

BEDROOM

ARCHED
OPENING

WIC

LIVING ROOM

Remodeled Floor Plan

TERRACE

MASTER
BED RM.
13⁰x13⁶

SHOWER

BED RM.
10⁰x10⁰

BATH

BED RM.
10⁰x10⁰

GARAGE
23⁸x23⁴

WALK-IN
CL.

PDR.
RM.

LIN.

CL.

STORAGE

PANTRY

CL.

EATING

ENTRANCE
HALL

KIT.
10⁰x13⁶

LIVING RM.
19⁴x13⁶

DINING RM.
11⁰x10⁰

PORCH

Original Floor Plan

DESIGN R108

PROBLEM

◆ Master bedroom is too small and dark looking.

◆ The existing space is bland and lacks style.

SOLUTION

◆ Sliding glass doors open from the sitting room to the patio, inviting a bounty of natural light.

◆ The clerestory fan-shaped window and the column supporting the porch add pizazz to the rear elevation.

Remodeled Rendering

Complete Pella Window Specfications Provided With Every Home Plan

Pella® VIEWED TO BE THE BEST™

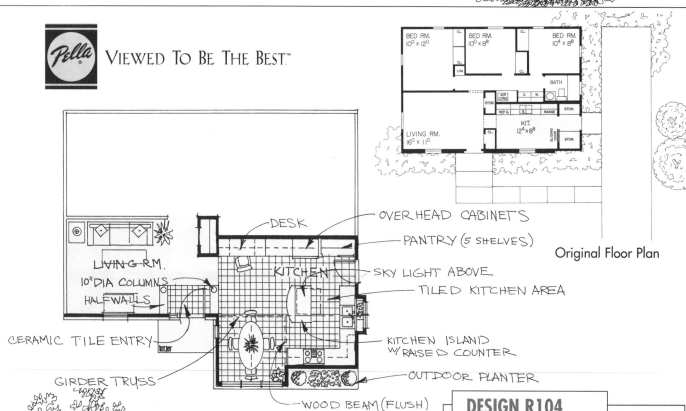

DESK

OVERHEAD CABINETS

PANTRY (5 SHELVES)

SKY LIGHT ABOVE

TILED KITCHEN AREA

KITCHEN ISLAND W/ RAISED COUNTER

OUTDOOR PLANTER

WOOD BEAM (FLUSH)

LIVING RM.

10" DIA COLUMNS

HALF WALLS

CERAMIC TILE ENTRY

GIRDER TRUSS

KITCHEN

Original Floor Plan

Remodeled Floor Plan

DESIGN R104

PROBLEM

◆ Window treatment on the front elevation demands special attention.
◆ Kitchen lacks light and space.

SOLUTION

◆ The Palladian window is an important design element, which gives the originally modest front elevation a much stronger presence.
◆ The new island eating bar is illuminated by a skylight, shedding a warm glow over the entire kitchen area.

Remodeled Rendering

Complete Pella Window Specfications Provided With Every Home Plan

WINDOWSCAPING®

Design by
Home Planners

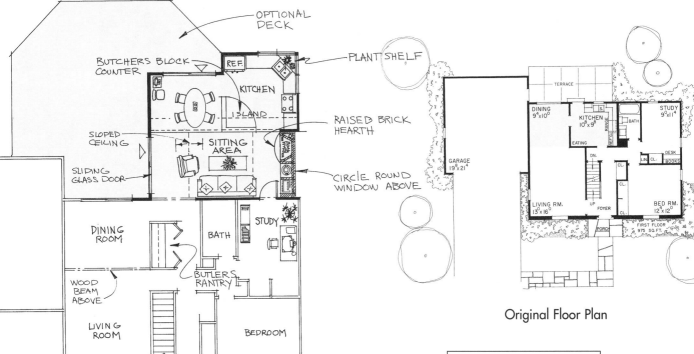

OPTIONAL DECK

BUTCHERS BLOCK COUNTER

REF.

PLANT SHELF

KITCHEN

ISLAND

SLOPED CEILING

SITTING AREA

RAISED BRICK HEARTH

SLIDING GLASS DOOR

CIRCLE ROUND WINDOW ABOVE

DINING ROOM

BATH

STUDY

WOOD BEAM ABOVE

BUTLERS PANTRY

LIVING ROOM

BEDROOM

UP

Remodeled Floor Plan

TERRACE

DINING 9⁴x10⁰

KITCHEN 10⁸x9⁰

RANGE

S.

BATH

STUDY 9⁰x11⁴

EATING

DN.

LIN. CL.

DESK

BOOKS

CL.

CL.

LIVING RM. 13⁴x16⁰

UP

FOYER

CL.

BED RM. 12⁴x12⁰

PORCH

FIRST FLOOR 975 SQ.FT.

GARAGE 19⁴x21⁴

Original Floor Plan

DESIGN R103

PROBLEM

◆ Kitchen and dining spaces lack windows and imagination with regard to design.
◆ Second-story windows limit addition height.

SOLUTION

◆ Corner windows light the space above the kitchen sink while sliding glass doors bring in additional light.
◆ Light streams through two new dormer windows, which, along with the stepped roof, helps balance the steep gables.

Remodeled Rendering

Complete Pella Window Specfications Provided With Every Home Plan

VIEWED TO BE THE BEST™

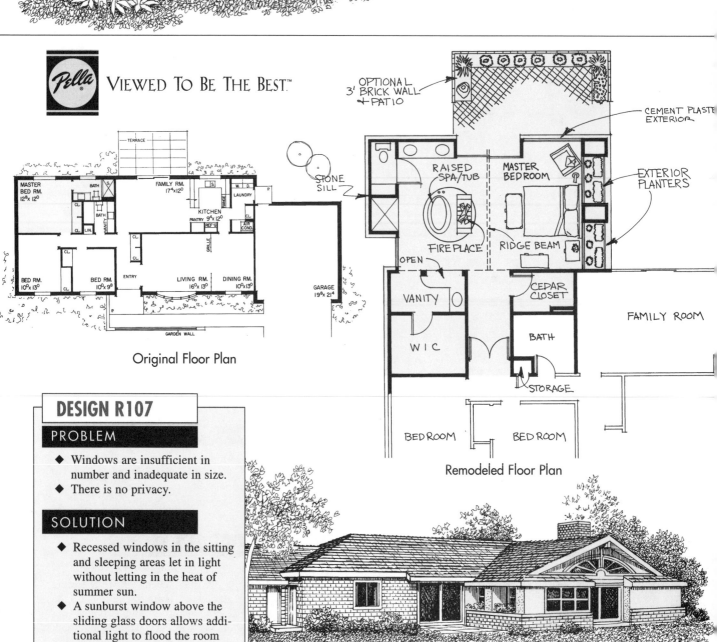

Original Floor Plan

OPTIONAL 3' BRICK WALL + PATIO

CEMENT PLASTER EXTERIOR

EXTERIOR PLANTERS

STONE SILL

RAISED SPA/TUB

MASTER BEDROOM

FIREPLACE

RIDGE BEAM

OPEN

VANITY

CEDAR CLOSET

FAMILY ROOM

W I C

BATH

STORAGE

BEDROOM

BEDROOM

Remodeled Floor Plan

DESIGN R107

PROBLEM

◆ Windows are insufficient in number and inadequate in size.
◆ There is no privacy.

SOLUTION

◆ Recessed windows in the sitting and sleeping areas let in light without letting in the heat of summer sun.
◆ A sunburst window above the sliding glass doors allows additional light to flood the room even if window coverings are closed.

Remodeled Rendering

Complete Pella Window Specfications Provided With Every Home Plan

WINDOWSCAPING®
Design by
Home Planners

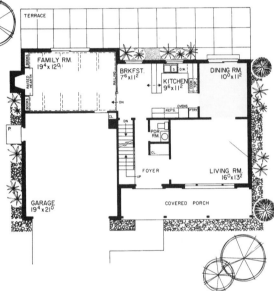

Original Floor Plan

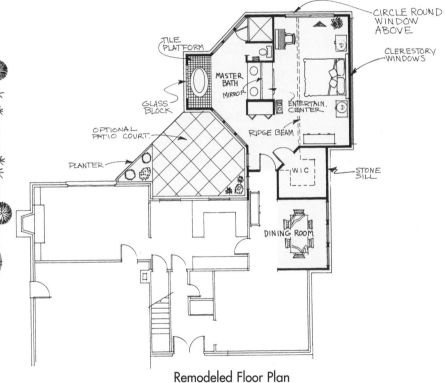

CIRCLE ROUND WINDOW ABOVE

CLERESTORY WINDOWS

TILE PLATFORM

MASTER BATH

MIRROR

GLASS BLOCK

ENTERTAIN. CENTER

OPTIONAL PATIO COURT

RIDGE BEAM

PLANTER

WIC

STONE SILL

DINING ROOM

Remodeled Floor Plan

DESIGN R106

PROBLEM

◆ Master bathroom is too small and too dark.
◆ Dining room is cramped and lacking windows for sunlight.

SOLUTION

◆ New bumped-out bath features a glass-block window topped by a clerestory to protect privacy.
◆ A wall of windows enhance the newly expanded dining room, incorporating nature's bounty into every occasion—formal or informal.

Complete Pella Window Specfications Provided With Every Home Plan

Remodeled Rendering

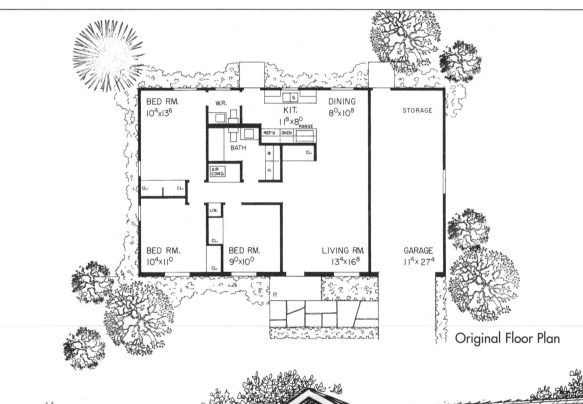

BED RM.
10⁴x13⁶

W.R.

KIT.
11⁸x8⁰

DINING
8⁰x10⁸

STORAGE

REF'G   OVEN   RANGE

BATH

CL.

AIR COND.

CL.   CL.

LIN.

CL.

BED RM.
10⁴x11⁰

BED RM.
9⁰x10⁰

CL.

LIVING RM.
13⁴x16⁸

GARAGE
11⁴x27⁴

P.

Original Floor Plan

Complete Pella Window Specfications Provided With Every Home Plan

Remodel Version A

WINDOWSCAPING®

Design by
Home Planners

Remodel Version B

DESIGN R125

PROBLEM

◆ Window treatment and front exterior are bland and uninteresting.
◆ There is no entry focal point.

SOLUTION

◆ The first solution adds brick veneer, coupled with horizontal banding and double-hung windows that give this house its substantial appearance.
◆ The second facelift brings a dramatic change with the over-sized gable. The upper sash of the new double-hung windows and garage door windows match, creating a rhythm to the facade.
◆ The third design solution, featuring tall windows with arched transoms, and gables that project over the garage and entry, adds a bit of spice to the brick facade.

VIEWED TO BE THE BEST™

Remodel Version C

Complete Pella Window Specfications Provided With Every Home Plan

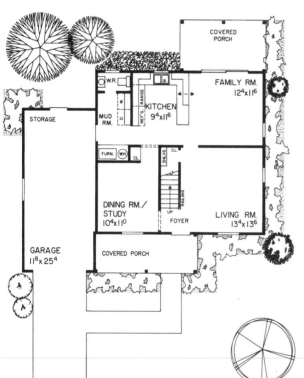

W.R.

COVERED
PORCH

FAMILY RM.
12⁴x11⁶

STORAGE

KITCHEN
9⁴x11⁶

MUD
RM.

REFG. RANGE

D

W

S

FURN. WH CL.

SHLVS. CL.

RAILING

DINING RM./
STUDY
10⁴x11⁰

UP
FOYER

LIVING RM.
13⁴x13⁶

GARAGE
11⁸x25⁴

COVERED PORCH

BEDROOM
10⁰x8⁰

CL.

BEDROOM
9⁰x11⁶

BATH

VANITY

CL.

CL.

LINEN

DN

RAIL.

BEDROOM
10⁴x11²

WALK-IN
CLOSET

MASTER
BEDROOM
13⁴x13⁶

Original Floor Plan

Pella®

VIEWED TO BE THE BEST™

Complete Pella Window Specifications Provided With Every Home Plan

Remodel Version A

WINDOWSCAPING®
Design by Home Planners

Remodel Version B

DESIGN R122

PROBLEM

◆ Home's entry is not inviting.
◆ Porch has awkward, unbalanced scale and skimpy posts.

SOLUTION

◆ In the first solution, projecting box-bays and an elliptical window on the second floor turn this ordinary home into a charming farmhouse.
◆ An inviting porch changes the second facade, minimizing the prominence of the garage. Addition of brick veneer enhances the existing first-floor windows.
◆ The third facelift adds sparkling windows to the new two-story pop-out to the right of the porch, creating a vertical element that balances the garage.

Remodel Version C

Complete Pella Window Specifications Provided With Every Home Plan

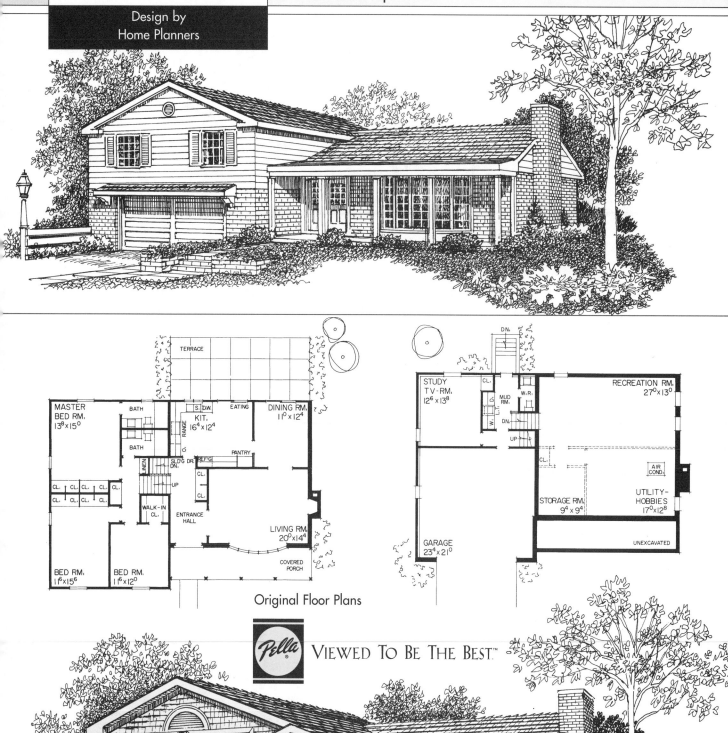

Original Floor Plans

Pella® VIEWED TO BE THE BEST™

Complete Pella Window Specifications Provided With Every Home Plan

Remodel Version A

WINDOWSCAPING®

Design by
Home Planners

Remodel Version B

DESIGN R124

PROBLEM

◆ Awkward two-story section is difficult to balance with less prominent one-story section.
◆ The front entrance in the one-story section is visually hard to find.

SOLUTION

◆ The first solution adds a strong front entry portico and larger
windows. The gabled roof extends to provide one side of the
entry portico, which balances the two sections of the house.
◆ The second design solution emphasizes the front porch. A projecting box-bay on the second story over the garage repeats the
column detail of the porch, creating balance.
◆ The third solution provides a gable accent above the living-
room window while a semi-circular window enhances the
entry. Sliding doors from upstairs bedrooms lead to a new
balcony over the garage.

Complete Pella Window Specifications Provided With Every Home Plan

Remodel Version C

This home, as shown in the photograph, may differ from the actual blueprints. For more detailed information, please check the floor plans carefully.

Photo by Elizabeth Brauer/Brauer Photography

DESIGN G207

PROBLEM

◆ A light, airy flex room is needed, but must allow space for the balcony on the existing house.

◆ New addition must blend well with the home's exterior while providing privacy and lots of light.

SOLUTION

◆ Abundant windows provide natural light, ideal for an in-law/guest bedroom, artist's studio, home office or private study.

◆ The bow window and unique window treatment contribute style to the exterior as well as enhancing the interior.

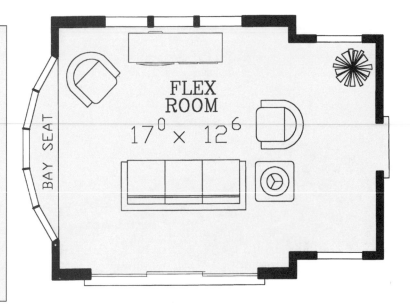

Remodeled Floor Plan

Pella VIEWED TO BE THE BEST™

Complete Pella Window Specfications Provided With Every Home Plan

WINDOWSCAPING®

Design by Home Planners

DESIGN R123

PROBLEM

◆ Window style of this split-foyer home dates the facade.
◆ There is no focal point to draw one's eye as they approach the home.

SOLUTION

◆ The first solution features box-bays that add definition to the first story. Wood banding under and over the first-floor windows reinforces the pattern. A horizontal band of square windows forms a transom over the front entry.
◆ The second facelift uses vertical accents at the windows and a gable roof to make the house stand tall. Dormers add "eyebrow" interest to the roofline.

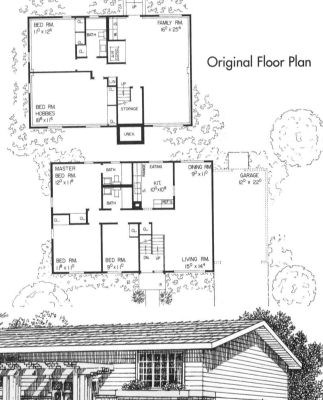

Original Floor Plan

Remodel Version A

Complete Pella Window Specifications Provided With Every Home Plan   Remodel Version B

WINDOWSCAPING®
Design by
Home Planners

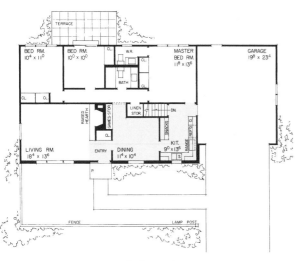

Original Floor Plan

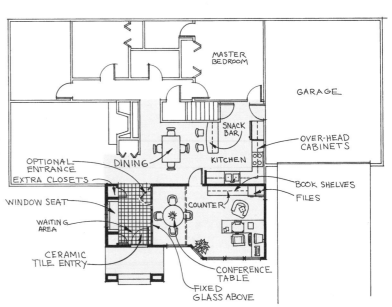

Remodeled Floor Plan

DESIGN R112

PROBLEM

◆ A dark entry opens directly onto the living room.
◆ There is no light-filled casual living area.

SOLUTION

◆ A clerestory window brightens the gable-roofed portico that provides a sheltered entry.
◆ Deep eaves provide variety and definition for the house as well as protection for the many new windows that enhance this home.

Pella
VIEWED TO BE THE BEST.™

Remodeled Rendering

Complete Pella Window Specifications Provided With Every Home Plan

WINDOWSCAPING®
Design by
Home Planners

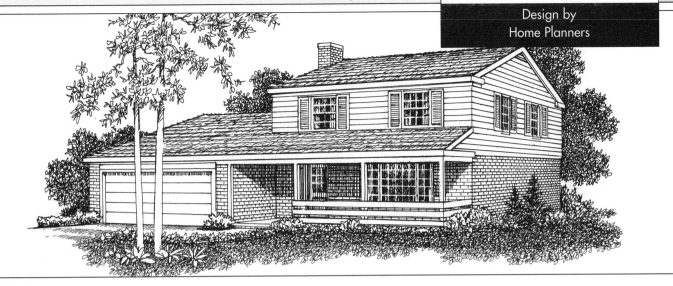

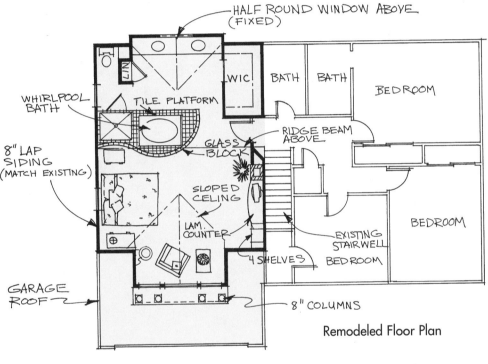

HALF ROUND WINDOW ABOVE
(FIXED)

WHIRLPOOL
BATH

TILE PLATFORM

WIC   BATH   BATH

BEDROOM

8" LAP
SIDING
(MATCH EXISTING)

GLASS
BLOCK

RIDGE BEAM
ABOVE

SLOPED
CELING

LAM.
COUNTER

EXISTING
STAIRWELL

BEDROOM

GARAGE
ROOF

4 SHELVES   BEDROOM

8" COLUMNS

Remodeled Floor Plan

BATH   BATH   MASTER
BED RM.
$15^0 \times 11^6$

DN.

CL.   CL. CL.   CL.

LIN.

CL.

BED RM.
$11^0 \times 10^0$ BED RM.
$11^0 \times 13^0$

Original Floor Plan

DESIGN R110

PROBLEM

◆ Existing master bedroom is dark and uninviting.
◆ Second-story addition will be a prominent addition, so it must be handled carefully.

SOLUTION

◆ The classic Palladian window on the projecting second-story dormer adds style and elegance.
◆ A half-circle window above the twin vanities in the master bath maintains privacy while providing natural light.

Remodeled Rendering

Complete Pella Window Specifications Provided With Every Home Plan

Original Floor Plan

VIEWED TO BE THE BEST™

DESIGN R111

PROBLEM

◆ There is no private master suite available, only a dimly lit bedroom.
◆ The remodeled addition must integrate with the various house levels.

SOLUTION

◆ The addition of the master bedroom and bath includes windows that surround the corner whirlpool tub.
◆ French doors open onto a deck that offers a transitional level that helps anchor and balance the existing, raised level of the house.

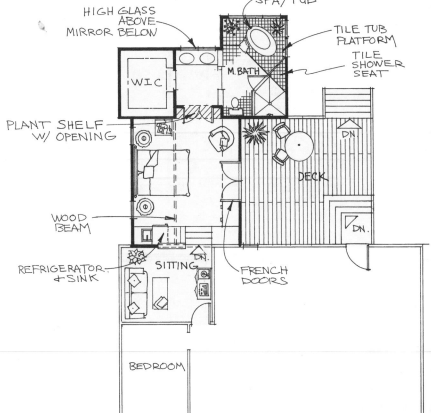

HIGH GLASS ABOVE MIRROR BELOW

SPA/TUB

TILE TUB PLATFORM

TILE SHOWER SEAT

WIC

M. BATH

PLANT SHELF W/ OPENING

DECK

DN

WOOD BEAM

DN.

REFRIGERATOR + SINK

SITTING

DN

FRENCH DOORS

BEDROOM

Remodeled Floor Plan

Complete Pella Window Specifications Provided With Every Home Plan

Remodeled Rendering

SIMPLY SENSATIONAL:
Stylish homes designed with a fresh point of view

This home, as shown in the photograph, may differ from the actual blueprints.
For more detailed information, please check the floor plans carefully.

Photo courtesy of Pella® Corporation

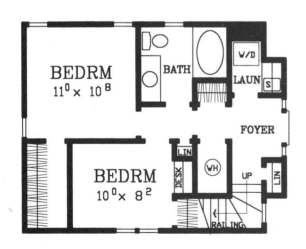

BEDRM
$11^0 \times 10^8$

BATH

W/D

LAUN   S

FOYER

BEDRM
$10^0 \times 8^2$

DESK   LIN   LIN

WH   UP   LIN

RAILING

REFG   PANT   S   WET BAR   STOR

RANGE   SNACK BAR   LIVING
$11^8 \times 16^0$ DECK

KITCHEN   S   RAILING

DV   S

PDR   DESK   DN   RAILING

RAILING

Width 26'-0"
Depth 20'-0"

DESIGN 4559

First Floor: 507 square feet
Second Floor: 438 square feet
Total: 945 square feet

■ Summers were spent with my aunt, who often described herself as she described her seaside home; with an exterior that had weathered and improved with age. Many hours were spent on the deck, where just a few steps took you from the comfortable living room to the outdoors. Here, breezes ruffled your hair and ocean spray settled on your skin. This home, with its shingled exterior and upstairs deck, recalls the joy of my childhood. Unique window treatments provide views from every room. The lifestyle is casual, including meals prepared in a kitchen separated by a snack-bar counter. A powder room and wet bar complete the upstairs. The first floor houses two bedrooms, a full bath and a laundry room. Built-ins make the most of compact space. After years of searching for the perfect design—it's good to be home!

Complete Pella Window Specifications Provided With Every Home Plan

DESIGN 3687

First Floor: 1,374 square feet
Second Floor: 600 square feet
Total: 1,974 square feet

L **D**

■ Balustrades and brackets, dual balconies and a wraparound porch create a country-style exterior reminiscent of soft summer evenings spent watching fireflies and sipping sun tea. An aura of hospitality prevails throughout the well-planned interior, starting with a tile foyer that opens to an expansive two-story great room filled with light from six windows, a fireplace with tile hearth, and a sloped ceiling. A sunny, bayed nook invites casual dining and shares its natural light with a snack counter and a well-appointed U-shaped kitchen. A spacious master suite occupies the bay on the front of the plan and offers a sumptuous bath with corner whirlpool, dual lavatories and walk-in closet. Upstairs, two family bedrooms, each with a private balcony and a walk-in closet, share a full bath that includes a double-bowl vanity.

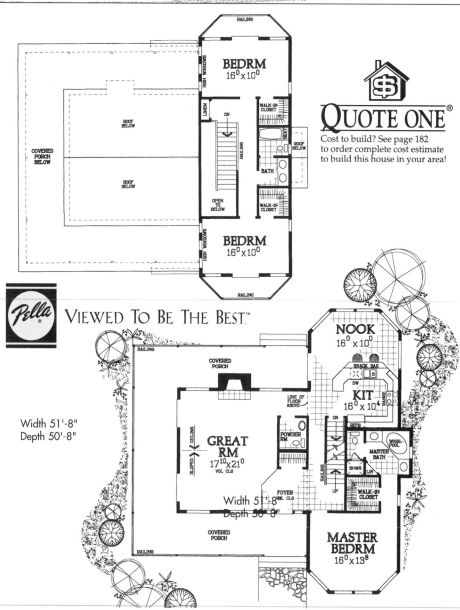

QUOTE ONE®
Cost to build? See page 182 to order complete cost estimate to build this house in your area!

Width 51'-8"
Depth 50'-8"

VIEWED TO BE THE BEST™

Complete Pella Window Specifications Provided With Every Home Plan

WINDOWSCAPING®

Design by
Home Planners

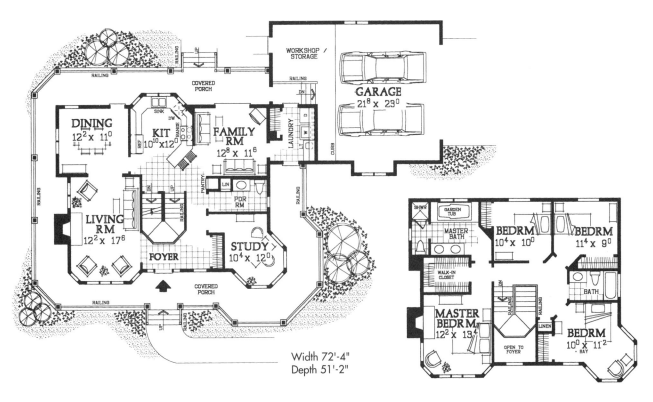

Width 72'-4"
Depth 51'-2"

DESIGN 3805

First Floor: 1,186 square feet
Second Floor: 988 square feet
Total: 2,174 square feet

L **D**

■ Reminisent of an era filled with lavender and lace, this Victorian-style exterior offers you the same wonderful details; such as a wraparound porch, muntin windows and turret-style bays. Inside, an impressive tile entry opens to the formal rooms, which nestle to the side of the plan and enjoy natural light from an abundance of windows. More than just a pretty face, the turret houses a secluded study on the first floor and provides a sunny bay window for a family bedroom upstairs. The second-floor master suite boasts its own fireplace, a dressing area with a walk-in closet, and a lavish bath with a garden tub and twin vanities. The two-car garage offers space for a workshop or extra storage.

Complete Pella Window Specifications Provided With Every Home Plan

WINDOWSCAPING®
Simply Sensational

Design by
Donald A. Gardner Architects, Inc.

DESIGN 9789

First Floor: 1,313 square feet
Second Floor: 525 square feet
Total: 1,838 square feet

■ Vaulted ceilings and daylit dormers will welcome your family home to open, contemporary living with comfortable country style. An airy foyer, emphasized by a grand staircase, flows into a great room differentiated from the dining room by accent columns. The breakfast room is conveniently located adjacent to the kitchen and provides access to the rear deck for outdoor entertaining. Located on the first floor for privacy, the master suite is highlighted by a vaulted ceiling and a private bath that features a garden tub with a double window. Upstairs, two family bedrooms—both with walk-in closets—share a full bath.

Complete Pella Window Specifications Provided With Every Home Plan

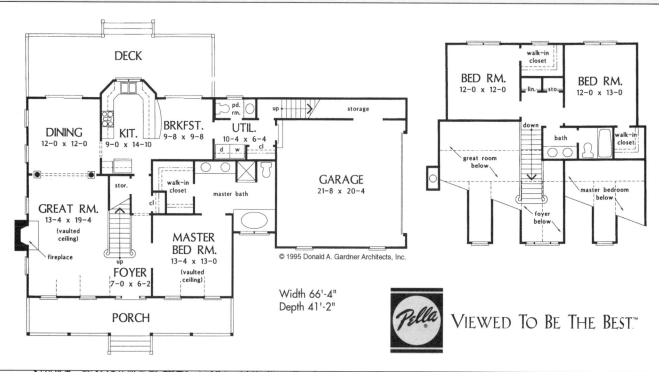

DECK

DINING
12-0 x 12-0

KIT.
9-0 x 14-10

BRKFST.
9-8 x 9-8

UTIL.
10-4 x 6-4

storage

pd. rm.

up

GREAT RM.
13-4 x 19-4
(vaulted ceiling)

fireplace

stor.

walk-in closet

cl

master bath

GARAGE
21-8 x 20-4

MASTER BED RM.
13-4 x 13-0
(vaulted ceiling)

FOYER
7-0 x 6-2

up

PORCH

© 1995 Donald A. Gardner Architects, Inc.

Width 66'-4"
Depth 41'-2"

BED RM.
12-0 x 12-0

BED RM.
12-0 x 13-0

walk-in closet

lin.

sto.

down

bath

walk-in closet

great room below

foyer below

master bedroom below

Pella

VIEWED TO BE THE BEST™

E. NATHAN © 1995 Donald A. Gardner Architects, Inc.

WINDOWSCAPING®

Design by
Donald A. Gardner Architects, Inc.

© 1995 Donald A. Gardner Architects, Inc.

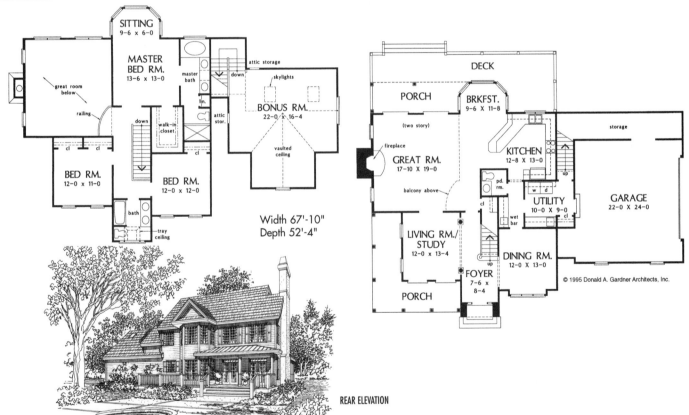

SITTING
9-6 x 6-0

MASTER
BED RM.
13-6 x 13-0

master
bath

attic storage

down

skylights

great room
below

railing

lin.

down

attic
stor.

BONUS RM.
22-0 x 16-4

walk-in
closet

cl

vaulted
ceiling

cl

cl

BED RM.
12-0 x 11-0

BED RM.
12-0 x 12-0

bath

tray
ceiling

Width 67'-10"
Depth 52'-4"

DECK

PORCH

BRKFST.
9-6 X 11-8

storage

(two story)

fireplace

KITCHEN
12-8 X 13-0

up

GREAT RM.
17-10 X 19-0

pd.
rm.

w d

UTILITY
10-0 x 9-0

GARAGE
22-0 X 24-0

balcony above

cl

wet
bar

cl

LIVING RM./
STUDY
12-0 x 13-4

DINING RM.
12-0 x 13-0

up

FOYER
7-6 x
8-4

PORCH

© 1995 Donald A. Gardner Architects, Inc.

REAR ELEVATION

DESIGN 9784

First Floor: 1,385 square feet
Second Floor: 1,008 square feet
Total: 2,393 square feet

■ In this traditional country home, a two-story great room accesses a porch and deck through French doors. Nine-foot ceilings throughout the first floor add extra volume and elegance. The great room is open to the kitchen. Here, a conveniently angled peninsula and a breakfast room with a bay window complement work space. For added flexibili-ty, a separate formal living room can double as a casual study. It features accent columns and French doors leading to the front porch. Upstairs, the roomy master suite features a sitting area, a spacious walk-in closet and a bath complete with a garden tub. An ample bonus room is highlighted by skylights and a vaulted ceiling.

Complete Pella Window Specifications Provided With Every Home Plan

© 1996 Donald A. Gardner Architects, Inc.
B. NATHAN

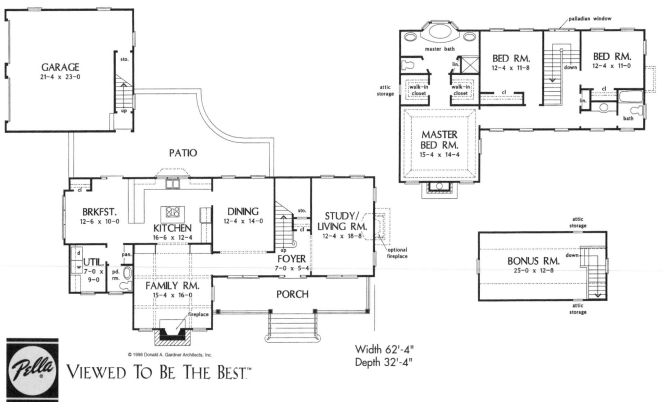

GARAGE
21-4 x 23-0

sto.

up

PATIO

BRKFST.
12-6 x 10-0

KITCHEN
16-6 x 12-4

DINING
12-4 x 14-0

STUDY/
LIVING RM.
12-4 x 18-8

optional
fireplace

UTIL.
7-0 x
9-0

FOYER
7-0 x 5-4

up

sto.

pd.
rm.

pan.

FAMILY RM.
15-4 x 16-0

PORCH

fireplace

© 1996 Donald A. Gardner Architects, Inc.

master bath

palladian window

BED RM.
12-4 x 11-8

BED RM.
12-4 x 11-0

down

attic
storage

walk-in
closet

walk-in
closet

cl

lin.

cl

lin.

bath

MASTER
BED RM.
15-4 x 14-4

attic
storage

BONUS RM.
25-0 x 12-8

down

attic
storage

Width 62'-4"
Depth 32'-4"

Pella

VIEWED TO BE THE BEST™

DESIGN 7620

First Floor: 1,413 square feet
Second Floor: 1,050 square feet
Total: 2,463 square feet
Bonus Room: 342 square feet

■ The welcoming covered porch on this home invites you to sit a spell—or to come in and visit. A large family room with fireplace completes the front of the house. Behind it is the kitchen with cooktop island and easy access to the breakfast room and formal dining room. The study/living room has an optional fireplace. Upstairs are three bedrooms, including the master suite with twin walk-in closets and a well-appointed master bath. You'll find plenty of attic storage space and a bonus room over the garage.

Complete Pella Window Specifications Provided With Every Home Plan

WINDOWSCAPING®

Design by
Donald A. Gardner Architects, Inc.

© 1994 Donald A. Gardner Architects, Inc.
B. HASKIN

DESIGN 9776

First Floor: 1,815 square feet
Second Floor: 689 square feet
Total: 2,504 square feet

■ Presenting a popular classic that makes a grand entrance—the quintessential country farmhouse with a covered porch. The floor plan features a two-story great room with a focal-point fireplace and double doors to the rear screened porch. The bumped-out breakfast bay leads to a rear deck with spa, and opens to the kitchen. Sleeping quarters include a first-floor master suite and two secondary bedrooms that share a compartmented bath and a balcony hall upstairs.

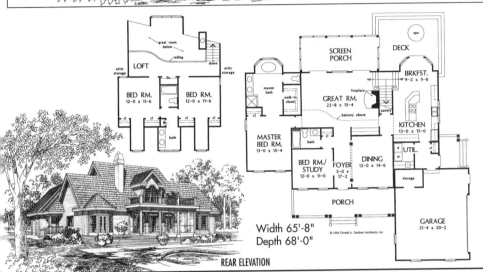

Width 65'-8"
Depth 68'-0"

REAR ELEVATION

© 1994 Donald A. Gardner Architects, Inc.

DESIGN 7623

Square Footage: 2,602
Bonus Room: 399 square feet

■ Classic brick and siding dress up this traditional home and introduce a well-cultivated interior. The foyer opens to an expansive great room with a centered fireplace flanked by built-in cabinets. The secluded master suite nestles to the rear of the plan and boasts a vaulted ceiling and a skylit master bath. Three additional bedrooms—or make one a study—share a full bath and a convenient powder room.

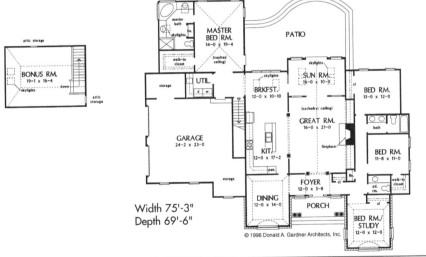

Width 75'-3"
Depth 69'-6"

© 1996 Donald A. Gardner Architects, Inc.

© 1996 Donald A. Gardner Architects, Inc.
B. HASKIN

Complete Pella Window Specifications Provided With Every Home Plan

B. NATHAN

© 1995 Donald A. Gardner Architects, Inc.

Pella VIEWED TO BE THE BEST™

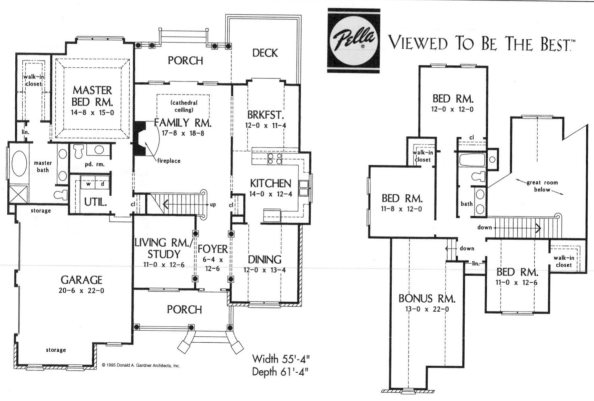

© 1995 Donald A. Gardner Architects, Inc.

Width 55'-4"
Depth 61'-4"

DESIGN 9790

First Floor: 1,799 square feet
Second Floor: 730 square feet
Total: 2,529 square feet
Bonus Room: 328 square feet

■ With its circle-top window and covered front porch, this plan is one everyone will want to call home. From the formal living room and formal dining room at the front of the plan, to the breakfast area and family room at the back, every need is well met. Secluded on the first floor, the master suite is lavish with amenities, including a huge walk-in closet, a separate shower and tub and a dual-bowl vanity. Upstairs, three secondary bedrooms share a full bath. A large bonus room could be used for a storage or games room.

Complete Pella Window Specifications Provided With Every Home Plan

WINDOWSCAPING®
Design by
Donald A. Gardner Architects, Inc.

© 1996 Donald A. Gardner Architects, Inc.

DESIGN 7608

First Floor: 1,784 square feet
Second Floor: 657 square feet
Total: 2,441 square feet

■ This traditional family home allows you the option of a more formal plan by converting the master bedroom study to a front living room, complete with a fireplace. A cathedral ceiling, along with a delightful fireplace, lets the family room be a welcoming, yet fashionable, gathering room for family activities. The large, island kitchen has a sunny breakfast nook. The master bedroom has a compartmented bath and large walk-in closet. Three family bedrooms, a full hall bath and a bonus room round out the second floor.

Width 56'-8"
Depth 55'-5"

© 1996 Donald A. Gardner Architects, Inc.

© 1995 Donald A. Gardner Architects, Inc.

DESIGN 9786

First Floor: 1,894 square feet
Second Floor: 641 square feet
Total: 2,535 square feet

■ Here's a farmhouse with a fresh face, filled with ideas suited for an active family. Glass doors and clerestory windows fill formal and casual living areas with natural light and invite gatherings and planned occasions. A focal-point fireplace brightens the space beyond the great room, which like the formal dining room, is defined by columns. A first-floor master suite offers a generous bath with a whirlpool spa. Upstairs, two family bedrooms share a full bath and a gallery hall with a balcony overlook.

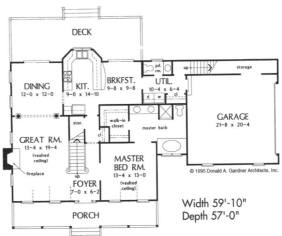

Width 59'-10"
Depth 57'-0"

© 1995 Donald A. Gardner Architects, Inc.

Complete Pella Window Specifications Provided With Every Home Plan

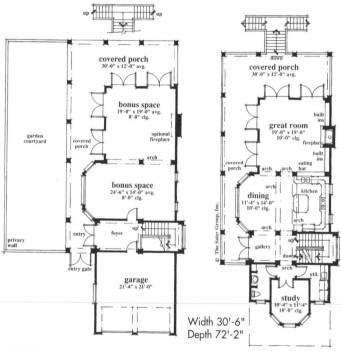

covered porch
30'-0" x 12'-0" avg.

bonus space
19'-0" x 19'-0" avg.
8'-0" clg.

optional fireplace

arch

bonus space
24'-6" x 14'-0" avg.
8'-0" clg.

garden courtyard

covered porch

entry

foyer

up'

privacy wall

entry gate

garage
21'-4" x 21'-0"

covered porch
30'-0" x 12'-0" avg.

great room
19'-0" x 19'-0"
10'-0" clg.

built ins

fireplace

built ins

eating bar

kitchen

dining
11'-4" x 14'-0"
10'-0" clg.

arch

covered porch

arch

gallery

up

down

util.

study
10'-4" x 11'-4"
10'-0" clg.

© The Sater Group, Inc.

Width 30'-6"
Depth 72'-2"

observation deck
30'-0" x 12'-0" avg.

master
19'-0" x 13'-8"
10'-0" tray clg.

sundeck

his

hers

his

br. 2
9'-6" x 12'-8"
9'-0" clg.

hers

arch

gallery

down

equip.

guest
10'-4" x 15'-8"
9'-0" clg.

© The Sater Group, Inc.

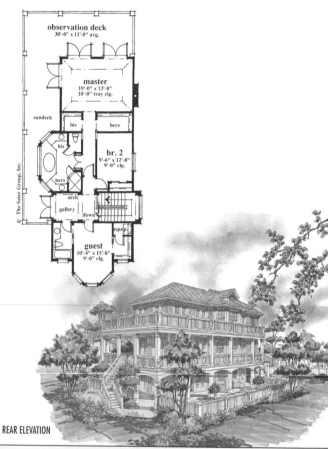

REAR ELEVATION

VIEWED TO BE THE BEST.™

DESIGN 6685

First Floor: 1,305 square feet
Second Floor: 1,215 square feet
Total: 2,520 square feet
Bonus Rooms: 935 square feet

■ This elegant Old Charleston Row design blends high vogue with a restful character that says shoes are optional. A flexible interior enjoys modern space that welcomes sunlight. Wraparound porticos on two levels offer views to the living areas, while a "sit and watch the stars" observation deck opens from the master suite. Four sets of French doors bring the outside in to the great room. The second-floor master suite features a spacious bath and three sets of doors that open to the observation deck. A guest bedroom on this level leads to a gallery hall with its own access to the deck. Bonus space awaits development on the lower level, which—true to its Old Charleston roots—opens gloriously to a garden courtyard.

Complete Pella Window Specifications Provided With Every Home Plan

WINDOWSCAPING®

Design by
Alan Mascord Design Associates, Inc.

DESIGN 7439

First Floor: 1,402 square feet
Second Floor: 848 square feet
Total: 2,250 square feet

Width 50'-0"
Depth 50'-0"

■ Palladian windows and clap-board siding blend to create a contemporary look to this comfortable home. Inside, formal rooms are open to one another, defined by lovely columns and archways. A vaulted family room enjoys a fireplace and built-in bookshelves. To the rear of the plan, Bedroom 4 easily converts to a den or guest room, with a nearby bath. Upstairs, the master suite has a vaulted ceiling and a deluxe bath. The width of the home is 40 feet with a two-car garage.

DESIGN 9573

First Floor: 1,502 square feet
Second Floor: 954 square feet
Total: 2,456 square feet

Width 50'-0"
Depth 35'-0"

■ Come home to the spectacular views and livability supplied by this lovely hillside home. It tucks a garage into the lower level; two full stories accommodate family living patterns. A two-story living room shares a through-fireplace with the formal dining room. Quiet time may be spent in the den, which opens through double doors to a deck. The sunken family room, adjacent to the kitchen and breakfast nook, also enjoys a fireplace. Upstairs, a vaulted master suite enjoys sunlight from the bumped-out window in the bedroom. Both of the family bedrooms access a full bath between.

Complete Pella Window Specifications Provided With Every Home Plan

© 1998 Donald A. Gardner, Inc.

B. NATHAN

DESIGN 7676

First Floor: 1,701 square feet
Second Floor: 543 square feet
Total: 2,235 square feet
Bonus: 274 square feet

■ Large multi-pane windows and a classic portico create a warm welcome to this attractive stucco home. The family room is impressive, with a fireplace, bookcases and views of the patio and beyond. Columns lead into the breakfast room, which opens off the kitchen. The dining room is at the front of the house, across the foyer from the living room, which is far enough from the main living areas to make a quiet study. The master suite is a fine retreat to the left of the plan, offering two walk-in closets and a deluxe bath to the homeowners. Two family bedrooms are on the second floor, along with a loft overlooking the downstairs and a bonus room with any number of possible uses.

Pella

VIEWED TO BE THE BEST™

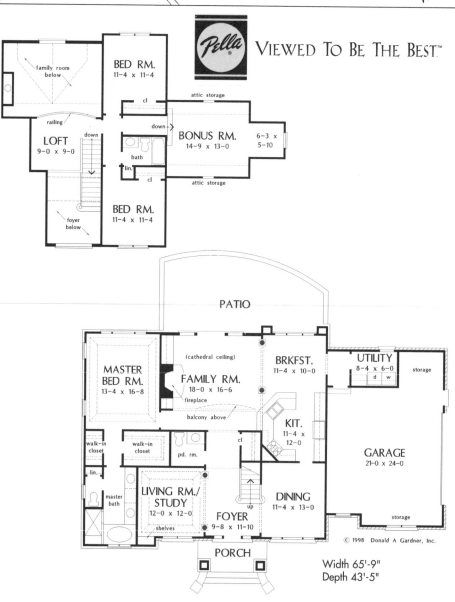

Second Floor

family room below

BED RM.
11-4 x 11-4

cl

attic storage

railing

down

down

BONUS RM.
14-9 x 13-0

6-3 x
5-10

LOFT
9-0 x 9-0

bath

lin.

cl

attic storage

foyer below

BED RM.
11-4 x 11-4

First Floor

PATIO

MASTER BED RM.
13-4 x 16-8

(cathedral ceiling)

FAMILY RM.
18-0 x 16-6

fireplace

balcony above

BRKFST.
11-4 x 10-0

UTILITY
8-4 x 6-0

storage

d   w

KIT.
11-4 x 12-0

GARAGE
21-0 x 24-0

walk-in closet

walk-in closet

pd. rm.

cl

lin.

master bath

LIVING RM./ STUDY
12-0 x 12-0

shelves

up

FOYER
9-8 x 11-10

DINING
11-4 x 13-0

storage

© 1998   Donald A Gardner, Inc.

PORCH

Width 65'-9"
Depth 43'-5"

54

WINDOWSCAPING®

Design by
Donald A. Gardner Architects, Inc.

© 1998 Donald A. Gardner, Inc.

Jenkins Chin Shue

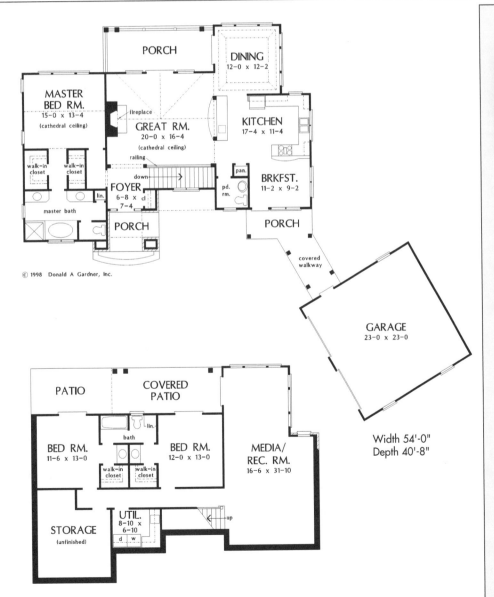

© 1998 Donald A Gardner, Inc.

Width 54'-0"
Depth 40'-8"

DESIGN 7665

Upper Level: 1,472 square feet
Lower Level: 1,211 square feet
Total: 2,683 square feet

■ This compact home presents an abundance of details on the outside and a great deal of livability on the inside. The stucco exterior is highlighted by an impressive stone entryway, keystone arches and wood accents on the gables. Inside, the main level focuses on the great room, with its impressive fireplace and cathedral ceiling. The U-shaped kitchen, separated from the great room by a snack bar, also easily serves a breakfast nook and the formal dining room. The master suite is on this level, and includes His and Hers walk-in closets and vanities. A rear porch can be reached from either the great room or the dining room. On the lower level, a bath is shared by two bedrooms, each with its own vanity area and a walk-in closet. A utility room, a media/recreation room and a storage room complete the plan.

Complete Pella Window Specifications Provided With Every Home Plan

Width 56'-4"
Depth 36'-5"

VIEWED TO BE THE BEST™

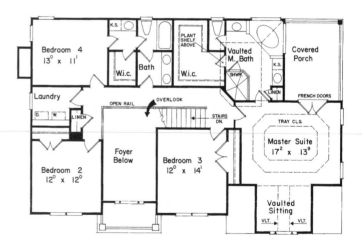

DESIGN P137

First Floor: 1,249 square feet
Second Floor: 1,436 square feet
Total: 2,685 square feet

■ This traditional home will be a joy to come home to after a long day at work. From the pleasing covered porch, the two-story foyer leads, through arched openings, to the formal dining room on the right and the formal living room on the left. Another arch opens to the family zone with a large family room and an island kitchen with a corner desk. The breakfast room includes French-door access to the outside. The sleeping zone is located upstairs. Three bedrooms surround the foyer overlook. The master suite features a tray ceiling, a separate vaulted sitting room, a master bath with individual sinks and a private covered porch. Please specify basement or crawlspace foundation when ordering.

Complete Pella Window Specifications Provided With Every Home Plan

DESIGN P175

First Floor: 1,948 square feet
Second Floor: 544 square feet
Total: 2,492 square feet
Bonus Room: 400 square feet

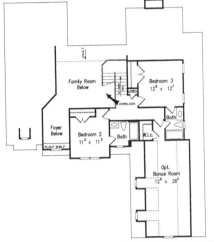

Width 56'-0"
Depth 65'-4"

■ High ceilings and big windows combine to produce openness and light. Arched openings outline the formal dining room and offer easy access from kitchen to vaulted family room. The kitchen features an island work area, built-in desk, pantry and plenty of counter space. The master suite includes a sitting room, large walk-in closet and a compartmented bathroom with a garden tub. Two family bedrooms and bathrooms are upstairs, as well as an optional bonus room. Please specify basement, slab or crawlspace foundation when ordering.

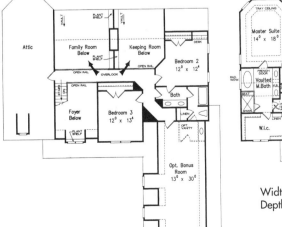

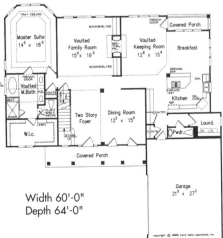

DESIGN P171

First Floor: 1,950 square feet
Second Floor: 679 square feet
Total: 2,629 square feet
Bonus Room: 444 square feet

■ There are plenty of extras in this well-designed house, including two covered porches, a through-fireplace between the vaulted family and keeping rooms, built-in bookcases, and a large work island and serving bar in the kitchen. The master suite includes a large walk-in closet and a compartmented bath with a garden tub, twin vanities and a plant shelf. Upstairs, two more bedrooms share a hall bath. There is also attic storage space plus an optional bonus room. Please specify basement or crawlspace foundation when ordering.

Width 60'-0"
Depth 64'-0"

Complete Pella Window Specifications Provided With Every Home Plan

Design by
Design Basics Inc.

DESIGN 7232

Square Footage: 2,512

■ Repeating arches and brick detail complement this stately one-story home. Impressive tapered columns define the formal dining room while, in the entry, a domed ceiling lies above the curved stairway to the basement. The sun-filled casual living area includes a great room, which shares its light with the open hearth room, the island kitchen and the gazebo-shaped breakfast nook. The master bedroom features access to the rear yard, a skylit walk-in closet and a luxurious bath with a wall of windows surrounding the curved whirlpool tub.

Width 74'-0"
Depth 67'-8"

QUOTE ONE®
Cost to build? See page 182 to order complete cost estimate to build this house in your area!

Pella
VIEWED TO BE THE BEST™

DESIGN 7233

Square Footage: 2,538

■ The grand front porch gives this home a unique style and majestic curb appeal. Inside, the 12' entry centers on the stately dining room with a bowed window. The island kitchen features abundant pantries and a snack bar. A sun-filled breakfast area opens to the large family room with a cathedral ceiling and fireplace. The bedroom wing has two family bedrooms and a master suite with a spacious walk-in closet and private access to the backyard. It also has a vaulted ceiling, whirlpool and dual vanities in the master bath.

Width 68'-8"
Depth 64'-8"

WINDOWSCAPING®

Design by
Frank Betz Associates, Inc.

DESIGN P147

First Floor: 1,205 square feet
Second Floor: 1,277 square feet
Total: 2,482 square feet

■ A taste of Europe is reflected in arched windows topped off by keystones in this traditional design. Formal rooms flank the foyer, which leads to a two-story family room with a focal-point fireplace. The sunny bayed breakfast nook opens to a private covered porch through a French door. A spacious, well-organized kitchen features angled, wrapping counters, double ovens and a walk-in panty. The garage offers a service entrance to the utility area and pantry. An angled staircase leads from the two-story foyer to sleeping quarters upstairs, where a gallery hall with balcony overlooks the foyer and living room. This hall connects family bedrooms. A private hall leads to the master bedroom. It boasts a well-lit sitting area, a walk-in closet with linen storage and a lavish bath with a vaulted ceiling and plant shelves. Please specify basement or crawlspace foundation when ordering.

Complete Pella Window Specifications Provided With Every Home Plan

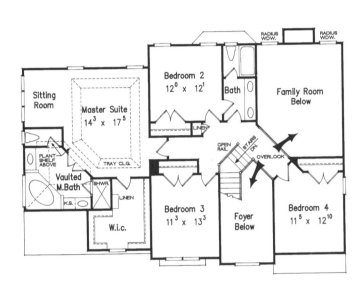

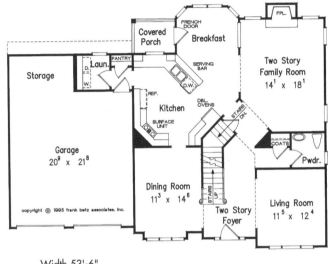

Width 53'-6"
Depth 41'-4"

DESIGN 7219

First Floor: 1,875 square feet
Second Floor: 687 square feet
Total: 2,562 square feet

■ Beyond the entry of this attractive two-story home, fifteen-foot arched openings frame the great room. French doors in the breakfast room open onto a versatile office with a sloping ten-foot ceiling. A private entrance into the master suite reveals a volume ceiling, a built-in dresser and linen storage area, two closets and a corner whirlpool tub with a dramatic window treatment. Upstairs, three family bedrooms share a bath.

Width 60'-0"
Depth 59'-4"

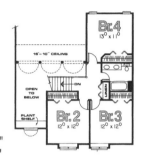

VIEWED TO BE THE BEST™

DESIGN 7264

First Floor: 1,415 square feet
Second Floor: 1,274 square feet
Total: 2,689 square feet

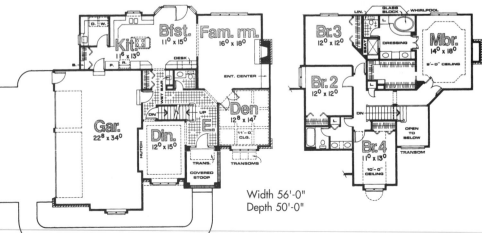

■ Handsome rooflines balance with brick and siding to provide appeal to this amenity-filled home. A two-story foyer leads to double doors opening into a den featuring tall windows and a spider-beam ceiling. An open family room is graced by a fireplace and a large built-in media center. The bayed breakfast room has access to the outdoors and offers a planning desk. Upstairs, angled double doors lead to a secluded master bedroom with a boxed ceiling, a huge walk-in closet and a lavish bath featuring dual vanities and a whirlpool tub. Three secondary bedrooms are well removed from the master suite and share a full bath.

Width 56'-0"
Depth 50'-0"

Complete Pella Window Specifications Provided With Every Home Plan

WINDOWSCAPING®

Design by
Living Concepts Home Planning

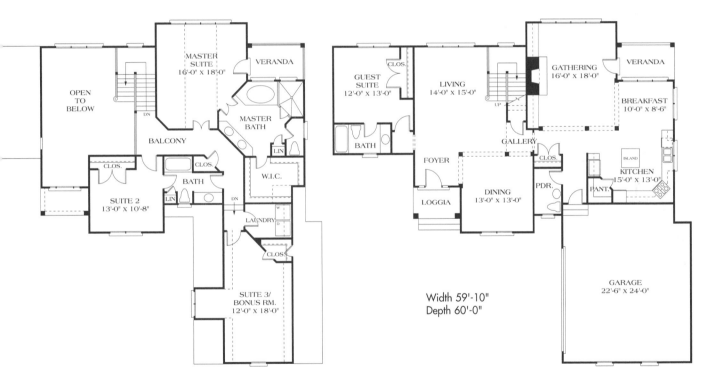

MASTER SUITE 16'-0" X 18'-0"

VERANDA

OPEN TO BELOW

DN

MASTER BATH

BALCONY

LIN

CLOS.

CLOS.

W.I.C.

BATH

SUITE 2 13'-0" X 10'-8"

LIN

DN

LAUNDRY

W
D

CLOS.

SUITE 3/ BONUS RM. 12'-0" X 18'-0"

GUEST SUITE 12'-0" X 13'-0"

CLOS.

LIVING 14'-0" X 15'-0"

UP

GATHERING 16'-0" X 18'-0"

VERANDA

BREAKFAST 10'-0" X 8'-6"

BATH

GALLERY

FOYER

CLOS.

ISLAND

KITCHEN 15'-0" X 13'-0"

LOGGIA

DINING 13'-0" X 13'-0"

PDR.

PANT.

Width 59'-10"
Depth 60'-0"

GARAGE 22'-6" X 24'-0"

DESIGN A161

First Floor: 1,644 square feet
Second Floor: 945 square feet
Total: 2,589 square feet
Bonus Room: 320 square feet

■ Multi-pane windows and an elegant two-story entrance add warmth to the exterior of this three-bedroom design with secluded guest suite on the first level. The living room and dining room share a large open area defined by columns. The large gathering room with fireplace and built-in bookshelves has access to the covered veranda and is open to the island kitchen and breakfast room. The spacious second-floor master bedroom suite features a sloped ceiling, a private covered veranda, a bath with a dual vanity and a large walk-in closet. A second bedroom on this level shares a full bath with a generous bonus room or additional suite over the garage.

Complete Pella Window Specifications Provided With Every Home Plan

QUOTE ONE®

Cost to build? See page 182
to order complete cost estimate
to build this house in your area!

Width 116'-3"
Depth 55'-1"

Pella — VIEWED TO BE THE BEST™

DESIGN 3622

First Floor: 1,566 square feet
Second Floor: 837 square feet
Total: 2,403 square feet
Apartment: 506 square feet

L

■ This sensational design is sweetly luxurious and simply elegant. A tile foyer opens to a two-story great hall that offers a warming fireplace for the living and dining areas and dual window seats that look out onto a rear covered veranda. The floor plan enjoys the fine detailing coveted in older homes: an extended-hearth fireplace in the master suite offers a place for nestling and a secluded window seat allows quiet reflection.

The master bath boasts a garden tub, a roomy walk-in closet, dual vanities and linen storage. Friends and family will feel at home in the sunny, bayed breakfast nook with its adjoining screened porch. Upstairs, three family bedrooms share a balcony hall and two full baths. This plan offers an optional apartment, which might be used as income property, a guest suite or separate lodging for relatives.

Complete Pella Window Specifications Provided With Every Home Plan

WINDOWSCAPING®
Design by
Home Planners

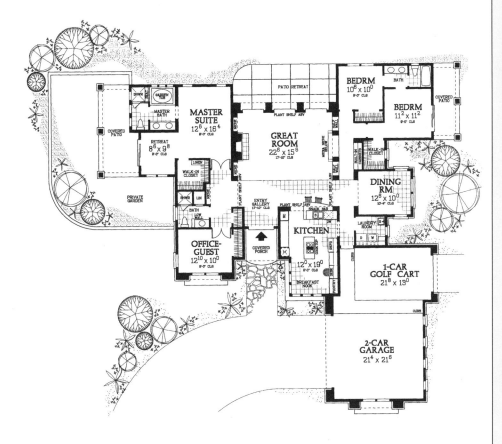

Width 86'-4"
Depth 80'-2"

QUOTE ONE®

Cost to build? See page 182
to order complete cost estimate
to build this house in your area!

DESIGN 3664

Square Footage: 2,471

L

■ Keystones, quoins and gentle arches lend an unpretentious spirit to this European-style plan. A vaulted entry introduces an unrestrained floor plan designed for comfort. The tiled gallery opens to a sizable great room that invites casual entertaining and features a handsome fireplace with an extended hearth, framed with decorative niches. The kitchen features a cooktop island and a built-in desk, and opens to a windowed breakfast bay which lets in natural light. For formal occasions, a great dining room permits quiet, unhurried evening meals. Relaxation awaits the homeowner in a sensational master suite, with an inner retreat and a private patio. Two family bedrooms share a private bath, and one room opens to a covered patio. A golf cart will easily fit into a side garage, which adjoins a roomy two-car garage that loads from the opposite side.

Complete Pella Window Specifications Provided With Every Home Plan

© 1996 Donald A. Gardner Architects, Inc.   B. NATHAN

DESIGN 7616

Square Footage: 2,450
Bonus Room: 423 square feet

■ This elegant home's understated Early American country theme introduces an interior plan that represents the height of style—but never at the expense of comfort. The foyer opens on either side to quiet formal rooms—or make one a bedroom—and leads to a central gallery hall. Wide open living space with a cathedral ceiling is defined by a double fireplace, with an extended hearth on each side. An L-shaped kitchen enjoys views of the outdoors and interior vistas of the family room over a centered island counter. The nearby breakfast room leads to a private porch and to the two-car garage, which offers a workshop and additional storage. Twin walk-in closets, a dressing area and a bumped-out tub highlight the master bath, which also features a vaulted ceiling. A secondary bedroom shares access to linen storage and offers its own bath.

VIEWED TO BE THE BEST™

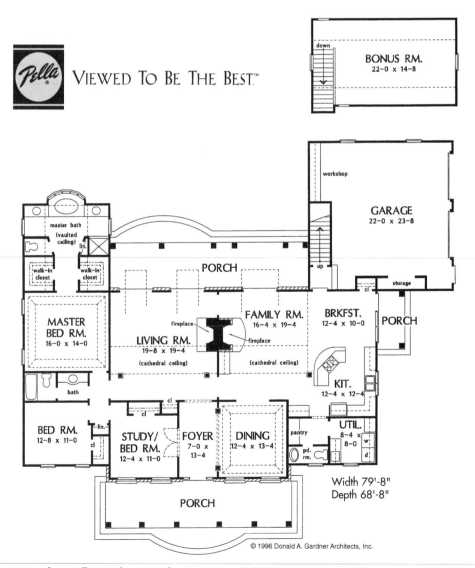

Width 79'-8"
Depth 68'-8"

© 1996 Donald A. Gardner Architects, Inc.

Complete Pella Window Specifications Provided With Every Home Plan

FORM AND FUNCTION:
Innovative homes that enjoy indoor-outdoor relationships

COPYRIGHT LARRY E. BELK

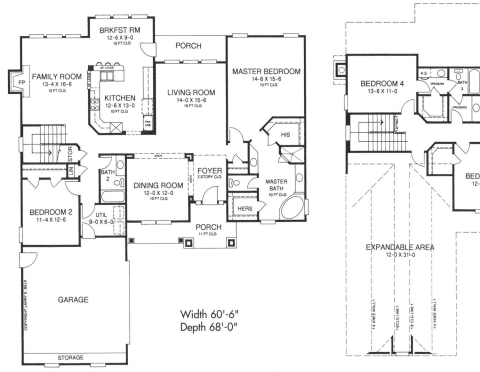

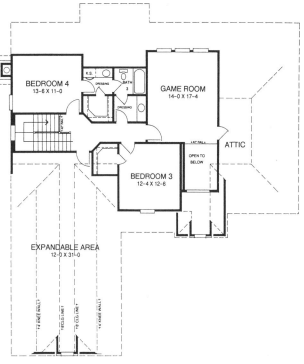

Width 60'-6"
Depth 68'-0"

DESIGN 8125

First Floor: 2,134 square feet
Second Floor: 863 square feet
Total: 2,997 square feet
Bonus Room: 372 square feet

■ A country French flair distinguishes this home. The two-story foyer opens to both the formal dining room and the formal living room. The kitchen, the breakfast room and the family room are grouped for great casual living. A nearby bedroom and bath would make a nice guest suite. The master suite is designed for privacy and relaxation. An amenity-filled bath features His and Hers walk-in closets and vanities, a corner whirlpool tub and separate shower. Two bedrooms and a bath with two private vanity areas are located upstairs. A large game room has a loft overlooking the foyer. An expandable area can be finished as needed. Please specify crawlspace or slab foundation when ordering.

Complete Pella Window Specifications Provided With Every Home Plan

Design by
Design Basics Inc.

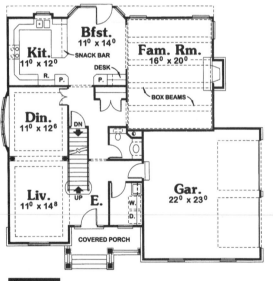

Kit.	11⁰ x 12⁰
Bfst.	11⁰ x 14⁰
Fam. Rm.	16⁰ x 20⁰
Din.	11⁰ x 12⁶
Liv.	11⁰ x 14⁸
Gar.	22⁰ x 23⁰

Kit. 11⁰ x 12⁰
Bfst. 11⁰ x 14⁰
SNACK BAR
DESK
Fam. Rm. 16⁰ x 20⁰
BOX BEAMS
R. P. P.
Din. 11⁰ x 12⁶
DN
Liv. 11⁰ x 14⁸
UP E.
W. D.
Gar. 22⁰ x 23⁰
COVERED PORCH

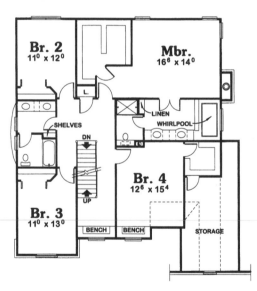

Br. 2 11⁰ x 12⁰
Mbr. 16⁶ x 14⁰
SHELVES
L.
LINEN
WHIRLPOOL
DN
Br. 4 12⁶ x 15⁴
Br. 3 11⁰ x 13⁰
UP
BENCH BENCH
STORAGE

Unfinished Attic 24⁸ x 16⁸
DN
DOWNDRAFT FURNACE
OPTIONAL STORAGE

VIEWED TO BE THE BEST™

Width 48'-0"
Depth 46'-0"

DESIGN 7001

First Floor: 1,304 square feet
Second Floor: 1,504 square feet
Total: 2,808 square feet
Bonus Room: 209 square feet

A glass-paneled entry introduces an interior rich with reminiscent detailing, including the home's signature trait: lovely French doors that open to the formal dining room from the central hall. Classic window benches in the upstairs landing and in Bedroom 4 add to the subtle charm of this design. Round columns define the formal rooms, while a box-beam ceiling and a fireplace make the family room cozy.

Complete Pella Window Specifications Provided With Every Home Plan

WINDOWSCAPING®

Design by
Design Basics Inc.

DESIGN 7002

First Floor: 1,901 square feet
Second Floor: 837 square feet
Total: 2,738 square feet
Bonus Room: 471 square feet

■ This uncomplicated elevation complements an open floor plan. Time-honored details flavor the interior, starting with space for a china hutch in the formal dining room. The master suite offers a sitting room, which has a wide cased opening that recalls the trimwork of the Arts and Crafts era. The front staircase has elaborate detailing and offers a beautiful focal point in the entry, while the rear staircase is convenient for everyday use.

Complete Pella Window Specifications Provided With Every Home Plan

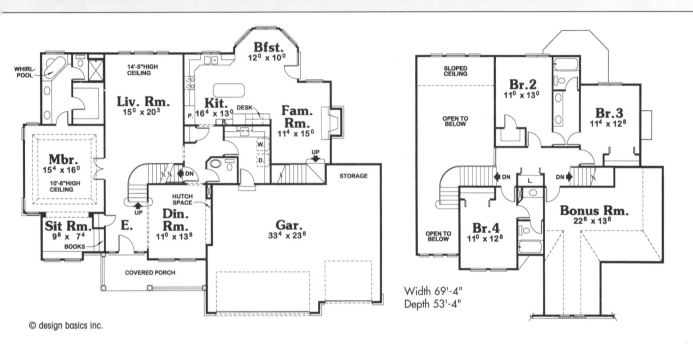

© design basics inc.

Width 69'-4"
Depth 53'-4"

DESIGNERS'INK

DESIGN 8003

First Floor: 1,961 square feet
Second Floor: 791 square feet
Total: 2,752 square feet

■ The combination of stacked stone, brick and siding add warmth to this eye-catching elevation. Inside, the large, angled foyer provides unobstructed views into the great room and dining room. A see-through fireplace between the great room and dining room adds elegance and completes a stunning dining room separated from the foyer by large arches supported by round columns. The kitchen includes a bay window and continues with the ten-foot ceilings found throughout the kitchen area. The home is designed with two bedrooms downstairs. The second bedroom is multi-functional and can be used as a nursery or office/study. All bedrooms downstairs have nine-foot ceilings. The second floor features two bedrooms and a large game room. Please specify crawlspace or slab foundation when ordering.

Width 64'-4"
Depth 62'-0"

COPYRIGHT 1991 LARRY E. BELK

VIEWED TO BE THE BEST™

Complete Pella Window Specifications Provided With Every Home Plan

WINDOWSCAPING®

Design by
Larry E. Belk Designs

DESIGN 8004

First Floor: 2,154 square feet
Second Floor: 845 square feet
Total: 2,999 square feet

■ This home's stacked bay windows create a turret effect and add drama to the facade. A through-fireplace warms the great room and the formal dining room, which is enhanced by a ten-foot ceiling and arches framed with round column supports. The kitchen is designed with a large walk-in pantry and a multi-windowed breakfast nook that fills that area with natural light. Two first-floor bedrooms include the inviting master suite and a bedroom that offers flexibility as an office or nursery. The second floor holds two family bedrooms, a bath and a game room. Please specify crawlspace or slab foundation when ordering.

Complete Pella Window Specifications Provided With Every Home Plan

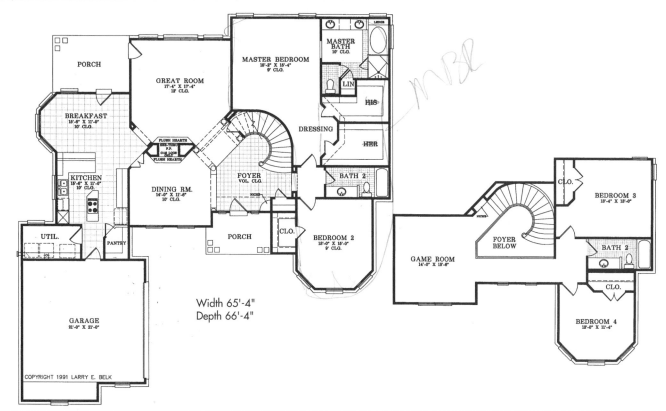

COPYRIGHT 1993 LARRY E. BELK

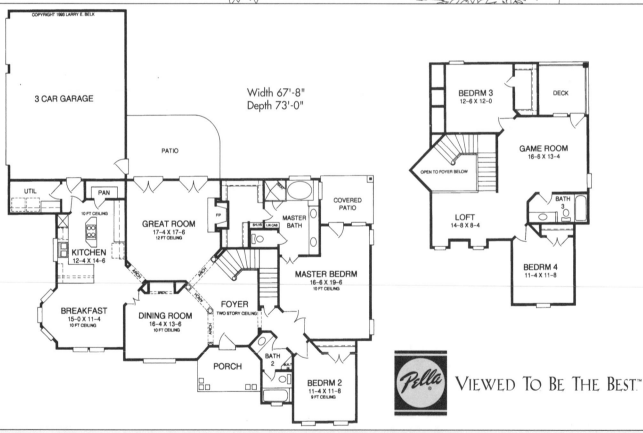

COPYRIGHT 1993 LARRY E. BELK

3 CAR GARAGE

Width 67'-8"
Depth 73'-0"

PATIO

UTIL

PAN

10 FT CEILING

GREAT ROOM
17-4 X 17-6
12 FT CEILING

FP

SHLVS LIN CAB

MASTER
BATH

COVERED
PATIO

KITCHEN
12-4 X 14-6

MASTER BEDRM
16-6 X 19-6
10 FT CEILING

BREAKFAST
15-0 X 11-4
10 FT CEILING

DINING ROOM
16-4 X 13-6
10 FT CEILING

FOYER
TWO STORY CEILING

PORCH

BATH
2

BEDRM 2
11-4 X 11-8
9 FT CEILING

BEDRM 3
12-6 X 12-0

DECK

OPEN TO FOYER BELOW

GAME ROOM
16-6 X 13-4

LOFT
14-8 X 8-4

BATH
3

BEDRM 4
11-4 X 11-8

Pella®
VIEWED TO BE THE BEST™

DESIGN 8054

First Floor: 2,012 square feet
Second Floor: 832 square feet
Total: 2,844 square feet

■ A large arched window, twin dormers and an entry accented by a swoop roof add detail and charm to this two-story home. A grand entry opening to the formal dining room and great room with a fireplace as its focal point provides added elegance with arched openings and columns marking each of these rooms. Busy cooks will appreciate the roomy kitchen featuring a large pantry, cook-top island and snack bar area. Lots of natural sunlight streams in from the bay window in the breakfast area. The master bedroom provides access to a covered patio offering a quiet outdoor retreat. The master bath features an enormous walk-in closet. An adjacent secondary bedroom and full bath is easily converted to a nursery, or a study. The second floor contains two secondary bedrooms, a full bath, a large game room and a deck. A sunny loft completes the plan and provides the perfect quiet retreat to curl up with a good book. This plan is available with either a crawlspace or slab foundation. Please specify when ordering.

WINDOWSCAPING®

Design by
Larry E. Belk Designs

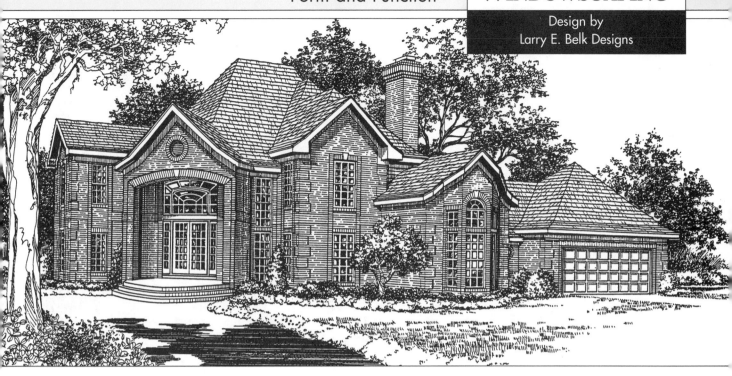

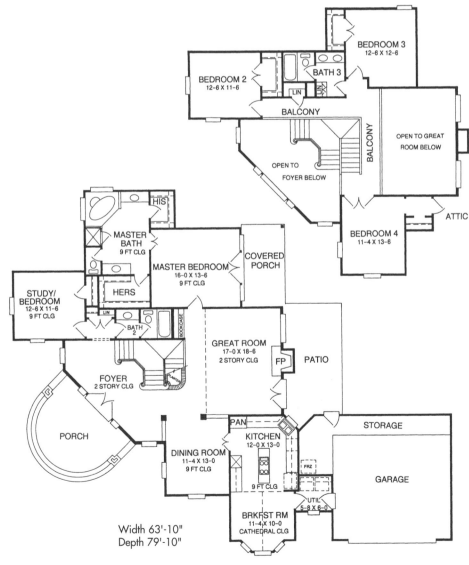

BEDROOM 3
12-6 X 12-6

BATH 3

BEDROOM 2
12-6 X 11-6

LIN

BALCONY

OPEN TO GREAT
ROOM BELOW

BALCONY

OPEN TO
FOYER BELOW

ATTIC

BEDROOM 4
11-4 X 13-6

HIS

MASTER
BATH
9 FT CLG

COVERED
PORCH

MASTER BEDROOM
16-0 X 13-6
9 FT CLG

HERS

STUDY/
BEDROOM
12-6 X 11-6
9 FT CLG

LIN

BATH
2

GREAT ROOM
17-0 X 18-6
2 STORY CLG

FP

PATIO

BOOKCASE

FOYER
2 STORY CLG

PORCH

PAN

STORAGE

KITCHEN
12-0 X 13-0

DINING ROOM
11-4 X 13-0
9 FT CLG

FRZ

GARAGE

9 FT CLG

UTIL
5-8 X 6-0

BRKFST RM
11-4 X 10-0
CATHEDRAL CLG

Width 63'-10"
Depth 79'-10"

DESIGN 8179

First Floor: 1,966 square feet
Second Floor: 872 square feet
Total: 2,838 square feet

■ This elegant brick two-story home, with its corner quoin detail, varied rooflines and multi-pane windows, has so many amenities to offer. Enter into the two-story foyer graced by an elegant, curved staircase. The formal dining room, defined by columns, is to the right and has double-door access to the efficient island kitchen. The large great room is enhanced by direct access to the rear patio and a warming fireplace. The first-floor master suite is secluded for privacy and is enhanced with a pampering, spa-style bath, His and Her walk-in closets, and a private covered porch. Upstairs, a balcony hall overlooking the great room leads to three family bedrooms, each with walk-in closets. Please specify crawl-space or slab foundation when ordering.

Complete Pella Window Specifications Provided With Every Home Plan

GARAGE
22'-6" x 20'-0"

UTILITY

D
W

PANT.

TERRACE/
DECK

BREAKFAST
9'-0" x 11'-0"

OPTIONAL ISLAND

KITCHEN
13'-0" x 13'-0"

DINING
ROOM
12'-0" x 12'-0"

PDR.

CLOS.

LIVING
ROOM
12'-0" x 12'-6"

GATHERING
ROOM
15'-0" x 21'-6"

UP

FOYER

Width 52'-2"
Depth 56'-6"

LOGGIA

COVERED PORCH

ACCESS W.I.C. ACCESS W.I.C.

SUITE 3
12'-0" x 12'-0"

SUITE 2
12'-0" x 10'-8"

MASTER
BATH

BATH

W.I.C.   W.I.C.

BATH

CLOS.

SUITE 4
12'-0" x 12'-0"

DN

OPEN

MASTER
SUITE
14'-6" x 18'-0"

SITTING
AREA

COVERED
PORCH

Pella
VIEWED TO BE THE BEST™

DESIGN A134

First Floor: 1,355 square feet
Second Floor: 1,442 square feet
Total: 2,797 square feet

■ This romantic Southern four-bedroom home is as beautiful on the outside as it is comfortable on the inside. Brick with wood balustrades on the porches, arched and Palladian windows and a recessed door are immediately appreciated. Inside, the foyer divides formal and informal living areas, with the gigantic gathering room on one side and the formal living and dining rooms on the other. The kitchen and breakfast nook lie to the back of the plan and overlook a delightful deck. Upstairs are three family bedrooms. Two have walk-in closets; one has a private bath. The master suite is also on this floor. It has double walk-ins, a coffered ceiling and a private porch. Of special interest is the sitting area just outside the master suite.

Complete Pella Window Specifications Provided With Every Home Plan

WINDOWSCAPING®

Design by
Living Concepts Home Planning

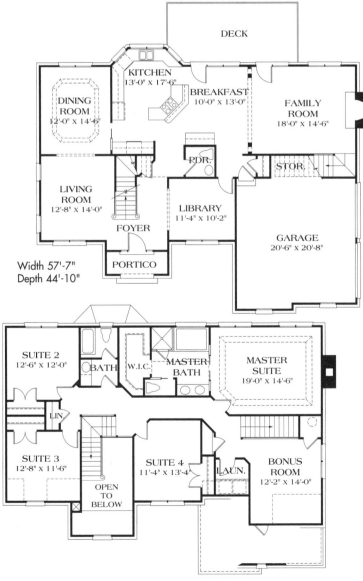

DECK

KITCHEN
13'-0" x 17'-6"

BREAKFAST
10'-0" x 13'-0"

FAMILY
ROOM
18'-0" x 14'-6"

DINING
ROOM
12'-0" x 14'-6"

LIVING
ROOM
12'-8" x 14'-0"

PDR.

STOR.

LIBRARY
11'-4" x 10'-2"

FOYER

GARAGE
20'-6" x 20'-8"

Width 57'-7"
Depth 44'-10"

PORTICO

SUITE 2
12'-6" x 12'-0"

BATH

W.I.C.

MASTER
BATH

MASTER
SUITE
19'-0" x 14'-6"

LIN

SUITE 3
12'-8" x 11'-6"

OPEN
TO
BELOW

SUITE 4
11'-4" x 13'-4"

LAUN.

BONUS
ROOM
12'-2" x 14'-0"

DESIGN A164

First Floor: 1,426 square feet
Second Floor: 1,315 square feet
Total: 2,741 square feet
Bonus Room: 200 square feet

■ The handsome facade of this outstanding two-story traditional home is equalled by its efficient interior design. A library with multi-pane windows is to the right of the entryway. The living room on the left adjoins a formal dining room with an octagonal tray ceiling. The island kitchen fills a bay window that looks out onto the rear deck. A large break-fast room is adjacent to the family room with fireplace and hearth. The master suite with cove ceiling, private bath and walk-in closet is on the second floor, along with three additional bedrooms and full bath. A corner bonus room and laundry facilities are also on this level.

Complete Pella Window Specifications Provided With Every Home Plan

DESIGN P192

First Floor: 2,137 square feet
Second Floor: 750 square feet
Total: 2,887 square feet

■ Enjoy the look of Europe with multiple rooflines, stucco detailing, copper roofs and an elegant entryway. Inside, the vaulted foyer is flanked by formal living and dining rooms, providing ease in serving dinner parties and offering after-dinner gathering space. To the rear of the home, a spacious family room with a warming fireplace is divided from the nearby kitchen and breakfast room by graceful columns. An office or den is located beyond the kitchen, ideal for working or relaxing at home. Also positioned for privacy, the deluxe master suite includes two walk-in closets and a sumptuous bath. The upstairs provides two bedrooms (and the possibility of a third), a full hall bath and a loft for games or computers. Please specify basement or crawlspace foundation when ordering.

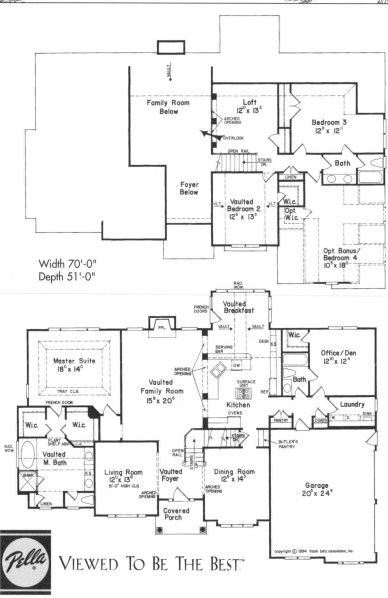

Pella VIEWED TO BE THE BEST.™

Complete Pella Window Specifications Provided With Every Home Plan

WINDOWSCAPING®

Design by
Frank Betz Associates, Inc.

DESIGN P118

First Floor: 2,044 square feet
Second Floor: 896 square feet
Total: 2,940 square feet
Bonus Room: 197 square feet

■ A gracious front porch off the formal dining room and a two-story entry set the tone for this elegant home. A front living room is set to the front of the plan, thoughtfully separated from casual family areas. The two-story family room is framed by a balcony hall and accented with a fireplace and serving bar. The first-floor master suite features a sitting area, lush bath and a walk-in closet. Upstairs, two family bedrooms share a hall bath while a third enjoys a private bath. Please specify basement or crawlspace foundation when ordering.

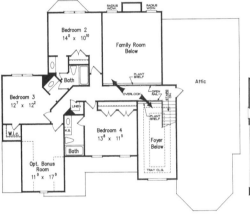

Width 63'-0"
Depth 54'-0"

DESIGN P141

First Floor: 2,211 square feet
Second Floor: 719 square feet
Total: 2,930 square feet
Bonus Room: 331 square feet

■ Stucco, stone and intricate detailing give this home a pleasing facade. Inside, the two-story foyer leads to a family room with a welcoming fireplace. The kitchen shares open space with a sunlit, bayed breakfast room with French-door access to the backyard. A luxurious master suite and a corner office complete the first floor. Upstairs, two bedrooms share a full bath, and a loft overlooks the family room. Please specify basement or crawlspace foundation when ordering.

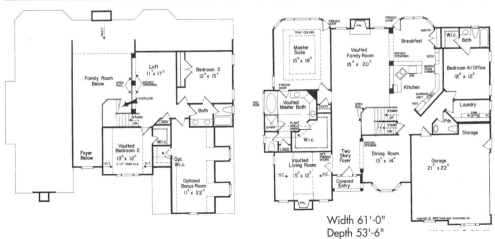

Width 61'-0"
Depth 53'-6"

Complete Pella Window Specifications Provided With Every Home Plan

© 1997 Donald A. Gardner Architects, Inc.

B. NATHAN

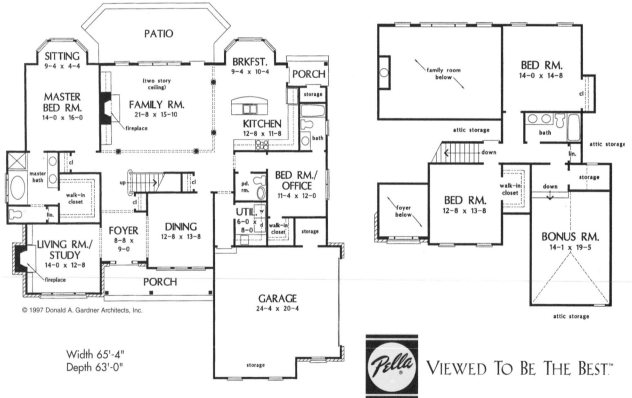

PATIO

SITTING
9-4 x 4-4

MASTER BED RM.
14-0 x 16-0

(two story ceiling)

FAMILY RM.
21-8 x 15-10

fireplace

BRKFST.
9-4 x 10-4

PORCH

storage

KITCHEN
12-8 x 11-8

bath

master bath

cl

walk-in closet

lin.

up

cl

cl

BED RM./OFFICE
11-4 x 12-0

pd. rm.

UTIL
6-0 x 8-0

walk-in closet

storage

LIVING RM./STUDY
14-0 x 12-8

fireplace

FOYER
8-8 x 9-0

DINING
12-8 x 13-8

PORCH

GARAGE
24-4 x 20-4

storage

© 1997 Donald A. Gardner Architects, Inc.

Width 65'-4"
Depth 63'-0"

family room below

BED RM.
14-0 x 14-8

cl

attic storage

bath

attic storage

down

lin.

foyer below

BED RM.
12-8 x 13-8

walk-in closet

storage

down

BONUS RM.
14-1 x 19-5

attic storage

Pella®

VIEWED TO BE THE BEST™

DESIGN 7633

First Floor: 2,293 square feet
Second Floor: 623 square feet
Total: 2,916 square feet
Bonus Room: 359 square feet

■ This four-bedroom design caters to a time when the family room was the heart of a home, and family gatherings were its soul. From the covered porch, the foyer leads either to a cozy living room/study on the left, to a formal dining room on the right, or straight ahead to this home's heart, a two-story family room with a fireplace and rear patio access. The adjacent kitchen features an island work-top, a bayed breakfast nook and access to a side porch. The private master bedroom features a bayed sitting area and a master bath with dual sinks, a separate tub and shower and a walk-in closet. Another bedroom on the first floor can be used as a guest room or an office. Two family bedrooms on the second floor share a full hall bath. A bonus room is available as needed.

Complete Pella Window Specifications Provided With Every Home Plan

WINDOWSCAPING®

Design by
Alan Mascord Design Associates, Inc.

DESIGN 9553

First Floor: 1,466 square feet
Second Floor: 1,369 square feet
Total: 2,835 square feet

■ Multi-pane windows and keystones enhance the beauty of this impressive two-story home. From the bay-windowed living room, to the casual family room, this plan caters to the active lifestyles of today's family. The large, U-shaped kitchen contains an island cooktop and a sunny nook nearby that supplies access to a covered porch. Upstairs, the master suite is designed for the ultimate in luxury. Three family bedrooms, a full bath and a den complete the second floor.

Complete Pella Window Specifications Provided With Every Home Plan

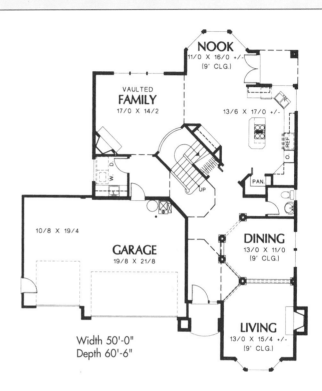

Width 50'-0"
Depth 60'-6"

DESIGN P354

First Floor: 2,165 square feet
Second Floor: 776 square feet
Total: 2,941 square feet
Bonus Room: 281 square feet

■ Stone adds texture and frames the gabled entry of an exterior that borrows design elements from the best of European style. Step inside to a foyer that soars to the second story, providing a grand entrance. Formal living and dining rooms are situated at the front of the plan, while the great room, kitchen and breakfast room—designed for casual gatherings—are located at the rear. A tray ceiling adds interest to the first-floor master bedroom; the master bath, with all its amenities invites relaxation. Secondary bedrooms—three in all—are found on the second floor. They share two full baths and enjoy a balcony that overlooks the spacious great room below. Please specify basement or crawlspace foundation when ordering.

Width 63'-0"
Depth 55'-0"

Complete Pella Window Specifications Provided With Every Home Plan

WINDOWSCAPING®

Design by
Living Concepts Home Planning

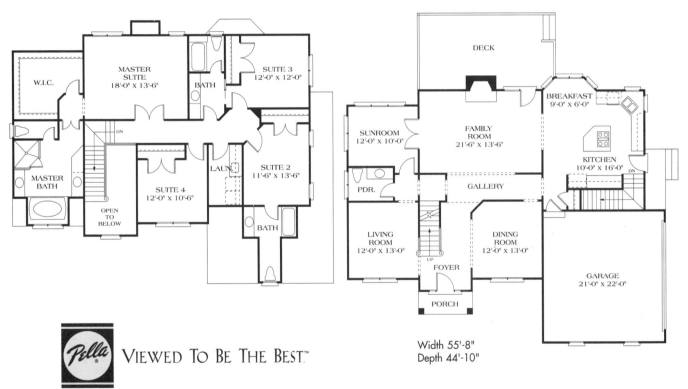

VIEWED TO BE THE BEST.

Width 55'-8"
Depth 44'-10"

DESIGN A137

First Floor: 1,458 square feet
Second Floor: 1,513 square feet
Total: 2,971 square feet

■ This classic French garden home exudes charm from every window. The columned porch opens into the entry foyer with open dining room on the right and stairs to the second level and the formal living room on the left. The large family room features a fireplace and access to the outside deck.

Abundant light enters through a glass-sided sunroom and the bay-windowed breakfast area adjacent to the corner kitchen. Upstairs, an enormous walk-in closet can be reached from either the bedroom or bath in the master suite. A laundry room and three additional bedrooms are also on this level.

Complete Pella Window Specifications Provided With Every Home Plan

WINDOWSCAPING®

Form and Function

Design by
Alan Mascord Design Associates, Inc.

DESIGN 9597

First Floor: 1,470 square feet
Second Floor: 1,269 square feet
Total: 2,739 square feet

■ Symmetry, stucco, multi-pane windows and an elegantly covered front entry combine to give this design plenty of curb appeal. Inside, the grand two-story foyer presents a formal living room to the left, complete with warming fireplace and opening to the rear into the formal dining room. A cozy den to the right of the foyer is entered through double doors. A large island kitchen awaits the gourmet of the family and offers a walk-in pantry, a corner sink with windows and plenty of counter and cabinet space. Access to the rear yard is available from the nearby bayed nook. A vaulted family room is perfect for casual gatherings and offers another fireplace. Upstairs, three family bedrooms share a full hall bath with twin vanities. The deluxe master suite reigns supreme and pampers with a walk-in closet, a spa tub, a separate shower, a dual-sink vanity and a compartmented toilet.

Complete Pella Window Specifications Provided With Every Home Plan

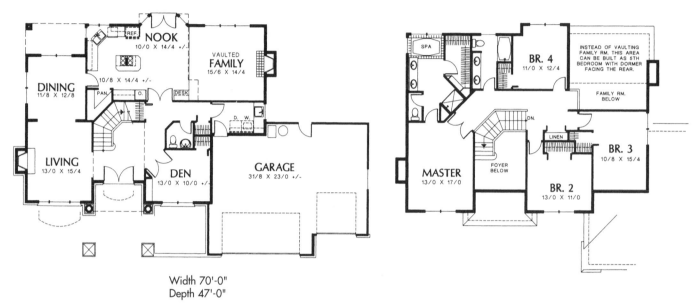

Width 70'-0"
Depth 47'-0"

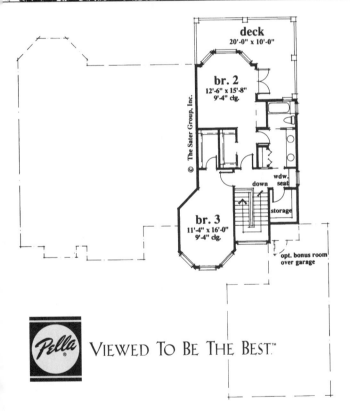

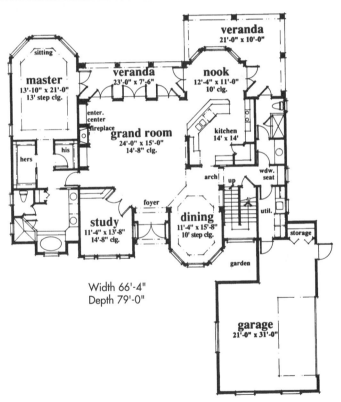

deck
20'-0" x 10'-0"

br. 2
12'-6" x 15'-8"
9'-4" clg.

© The Sater Group, Inc.

down

wdw. seat

storage

br. 3
11'-4" x 16'-0"
9'-4" clg.

opt. bonus room over garage

sitting

master
13'-10" x 21'-0"
13' step clg.

enter. center fireplace

hers

his

veranda
23'-0" x 7'-6"

grand room
24'-0" x 15'-0"
14'-8" clg.

arch

foyer

study
11'-4" x 13'-8"
14'-8" clg.

dining
11'-4" x 15'-8"
10' step clg.

garden

veranda
21'-0" x 10'-0"

nook
12'-4" x 11'-0"
10' clg.

kitchen
14' x 14'

wdw. seat

up

util.

storage

garage
21'-0" x 31'-0"

Width 66'-4"
Depth 79'-0"

Pella
VIEWED TO BE THE BEST™

DESIGN 6652

First Floor: 2,181 square feet
Second Floor: 710 square feet
Total: 2,891 square feet

■ An arched, covered porch presents fine double doors leading to a spacious foyer in this decidedly European home. A two-story tower contains an elegant formal dining room on the first floor and a spacious bedroom on the second floor. The grand room is aptly named with a fireplace, a built-in entertainment center and three sets of doors opening onto the veranda. A large kitchen is ready to please the gourmet of the family with a big walk-in pantry and a sunny, bay-windowed eating nook. The secluded master suite is luxury in itself. A bay-windowed sitting area, access to the rear veranda, His and Hers walk-in closets and a lavish bath are all set to pamper you. Upstairs, two bedrooms, both with walk-in closets, share a full hall bath with twin vanities. Please specify basement or slab foundation when ordering.

Complete Pella Window Specifications Provided With Every Home Plan

DESIGN 8254

First Floor: 1,718 square feet
Second Floor: 1,089 square feet
Total: 2,807 square feet

■ Inside this charming Victorian-style home a bay window frames the formal dining room to the left of the foyer. Casual meals can be enjoyed in the adjacent kitchen and breakfast room which offers easy access to the front covered porch. The first-floor master suite is filled with amenities that include a sun-filled sitting room, two walk-in closets and a bath designed for relaxation. Upstairs, two family bedrooms offer access to outdoor balconies and share a full bath. Please specify crawlspace or slab foundation when ordering.

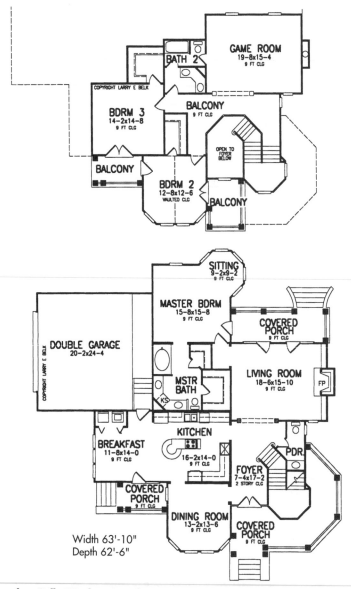

Width 63'-10"
Depth 62'-6"

Complete Pella Window Specifications Provided With Every Home Plan

WINDOWSCAPING®

Design by
Alan Mascord Design Associates, Inc.

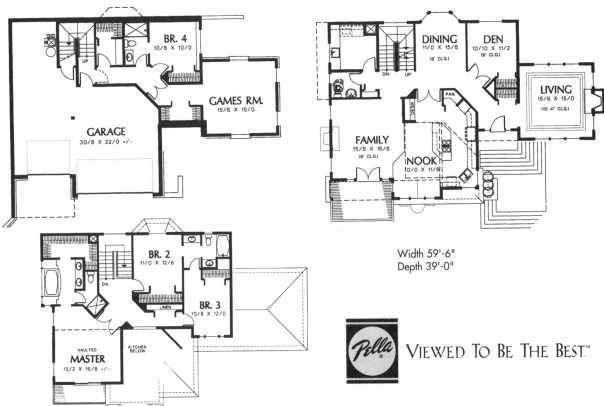

BR. 4
10/8 X 10/0

GAMES RM.
15/6 X 15/0

GARAGE
30/8 X 22/0 +/-

DINING
11/0 X 15/6
(9' CLG.)

DEN
10/10 X 11/2
(9' CLG.)

LIVING
15/6 X 15/0
(10'-4" CLG.)

FAMILY
15/6 X 16/6
(9' CLG.)

NOOK
10/0 X 11/6

BR. 2
11/0 X 12/6

BR. 3
10/8 X 12/0

LINEN

VAULTED
MASTER
15/2 X 16/8 +/-

KITCHEN
BELOW

Width 59'-6"
Depth 39'-0"

Pella
VIEWED TO BE THE BEST™

DESIGN 7417

Main Level: 1,594 square feet
Upper Level: 1,038 square feet
Lower Level: 88 square feet
Total: 2,720 square feet
Basement Development: 662 square feet

■ Besides being a truly attractive design, this home is comfortable and makes an excellent use of space. The main living area is on the first floor and is designed to hold formal living and dining rooms, a large family room and a private den. The island kitchen and nook serve as the hub of this floor. Upstairs are two family bedrooms sharing a full bath, and a vaulted master suite. For additional space, the lower level offers a bedroom and full bath plus a games room.

Complete Pella Window Specifications Provided With Every Home Plan

DESIGN 6698

First Floor: 1,684 square feet
Second Floor: 1,195 square feet
Total: 2,879 square feet

■ Stunning New South charm flavors this reinterpretation of Key West island style. Asymmetrical rooflines set off a grand turret and a two-story bay that allows glorious views from within. Glass doors open the great room to a deck, while arch-top clerestory windows enhance the casual atmosphere with natural light. The gourmet kitchen boasts a center island with an eating bar for easy meals, plus a windowed wrapping counter. A winding staircase leads to a luxurious master suite that features a morning kitchen and opens onto a master balcony. The gallery hall leads to a study, which enjoys wide views through a front bay window.

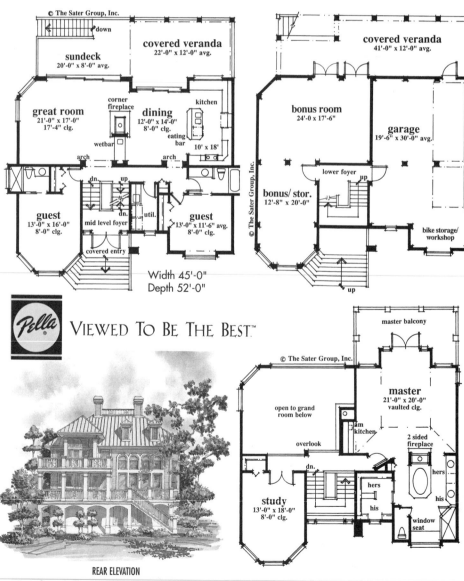

© The Sater Group, Inc.

sundeck
20'-0" x 8'-0" avg.

covered veranda
22'-0" x 12'-0" avg.

great room
21'-0" x 17'-0"
17'-4" clg.

corner fireplace

dining
12'-0" x 14'-0"
8'-0" clg.

kitchen

wetbar

eating bar

10' x 18'

arch

arch

dn.

up

guest
13'-0" x 16'-0"
8'-0" clg.

mid level foyer

dn.

util.

guest
13'-0" x 11'-6" avg.
8'-0" clg.

covered entry

Width 45'-0"
Depth 52'-0"

covered veranda
41'-0" x 12'-0" avg.

bonus room
24'-0 x 17'-6"

garage
19'-6" x 30'-0" avg.

lower foyer

up

bonus/ stor.
12'-8" x 20'-0"

bike storage/ workshop

up

© The Sater Group, Inc.

VIEWED TO BE THE BEST™

© The Sater Group, Inc.

master balcony

master
21'-0" x 20'-0"
vaulted clg.

open to grand room below

am kitchen

overlook

2 sided fireplace

dn.

hers

hers

his

his

study
13'-0" x 18'-0"
8'-0" clg.

window seat

REAR ELEVATION

Complete Pella Window Specifications Provided With Every Home Plan

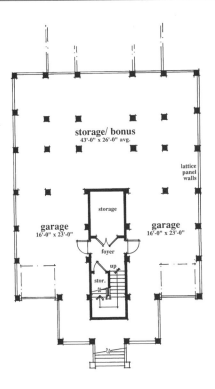

storage/ bonus
43'-0" x 26'-0" avg.

lattice
panel
walls

garage
16'-0" x 23'-0"

storage

garage
16'-0" x 23'-0"

foyer

up

stor.

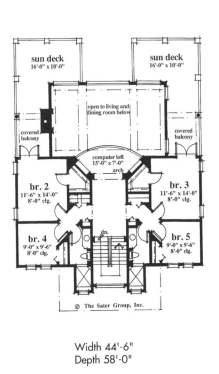

sun deck
16'-0" x 10'-0"

sun deck
16'-0" x 10'-0"

open to living and
dining room below

covered
balcony

covered
balcony

computer loft
15'-0" x 7'-0"

arch

br. 2
11'-6" x 14'-0"
8'-0" clg.

br. 3
11'-6" x 14'-0"
8'-0" clg.

dn.

br. 4
9'-0" x 9'-6"
8'-0" clg.

br. 5
9'-0" x 9'-6"
8'-0" clg.

© The Sater Group, Inc.

Width 44'-6"
Depth 58'-0"

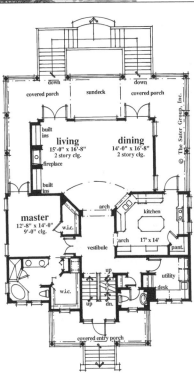

down

down

covered porch

sundeck

covered porch

built
ins

living
15'-0" x 16'-8"
2 story clg.

dining
14'-0" x 16'-8"
2 story clg.

fireplace

built
ins

arch

kitchen

master
12'-8" x 14'-0"
9'-0" clg.

w.i.c.

17' x 14'

arch

vestibule

pant.

w.i.c.

up

utility

up

dn.

desk

covered entry porch

© The Sater Group, Inc.

DESIGN 6689

Main Level: 1,642 square feet
Upper Level: 1,165 square feet
Lower Entry: 150 square feet
Total: 2,957 square feet

■ Prevailing summer breezes find their way through many joyful rooms in this Neoclassical Revival design. Inspired by 19th-Century Key West houses, the exterior is beautiful with Doric columns, lattice and fretwork, and a glass-paneled, arched entry. The mid-level foyer eases the trip from ground level to living and dining areas, which offer flexible space for planned events or cozy gatherings. Two sets of French doors lead out to the gallery and sundeck, and a two-story picture window invites natural light and a spirit of *bon vivant* to pour into the heart of the home.

Complete Pella Window Specifications Provided With Every Home Plan

**Design by
Donald A. Gardner Architects, Inc.**

DESIGN 7617

First Floor: 1,847 square feet
Second Floor: 964 square feet
Total: 2,811 square feet
Bonus Room: 413 square feet

■ Two covered porches will entice you outside, while the large multi-pane windows bring the outdoors in. The foyer opens directly into the formal living and dining rooms, with attractive columns framing their boundaries. The casual living area is spacious, flowing freely from the breakfast room to the family room, which boasts a fireplace and a cathedral ceiling. The master suite completes the first floor. The upstairs hallway overlooks the living room and foyer while connecting three bedrooms and a bonus room.

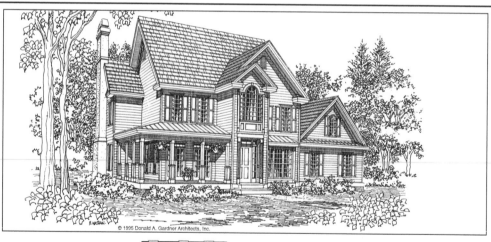

Width 61'-8"
Depth 64'-4"

DESIGN 9785

First Floor: 1,989 square feet
Second Floor: 854 square feet
Total: 2,843 square feet

■ A Palladian window set above the entry of this two-story home creates a new look in farmhouse exteriors. Natural light casts a warm glow on the foyer, which leads to formal rooms and casual living space. A gourmet kitchen serves the formal dining room through a butler's pantry, and leads out to a rear deck. The first-floor master suite offers a sizable walk-in closet and a skylit bath filled with amenities. Upstairs, three bedrooms share a full bath and a bonus room.

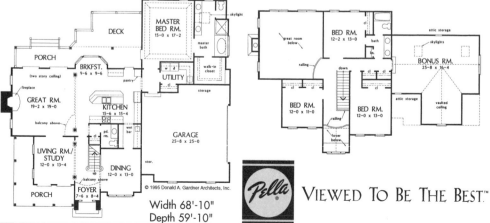

Width 68'-10"
Depth 59'-10"

Pella

VIEWED TO BE THE BEST™

Complete Pella Window Specifications Provided With Every Home Plan

WINDOWSCAPING®

Design by
Donald A. Gardner Architects, Inc.

DESIGN 9787

First Floor: 2,184 square feet
Second Floor: 678 square feet
Total: 2,862 square feet

■ A pillared, covered porch and circle-top windows lend a new spirit to the quaint, country charm of this great farmhouse-style home. Immediately off the foyer are a formal living room with a tiered ceiling, and a study or a guest room. The great room, located at the rear of the plan, is graced by a fireplace and access to the large rear deck and opens to a formal dining room. The large country kitchen is further enhanced by an attractive breakfast area. Designed for privacy, the master suite offers an abundance of walk-in closet space and a luxurious bath. Upstairs, two family bedrooms share a full bath and access to a large bonus room over the two-car garage.

Complete Pella Window Specifications Provided With Every Home Plan

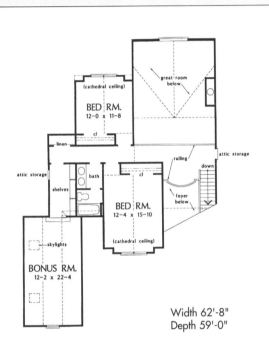

Width 62'-8"
Depth 59'-0"

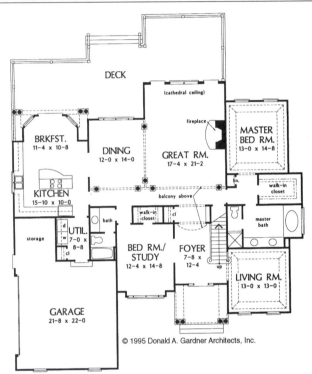

© 1995 Donald A. Gardner Architects, Inc.

B. NATHAN © 1995 Donald A. Gardner Architects, Inc.

WINDOWSCAPING®

Design by
Living Concepts Home Planning

DESIGN A132

Square Footage: 2,774
Bonus Room: 367 square feet

■ Warm and welcoming, this compact three-bedroom home includes an optional bonus room in the attic. Three bay windows across the rear of the plan highlight the master bedroom, breakfast nook and large gathering room. An adjacent kitchen easily serves all living areas. Two family bedroom suites have private baths and large closets. The master suite features His and Hers walk-in closets, dual vanities and an oval garden tub.

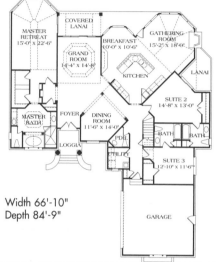

Width 66'-10"
Depth 84'-9"

Design by
Living Concepts Home Planning

Pella VIEWED TO BE THE BEST™

Design by
Design Basics Inc.

DESIGN 7339

First Floor: 2,098 square feet
Second Floor: 790 square feet
Total: 2,888 square feet

■ Outside, the symmetry of this home creates a strong impression. Inside, varying levels and textures generate interest. To the left of the entry, the living room boasts an eleven-foot ceiling. Further inside, the tiled area forms a right angle around a curved dining room. The master suite features access to the covered porch, a whirlpool tub and compartmented bathroom. The secondary bedrooms are nicely appointed. Bedroom 4 enjoys a private bathroom while Bedrooms 2 and 3 share a full bath.

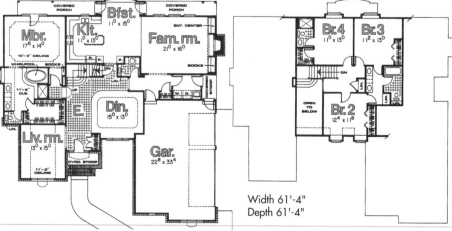

Width 61'-4"
Depth 61'-4"

Complete Pella Window Specifications Provided With Every Home Plan

Width 94'-1"
Depth 67'-4"

Quote One®

Cost to build? See page 182
to order complete cost estimate
to build this house in your area!

DESIGN 3612

Square Footage: 2,946

L

■ Varying hip roof planes complement a glass-paneled entry and divided-light transoms that reflect a well-articulated style and make a bold statement. The tiled foyer opens to formal and casual living areas, defined by arched colonnades and set off by an extended-hearth fireplace in the family room. The gourmet kitchen boasts a food preparation island, an angled snack bar and a walk-in pantry. A guest suite, or study, resides just off the living area. The secluded master suite enjoys a private patio with a spa, as well as a spacious bath with a box-bay whirlpool tub, twin lavatories and a knee-space vanity. A home office or den with a separate entry and porch, and two family bedrooms with a full bath complete the plan.

Complete Pella Window Specifications Provided With Every Home Plan

DESIGN 3631

Square Footage: 2,831

L

■ A triple-arched portico frames the entry to this Mediterranean design, while turrets on either side feature multi-pane windows with circle-head tops. The rear of the home is open; here the family room and U-shaped kitchen offer access to a covered patio for enhanced indoor-outdoor relationships. Filled with amenities, the master suite offers walk-in closets, a private office with a covered porch, an exercise area and access to a deck where a spa awaits. Three family bedrooms—one with a private porch—share a full bath.

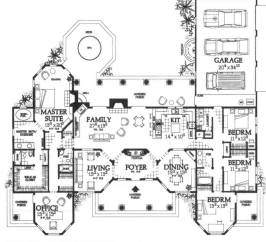

QUOTE ONE®

Cost to build? See page 182
to order complete cost estimate
to build this house in your area!

Width 84'-0"
Depth 77'-0"

Design by
The Sater Design Collection

DESIGN 6663

Square Footage: 2,978

■ This gracious home features a series of arched windows and a deep hipped roof that are reminiscent of historical styles yet have the flavor of a contemporary sun-country home. The high entry porch opens to the gallery foyer, the living room and dining area—both share sliding glass doors to the veranda. Casual living is simply elegant in the demonstration kitchen with a breakfast nook and adjoining leisure room. Two family bedrooms share a full hall bath. The master suite is well appointed with a private garden, spa-style bath and twin closets.

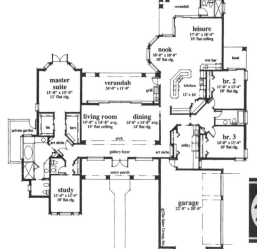

Width 84'-0"
Depth 90'-0"

VIEWED TO BE THE BEST™

Complete Pella Window Specifications Provided With Every Home Plan

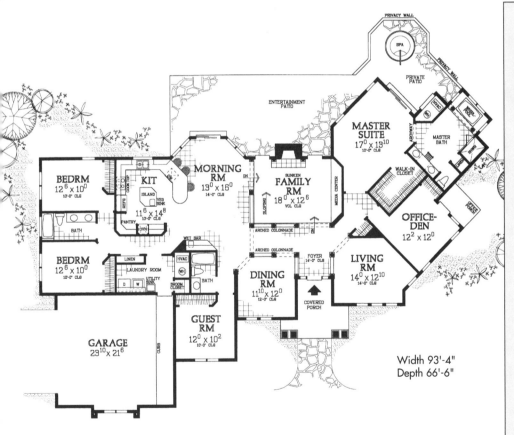

Width 93'-4"
Depth 66'-6"

QUOTE ONE®

Cost to build? See page 182
to order complete cost estimate
to build this house in your area!

DESIGN 3638

Square Footage: 2,861

L

■ Double columns and an arched entry create a grand entrance to this elegant one-story home. Inside, arched colonnades add grace and definition to the formal living and dining rooms as well as the family room. The master suite occupies a separate wing, providing a private retreat. Treat yourself to luxury in the master bath which includes a bumped-out whirlpool tub, a separate shower and twin vanities. An office/den located nearby easily converts to a nursery. A snack bar provides space for meals on-the-go and separates the island kitchen from the bay-windowed morning room. Two family bedrooms share a full hall bath with dual vanities. The central guest bedroom has an adjacent full bath.

Complete Pella Window Specifications Provided With Every Home Plan

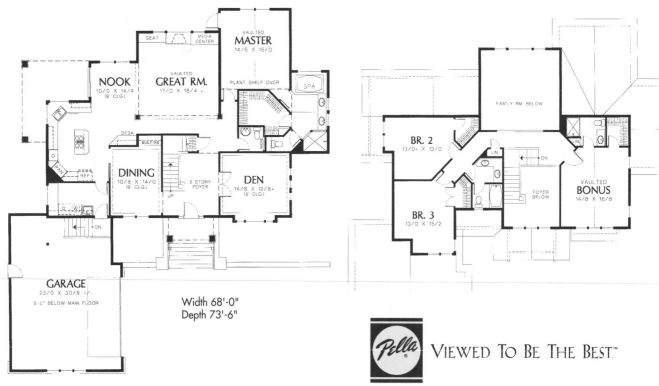

NOOK
10/0 X 14/4
(9' CLG.)

SEAT — MEDIA CENTER

VAULTED
MASTER
14/6 X 16/0

VAULTED
GREAT RM.
17/0 X 18/4 +

PLANT SHELF OVER

SPA

DESK
BUILT-INS

DINING
10/8 X 14/0
(9' CLG.)

2 STORY
FOYER

UP

DEN
14/8 X 12/8+
(9' CLG.)

PAN
REF

DN

GARAGE
23/0 X 30/8 +/-
5'-0" BELOW MAIN FLOOR

Width 68'-0"
Depth 73'-6"

FAMILY RM. BELOW

BR. 2
13/0+ X 13/0

LIN

DN.

LIN

BR. 3
13/0 X 15/2

FOYER
BELOW

VAULTED
BONUS
14/8 X 16/8

Pella® VIEWED TO BE THE BEST™

DESIGN 7474

First Floor: 2,005 square feet
Second Floor: 689 square feet
Total: 2,694 square feet
Bonus Room: 356 square feet

■ Incorporating elements from the Arts and Crafts era, this Craftsman-style home is designed to retain the original charm of the period, while providing an amenity-filled floor plan that fits today's lifestyles. From the two-story foyer, you may enter the den for a contemplative moment, or enter the formal dining room. An adjacent U-shaped kitchen shares space with a sun-filled nook. Combined with the kitchen area is a vaulted great room that enjoys warmth from a fireplace framed by a built-in seat and a media center. Completing the first floor is a master suite designed with luxury in mind. Upstairs, an angled hallway leads to two family bedrooms and a shared bath. A large bonus room with its own bathroom and walk-in closet offers flexibility as an additional bedroom.

Complete Pella Window Specifications Provided With Every Home Plan

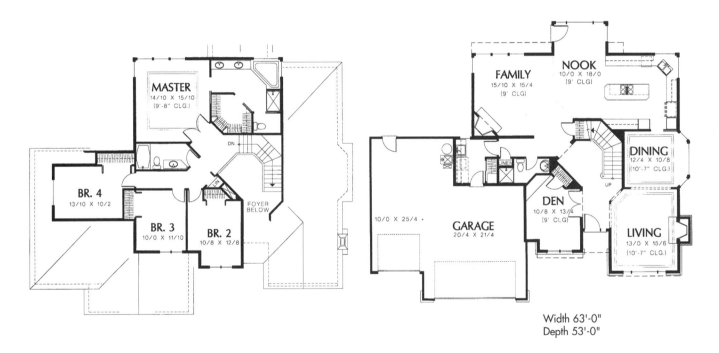

Width 63'-0"
Depth 53'-0"

DESIGN 7473

First Floor: 1,578 square feet
Second Floor: 1,159 square feet
Total: 2,737 square feet

■ It's often said that everything old is new again. The pioneering spirit of the Arts and Crafts movement went beyond simply defining a new trend in home design—it embraced and encouraged a total lifestyle. This adaptation of Craftsman style would certainly please the brothers Greene and Greene. Stone piers, rafter tails that dress up overhanging eaves, and unique window treatments frame an exterior that houses a contemporary floor plan. Open planning cleverly combines the living room and dining room, creating a wealth of space that accommodates any formal occasion. The adjacent kitchen serves the sun-filled nook and family room with equal ease. A conveniently placed laundry room completes the first floor. Upstairs, you'll find four bedrooms—including a grand master suite—and a hall bath.

Complete Pella Window Specifications Provided With Every Home Plan

DESIGN 9798

First Floor: 1,483 square feet
Second Floor: 1,349 square feet
Total: 2,832 square feet
Bonus Room: 486 square feet

■ This country home displays a quaint rural character outside and a savvy sophistication within. The foyer opens on either side to elegant formal areas, beautifully lit with natural light from multi-pane windows. A casual living area opens to the U-shaped kitchen and bayed breakfast nook, and features a focal-point fireplace. The master suite offers a sumptuous bath with a bumped-out whirlpool tub, twin vanities and a generous walk-in closet. Three family bedrooms share a gallery hall that leads to a spacious bonus room.

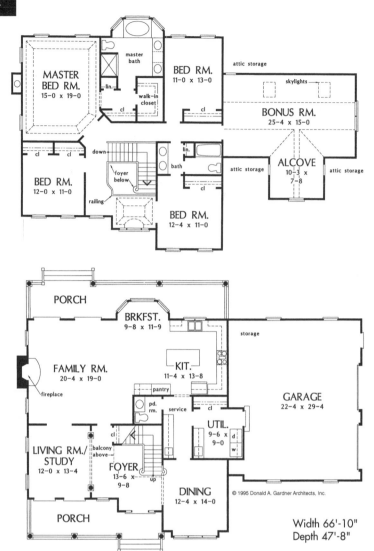

MASTER BED RM.
15-0 x 19-0

master bath

BED RM.
11-0 x 13-0

attic storage

skylights

walk-in closet

BONUS RM.
25-4 x 15-0

BED RM.
12-0 x 11-0

down

foyer below

railing

bath

attic storage

ALCOVE
10-3 x 7-8

attic storage

BED RM.
12-4 x 11-0

PORCH

BRKFST.
9-8 x 11-9

storage

FAMILY RM.
20-4 x 19-0

KIT.
11-4 x 13-8

fireplace

pantry

GARAGE
22-4 x 29-4

pd. rm.

service

cl

UTIL.
9-6 x 9-0

LIVING RM./STUDY
12-0 x 13-4

balcony above

FOYER
13-6 x 9-8

up

DINING
12-4 x 14-0

© 1995 Donald A. Gardner Architects, Inc.

Width 66'-10"
Depth 47'-8"

© 1995 Donald A. Gardner Architects, Inc.

ELEGANT TRADITIONS;
Graceful homes produce a clear choice of styles

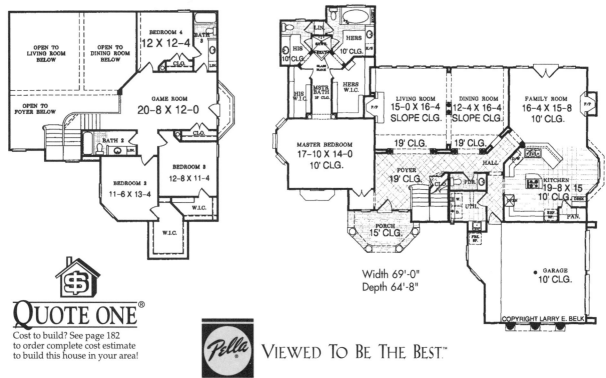

QUOTE ONE®

Cost to build? See page 182
to order complete cost estimate
to build this house in your area!

Pella VIEWED TO BE THE BEST™

Width 69'-0"
Depth 64'-8"

COPYRIGHT LARRY E. BELK

DESIGN 8026

First Floor: 2,188 square feet
Second Floor: 1,110 square feet
Total: 3,298 square feet

■ This brick and stucco home with European style showcases an arched entry and presents a commanding presence from the curb. Inside, the living room, the dining room and the family room are located at the rear of the home to provide wide open views of the rear grounds beyond. A colonnade with connecting arches defines the space for a living room with a fireplace and the dining room. The spacious master suite features a relaxing sitting area, His and Hers closets and an extravagant master bath. Take special note of the private His and Hers bathrooms. On the second floor, three bedrooms, two baths and a game room complete the home.

Complete Pella Window Specifications Provided With Every Home Plan

Design by
Larry E. Belk Designs

BRKFST ROOM
13-6 X 9-0
10 FT CLG

PORCH

HIS

MASTER
BATH
10 FT CLG

SEAT

LIVING ROOM
17-0 X 15-0
2 STORY CLG

KITCHEN
14-0 X 15-0
10 FT CLG

IC LEDGE

FAMILY ROOM
15-0 X 16-0
10 FT CLG

FP

K.S.

HERS

PANTRY

UTIL
6-0 X 6-6

STOR

MASTER BEDRM
13-4 X 15-6
10 FT CLG

ARCH

FOYER
2 STORY CLG

PWDR

DINING ROOM
11-6 X 12-0
10 FT CLG

COPYRIGHT LARRY E. BELK

PORCH

GARAGE

Width 64'-6"
Depth 55'-10"

ATTIC

OPEN TO LIVING ROOM BELOW

BEDROOM 3
13-8 X 12-0

BATH 2

LIN

DRESSING

GAME ROOM
14-6 X 16-4

BEDROOM 2
13-8 X 12-0

OPEN TO
FOYER
BELOW

BATH
3

DRESSING

BEDROOM 4
11-6 X 12-4

EXPANDABLE AREA
13-0 X 22-0

Pella

VIEWED TO BE THE BEST.™

DESIGN 8186

First Floor: 1,919 square feet
Second Floor: 1,190 square feet
Total: 3,109 square feet

■ A uniquely beautiful entrance is framed by huge columns topped by elegant arches to welcome you into this classic European-style home. Inside, the formal dining room to the right of the foyer is defined by yet another set of columns and arches. The appealing living room offers access to the rear yard via two sets of double French doors. A gourmet kitchen is conveniently located between the dining room and the sunny breakfast room. An inviting family room with a fireplace and access to the rear porch is also nearby. The deluxe master suite, with its lavish bath and His and Hers walk-in closets, completes the main level. Upstairs, one large bedroom includes its own full bath and may be used as a guest suite. Two other bedrooms share a full bath and access to a huge game room. Please specify crawlspace or slab foundation when ordering.

Complete Pella Window Specifications Provided With Every Home Plan

WINDOWSCAPING®

Design by
Larry E. Belk Designs

COPYRIGHT LARRY E. BELK

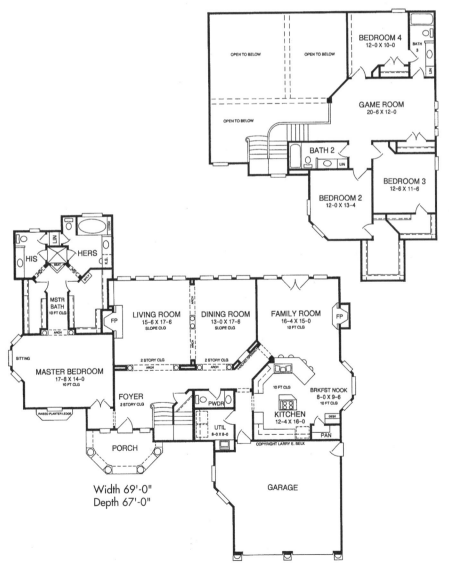

Width 69'-0"
Depth 67'-0"

DESIGN 8111

First Floor: 2,188 square feet
Second Floor: 1,110 square feet
Total: 3,298 square feet

■ Classic elegance supplies this home with its unique Old World style. Inside, all gathering and entertaining areas are combined at the rear, contributing to a plan that is ideal for a golf course or vacation site. Elegant columns on pedestals define the living room and the dining room. The first-floor master suite features separate His and Hers baths and a sitting area formed by a bay window. Three additional bedrooms, two full baths and an oversized game room are located on the second floor. Please specify crawlspace or slab foundation when ordering.

Complete Pella Window Specifications Provided With Every Home Plan

COPYRIGHT LARRY E. BELK

DESIGN 8110

First Floor: 2,469 square feet
Second Floor: 1,025 square feet
Total: 3,494 square feet

■ This design spotlights super entertaining areas with a columned dining and living room. Double sets of French doors lead out to the rear covered porch, making the living room even more versatile for gatherings. Informal areas take off with a combined kitchen, breakfast room and family room. A study or bedroom and a master suite complete the first floor. On the second floor, two bedrooms enjoy a nearby gameroom. Please specify crawlspace or slab foundation when ordering.

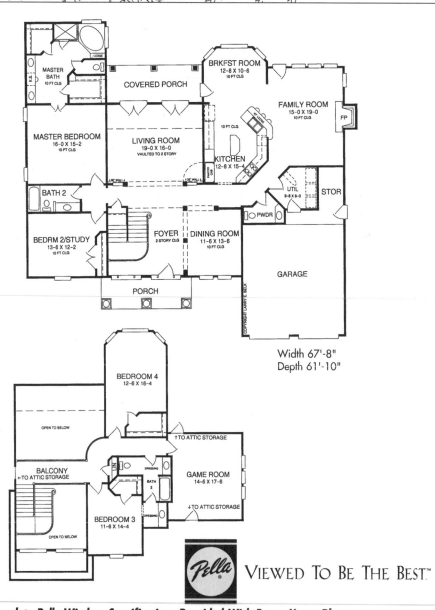

Width 67'-8"
Depth 61'-10"

VIEWED TO BE THE BEST.™

Complete Pella Window Specifications Provided With Every Home Plan

WINDOWSCAPING®

Design by
Design Basics Inc.

DESIGN 7243

First Floor: 2,235 square feet
Second Floor: 1,003 square feet
Total: 3,238 square feet
Bonus Room: 274 square feet

■ This traditional elevation is captivated by a dramatic bay, a stunning entrance and attractive window accents. The grand entry opens to a formal dining room with a bay window and to a formal living room with a through-fireplace to the hearth room. The cozy hearth room includes a sunny breakfast bay and is complemented by an island kitchen. French doors off the front stairs reveal a glorious mid-level master suite with a private den and an impressive master bath featuring a whirlpool tub, dual lavs and a large walk-in closet. On the upper level, Bedroom 2 is accented with ceiling details, a walk-in closet and a private bath, while Bedrooms 3 and 4 share a Hollywood bath. A bonus room is available for future expansion.

Complete Pella Window Specifications Provided With Every Home Plan

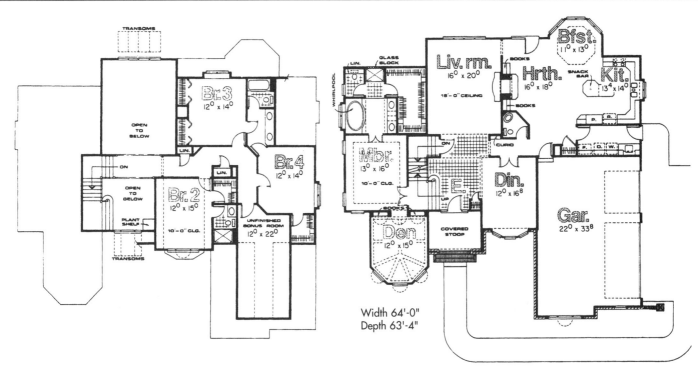

Width 64'-0"
Depth 63'-4"

DESIGN 7266

First Floor: 1,631 square feet
Second Floor: 1,426 square feet
Total: 3,057 square feet

■ Stucco accents and graceful window treatments enhance this charming elevation. Inside, French doors open to a private den with a bright, bayed window. A spacious living room provides natural light through two sets of transom windows, and opens to a vestibule with French doors to an expansive screened veranda. The gourmet kitchen enjoys a bayed breakfast nook and offers a snack bar. Upstairs, a fabulous master suite features a bay window, a dressing area with a built-in dresser, and a privite bath with a corner whirlpool tub. Bedroom 2 enjoys a private bath, while Bedrooms 3 and 4 share a full bath.

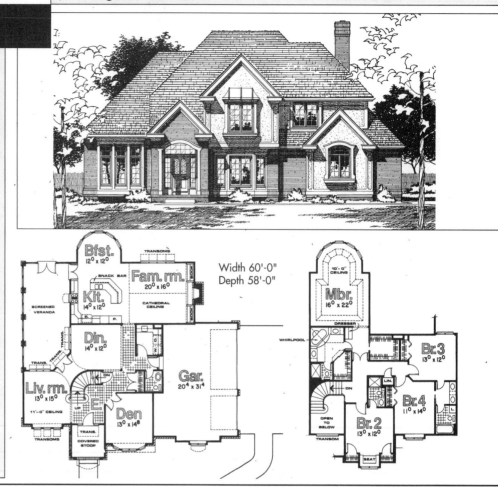

Width 60'-0"
Depth 58'-0"

Design by
Frank Betz Associates, Inc.

DESIGN P224

First Floor: 2,429 square feet
Second Floor: 654 square feet
Total: 3,083 square feet
Bonus Room: 420 square feet

■Keystones that cap each window, a terrace that dresses up the entrance, and a bay-windowed turret add up to a totally refined exterior. Inside, open planning employs columns to define the foyer, dining room and two-story family room. A first-floor master suite is designed with every amenity to answer your needs. Combining the casual living area; the kitchen, breakfast nook and keeping room. The second floor contains two bedrooms, two baths and an optional bonus room.

Width 63'-6"
Depth 71'-4"

Complete Pella Window Specifications Provided With Every Home Plan

WINDOWSCAPING®

Design by
Design Basics Inc.

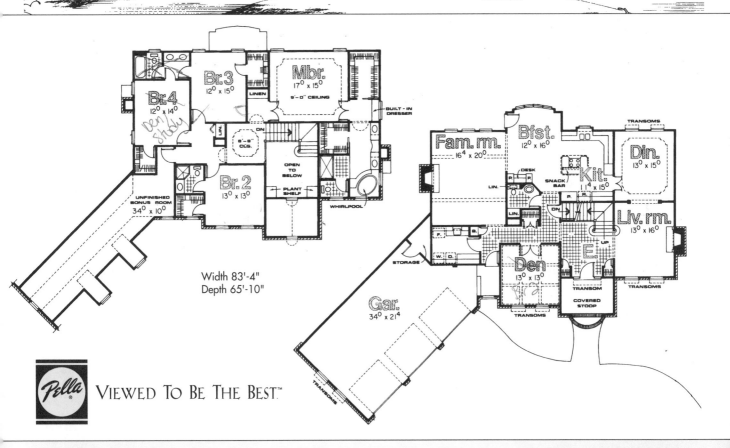

Width 83'-4"
Depth 65'-10"

Br. 4
12⁰ x 14⁰

Br. 3
12⁰ x 15⁰

Mbr.
17⁰ x 15⁰
9'-0" CEILING

LINEN

BUILT - IN DRESSER

8' - 8" CLG.

DN

OPEN TO BELOW

PLANT SHELF

WHIRLPOOL

Br. 2
13⁰ x 13⁰

UNFINISHED BONUS ROOM
34⁰ x 10⁰

Fam. rm.
16⁴ x 20⁰

Bfst.
12⁰ x 16⁰

Din.
13⁰ x 15⁰

Kit.
11⁴ x 15⁰

Liv. rm.
13⁰ x 16⁰

DESK

SNACK BAR

LIN.

LIN.

STORAGE

W./D.

Den
13⁰ x 13⁰

COVERED STOOP

Gar.
34⁰ x 21⁴

TRANSOMS

TRANSOMS

TRANSOMS

TRANSOM

Pella
VIEWED TO BE THE BEST™

DESIGN 7270

First Floor: 1,824 square feet
Second Floor: 1,580 square feet
Total: 3,404 square feet

■ Gabled roofs, numerous windows and an angled garage accent this magnificent elevation. The two-story entry opens to the formal living room with a fireplace and transom windows. The private den has a spider-beam ceiling and transom windows. French doors off the dining room lead to the spacious kitchen with an island cooktop range and a snack bar. In the master suite, two walk-in closets, a built-in dresser, dual lavs, a whirlpool and an open shower are appreciated enhancements. Bedrooms 3 and 4 share a convenient bath while Bedroom 2 features its own private bath. The unfinished bonus room above the garage is excellent for future expansion.

Complete Pella Window Specifications Provided With Every Home Plan

DESIGN 7485

First Floor: 2,532 square feet
Second Floor: 650 square feet
Total: 3,182 square feet
Bonus Room: 383 square feet

■ A garage with barn-like doors and unusual shingled dormers gives this French country home a true country look. Stone accents and wooden shutters add to the appeal. A recessed entry opens to the foyer, where columns and arches define the dining and living rooms. A butler's pantry leads to the island kitchen, part of a large open area that includes a sizable nook and a vaulted family room. Notice the built-ins, the through-fireplace and the wall of windows across the back of the house. To the right of the foyer are a den and the master suite, which offers a large walk-in closet and a fine bath. The second floor holds two more bedrooms, a bath, a bonus room and plenty of attic storage.

Width 80'-0"
Depth 77'-6"

Pella VIEWED TO BE THE BEST™

Complete Pella Window Specifications Provided With Every Home Plan

WINDOWSCAPING®

Design by
Alan Mascord Design Associates, Inc.

Width 90'-6"
Depth 84'-0"

DESIGN 7486

First Floor: 2,698 square feet
Second Floor: 819 square feet
Total: 3,517 square feet
Bonus Room: 370 square feet

■ If you've ever traveled the European country-side, past rolling hills that range in hue from apple green to deep, rich emerald, you may have come upon a home much like this one. Stone accents combined with stucco, and shutters that frame multi-pane windows add a touch of charm that introduces the marvelous floor plan found inside. The foyer opens onto a great room that offers a panoramic view of the veranda and beyond. To the left, a formal dining room; to the right, a quiet den. Just steps away is a sitting room that introduces the grand master suite. A kitchen with nook, laundry room and large shop area complete the first floor. The second floor contains two family bedrooms, two full baths and a bonus room.

Complete Pella Window Specifications Provided With Every Home Plan

Design by
Alan Mascord Design Associates, Inc.

DESIGN 7402

First Floor: 1,740 square feet
Second Floor: 1,477 square feet
Total: 3,217 square feet
Bonus Room: 382 square feet

■ If you have a lot that slopes slightly to the front, this design will accommodate your site with a garage that rests below the main level. The entry is grand, opening to a bay-windowed den on the left and a formal living room with fireplace on the right. Family bedrooms join the master suite on the second floor. Bedroom 3 has a private bath, while Bedrooms 2 and 4 share a hall bath.

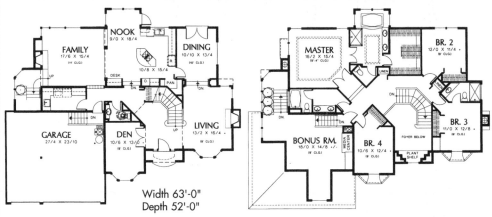

Width 63'-0"
Depth 52'-0"

DESIGN 7442

First Floor: 1,728 square feet
Second Floor: 1,477 square feet
Total: 3,205 square feet
Bonus Room: 382 square feet

■ A stone-and-stucco facade combines with multiple rooflines to give this home plenty of curb appeal. The two-story foyer is flanked by a quiet, bay-windowed den to the left and a formal living room to the right. At the rear of the house is a sunken dining room, spacious island kitchen, and large family room for entertaining ease. Upstairs, two family bedrooms share a full bath while a third bedroom has a private bath. The master bedroom suite has a lavish bath. The bonus room—down half a level—offers access to the family room.

Width 63'-0"
Depth 52'-0"

Complete Pella Window Specifications Provided With Every Home Plan

WINDOWSCAPING®

Design by
Alan Mascord Design Associates, Inc.

DESIGN 9559

First Floor: 1,763 square feet
Second Floor: 1,469 square feet
Total: 3,232 square feet
Bonus Room: 256 square feet

■ This European-style home's floor plan places the formal living and dining rooms together—creating an elegant area for entertaining—and the casual living area to the rear. Open to the breakfast nook and family room, the kitchen also offers easy access to the formal dining room. The family room has a corner fireplace and a built-in media center. A den and powder room complete this floor. Upstairs, the master suite is situated to one side for privacy. Three secondary bedrooms—two that share a private bath—a bonus room, a rear stair and a hall bath round out this floor.

Complete Pella Window Specifications Provided With Every Home Plan

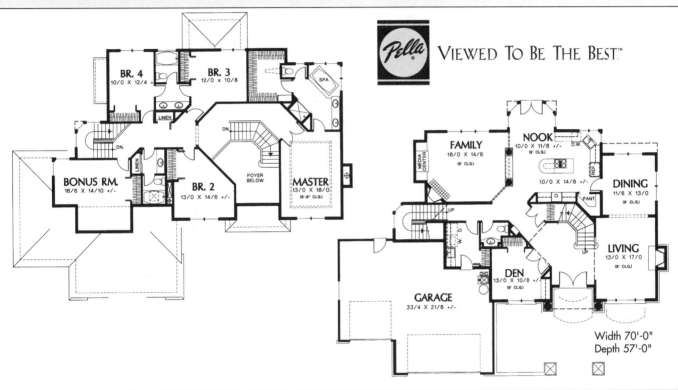

Pella® VIEWED TO BE THE BEST™

DESIGN 9563

First Floor: 1,509 square feet
Second Floor: 1,286 square feet
Bonus Room: 538 square feet
Total: 3,333 square feet

■ Classic French style brings a touch of *joie de vivre* to this exquisite two-story home. Space for formal entertaining is shared by the parlor with its warming fireplace and the baronial dining room. An adjacent gourmet kitchen serves the dining room and breakfast nook with equal ease. The family room features a fireplace, a corner media center, unobstructed views and access to the rear grounds. The second floor contains four bedrooms, including the grand master suite. Steps away, the master bath with a spa that invites relaxation awaits. A large bonus room provides additional space for expansion as it is needed.

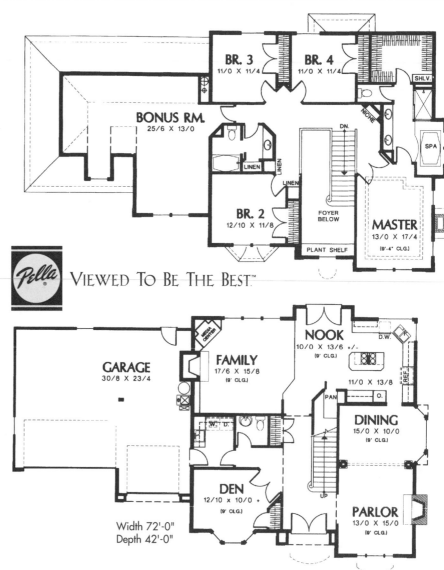

Pella

VIEWED TO BE THE BEST™

Complete Pella Window Specifications Provided With Every Home Plan

WINDOWSCAPING®

Design by
Alan Mascord Design Associates, Inc.

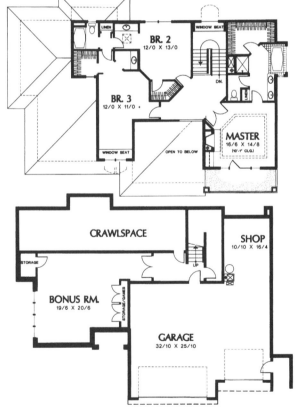

CRAWLSPACE

SHOP
10/10 X 16/4

STORAGE

BONUS RM.
19/6 X 20/6

GARAGE
32/10 X 25/10

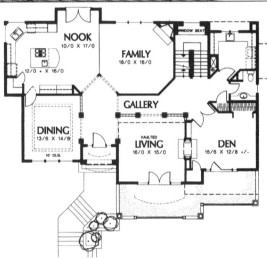

NOOK
10/0 X 17/0

FAMILY
18/0 X 16/0

BR. 2
12/0 X 13/0

WINDOW SEAT

BR. 3
12/0 X 11/0 +

GALLERY

DINING
13/6 X 14/8

LIVING
16/0 X 15/0

DEN
15/6 X 12/8 +/-

MASTER
16/6 X 14/8
(10'-1" CLG)

OPEN TO BELOW

WINDOW SEAT

Width 63'-0"
Depth 48'-0"

QUOTE ONE®

Cost to build? See page 182
to order complete cost estimate
to build this house in your area!

DESIGN 9554

Main Level: 1,989 square feet
Upper Level: 1,349 square feet
Lower Level: 105 square feet
Total: 3,443 square feet
Bonus Room: 487 square feet

■ Balconies and feature windows are as useful as they are luxurious in this roomy home. Inside, a through-fireplace warms the formal living room and den. Both living spaces open onto a balcony that's convenient for relaxing after dinner in the formal dining room. Second-floor sleeping quarters include two bedrooms that share a corner bath. Beyond a set of double doors, the master suite features an extended-hearth fireplace and a private balcony. The lower level accommodates a shop and a bonus room for future development.

Complete Pella Window Specifications Provided With Every Home Plan

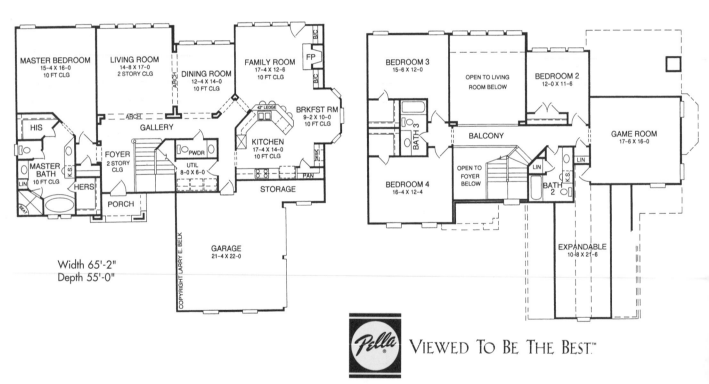

VIEWED TO BE THE BEST™

DESIGN 8225

First Floor: 2,006 square feet
Second Floor: 1,346 square feet
Total: 3,352 square feet

■ Multi-pane windows, mock-shutters and an arched entryway provide this home with a lot of curb appeal. Inside, the two-story foyer opens beneath the balcony to a grand living room where a wall of windows let natural light flow in. An arch leads from this room into an elegant formal dining room, defined by pillars. The large kitchen easily serves the bay-windowed breakfast room, the nearby family room and the formal dining room. In the family room a fireplace is flanked by built-in bookcases and another wall of windows helps to brighten family gatherings. Located on the first floor for privacy, the deluxe master bedroom suite offers many amenities. Upstairs, two bedrooms—each with a walk-in closet—share a full bath, while a third bedroom has access to a separate hall bath. A large game room is also on this level. Please specify crawlspace or slab foundation when ordering.

Complete Pella Window Specifications Provided With Every Home Plan

WINDOWSCAPING®
Design by
Living Concepts Home Planning

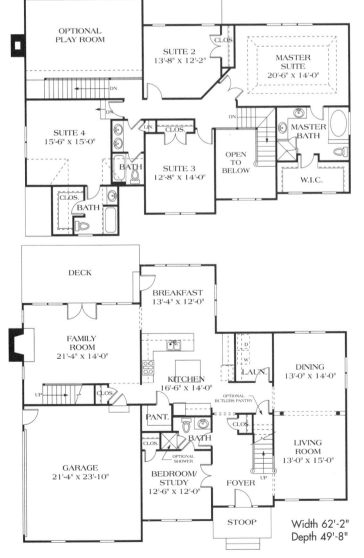

DESIGN A144

First Floor: 1,820 square feet
Second Floor: 1,474 square feet
Total: 3,294 square feet
Bonus Room: 308 square feet

■ Quoins and shutters add fine detailing to this two-story brick home. The study or optional fifth bedroom is to the left of the foyer; on the right a formal living room opens to the formal dining room. A central hall leads to the family room with fireplace and a second stairway to the optional playroom above. The island kitchen offers plenty of storage and is open to the breakfast room. Upstairs, the master suite has a sloped ceiling and large walk-in closet. Two of the three additional bedrooms have linear closets and share a hall bath. The remaining suite has a walk-in closet and private bath.

Complete Pella Window Specifications Provided With Every Home Plan

**Design by
Living Concepts Home Planning**

DESIGN A182

First Floor: 1,404 square feet
Second Floor: 1,613 square feet
Total: 3,017 square feet

■ A two-story foyer filled with light from the front entrance provides a fine introduction to this lovely brick home. Columns separate the formal living room and bay-windowed dining room. Conveniently located nearby, the kitchen contains a window sink, an angled cooktop island, a desk, a walk-in pantry and a multi-windowed breakfast area. The second floor contains a majestic master suite designed to make you feel like royalty. Three additional suites, two full baths and a laundry room complete the plan.

Complete Pella Window Specifications Provided With Every Home Plan

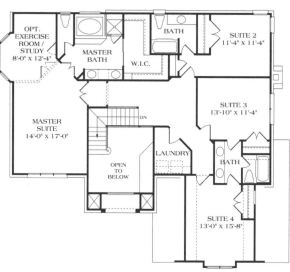

Width 55'-6"
Depth 46'-10"

VIEWED TO BE THE BEST™

WINDOWSCAPING®

Design by
Living Concepts Home Planning

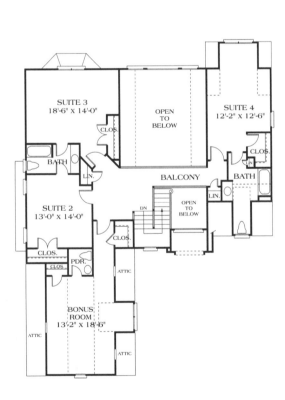

DECK

BREAKFAST
12'-2" x 8'-0"

MASTER SUITE
16'-0" x 18'-0"

GATHERING ROOM

KITCHEN
12'-2" x 13'-0"

PANT.   REF.

W.I.C.

UP

MASTER BATH

PDR.   **FOYER**

DINING ROOM
12'-2" x 13'-6"

LAUNDRY

LIN.

LOGGIA

GARAGE
21'-6" x 21'-0"

Width 52'-2"
Depth 66'-2"

SUITE 3
18'-6" x 14'-0"

OPEN TO BELOW

SUITE 4
12'-2" x 12'-6"

CLOS.

BATH

LIN

CLOS.

BATH

BALCONY

LIN

SUITE 2
13'-0" x 14'-0"

DN

OPEN TO BELOW

CLOS.

CLOS.

PDR.

ATTIC

CLOS

BONUS ROOM
13'-2" x 18'-6"

ATTIC

ATTIC

DESIGN A140

First Floor: 1,846 square feet
Second Floor: 1,249 square feet
Total: 3,095 square feet
Bonus Room: 394 square feet

■ A striking cove entrance sets the tone for this well-planned, two-story traditional design. Inside, the foyer leads directly into the spacious gathering room, open to the second floor, with double-door access to the large rear deck. To the right, the efficient kitchen is nestled between a formal dining room and 12'x8' breakfast nook. The master bedroom suite has a garden bath and large walk-in closet, plus direct access to the deck. Three additional bedrooms are arranged upstairs off the long balcony overlooking the gathering room. Two full baths and a large bonus room with half bath are also on this level.

Complete Pella Window Specifications Provided With Every Home Plan

Design by
Living Concepts Home Planning

DESIGN A122

First Floor: 1,583 square feet
Second Floor: 1,431 square feet
Total: 3,014 square feet

■ A wraparound porch offers additional outside living while giving this design, oriented for front and side views, a great informal feeling. Inside is an economical layout featuring a spacious gathering room and open living and dining room. The full kitchen is easily accessible from both the dining room and breakfast room. A vaulted ceiling gives added dimension to the large sun room. The upstairs master suite offers a spacious bedroom with a tray ceiling and His and Hers walk-in closets. Outside the master suite are a seating area and balcony. There are three additional suites upstairs, including a suite with a private bath.

Complete Pella Window Specifications Provided With Every Home Plan

Width 63'-8"
Depth 59'-4"

VIEWED TO BE THE BEST™

DESIGN A171

First Floor: 2,136 square feet
Second Floor: 1,201 square feet
Total: 3,337 square feet
Bonus Room: 482 square feet

■ From formal entertaining in the elegant front rooms to relaxing on the back deck, this home is perfect for all aspects of your life. The generously sized kitchen offers a cooktop island, pantry, and plenty of counter and cabinet space. It is open to the breakfast area and family room, both of which open onto the wood deck. The family room is large enough for any family gathering and, with its high ceiling and cheerful fireplace, it will be well used. The master bedroom features a tray ceiling and a view of the backyard. Upstairs, the hallway leads to three bedrooms and a bonus room that extends over the garage.

Complete Pella Window Specifications Provided With Every Home Plan

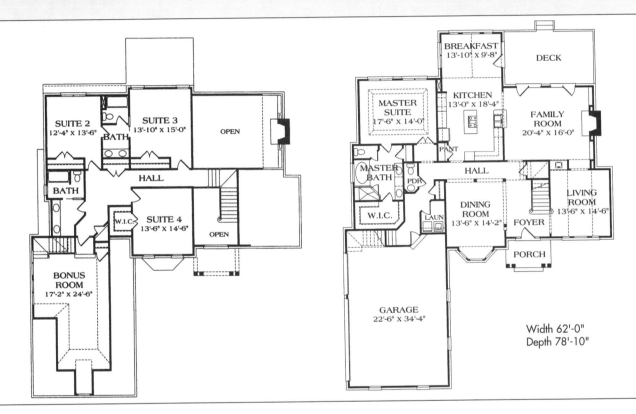

Width 62'-0"
Depth 78'-10"

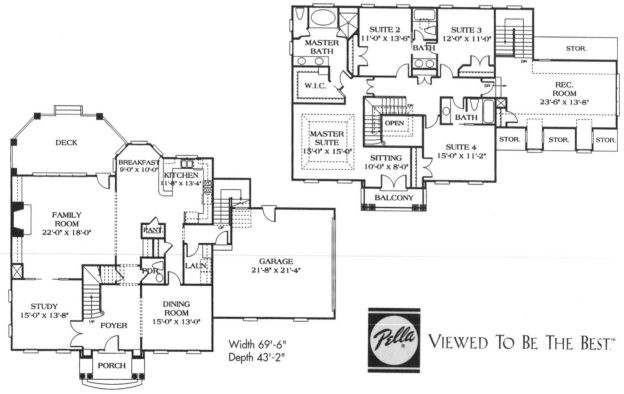

DECK

BREAKFAST
9'-0" x 10'-0"

KITCHEN
11'-8" x 13'-4"

FAMILY
ROOM
22'-0" x 18'-0"

PANT.

UP

PDR.

LAUN.

GARAGE
21'-8" x 21'-4"

STUDY
15'-0" x 13'-8"

UP

FOYER

DINING
ROOM
15'-0" x 13'-0"

PORCH

Width 69'-6"
Depth 43'-2"

MASTER
BATH

SUITE 2
11'-0" x 13'-6"

BATH

SUITE 3
12'-0" x 11'-0"

STOR.

W.I.C.

DN

REC.
ROOM
23'-6" x 13'-8"

DN

MASTER
SUITE
15'-0" x 15'-0"

OPEN

DN

BATH

SUITE 4
15'-0" x 11'-2"

STOR.

STOR.

STOR.

STOR.

SITTING
10'-0" x 8'-0"

BALCONY

Pella
®

VIEWED TO BE THE BEST™

DESIGN A193

First Floor: 1,715 square feet
Second Floor: 1,583 square feet
Total: 3,298 square feet
Bonus Room: 410 square feet

■ Double columns lend support to a balcony that also creates a sheltering entrance for this stately Colonial home. The interior begins with a formal dining room conveniently located adjacent to the sunny breakfast nook and kitchen, which makes entertaining a breeze, whether formal or informal. The family room invites a "put your feet up and relax" attitude that extends to the deck. A study—the ideal place to sort your thoughts—completes the first floor. The second floor contains the master suite. Here you can take a relaxing soak in the tub or curl up with a good book in the sitting room while enjoying the sweet scents of nature that waft across the balcony through French doors. Three additional bedrooms, two baths and a recreation room complete this great plan.

Complete Pella Window Specifications Provided With Every Home Plan

WINDOWSCAPING®

Design by
Home Planners

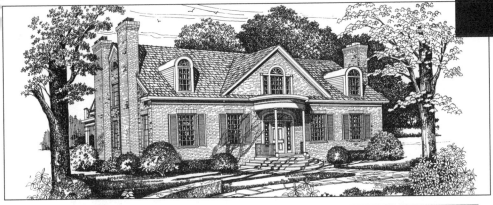

DESIGN 3513

First Floor: 1,855 square feet
Second Floor: 1,287 square feet
Total: 3,142 square feet

L **D**

■ This grand entrance is based on that of a home built in 1827 for William Thomas Buckner near Paris, Kentucky. Light from a Palladian window brightens the two-story foyer, which opens to the formal living and dining rooms—each with a fireplace. Informal living areas are situated to the rear of the plan. Here, a step-saving kitchen harmonizes well with the eating nook and the family room. The second floor holds two family bedrooms—one with balcony access—and the master suite.

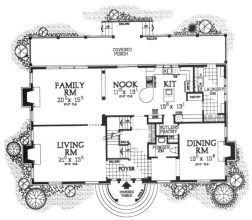

Width 56'-10"
Depth 53'-10"

QUOTE ONE®

Cost to build? See page 182
to order complete cost estimate
to build this house in your area!

Design by
Larry E. Belk Designs

DESIGN 8139

First Floor: 1,713 square feet
Second Floor: 1,430 square feet
Total: 3,143 square feet

■ The lovely curved porch of this classic Georgian home opens to a two-story foyer flanked by the formal living and dining rooms. A bright sun room is situated off the living room, creating a light, airy place for informal entertaining. The kitchen includes a large pantry and a small morning nook. The master suite includes a large bedroom and a His and Hers master bath. A sitting area with a walk-in cedar closet is shared with two family bedrooms. Please specify crawlspace or slab foundation when ordering.

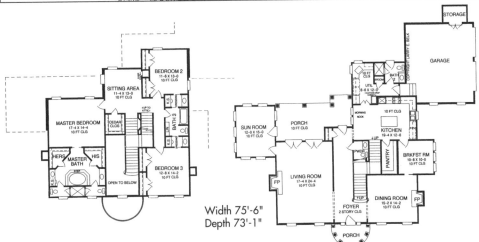

Width 75'-6"
Depth 73'-1"

Complete Pella Window Specifications Provided With Every Home Plan

Design by
Design Basics Inc.

DESIGN 7267

First Floor: 1,598 square feet
Second Floor: 1,675 square feet
Total: 3,273 square feet

■ Covered porches on both levels add interest to this Georgian exterior. The prominent entry opens to the formal living and dining rooms, both of which are brightened by transom windows. The family room is highlighted by a fireplace and views of a screened porch with a cozy window seat. Upstairs, French doors open to the master suite, which features decorative ceiling details, a large dressing area and a lavish bath. Three family bedrooms, two bathrooms and a bonus room complete the plan.

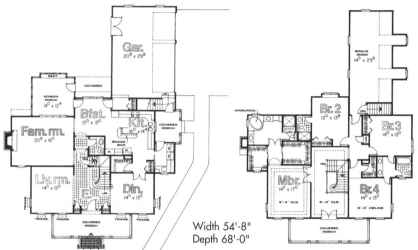

Width 54'-8"
Depth 68'-0"

Design by
Home Planners

DESIGN 2989

First Floor: 1,972 square feet
Second Floor: 1,533 square feet
Total: 3,505 square feet

L

■ This home recalls the Longfellow House in Cambridge, Massachusetts, residence of the poet for forty-five years. It was built in 1759 by Major John Vassall, an ardent Tory who was driven out of the house in 1774. On the first floor are the formal living and dining rooms, each with a fireplace. A front study connects to the family room. Upstairs are three bedrooms, including a wonderful master suite with a sitting room and a private bath.

Width 66'-4"
Depth 66'-4"

QUOTE ONE®
Cost to build? See page 182 to order complete cost estimate to build this house in your area!

Complete Pella Window Specifications Provided With Every Home Plan

WINDOWSCAPING®

Design by
Home Planners

A.J. YOUNG
FUQUAY VARINA N.C.

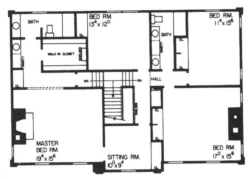

DESIGN 2522

First Floor: 1,835 square feet
Second Floor: 1,625 square feet
Total: 3,460 square feet

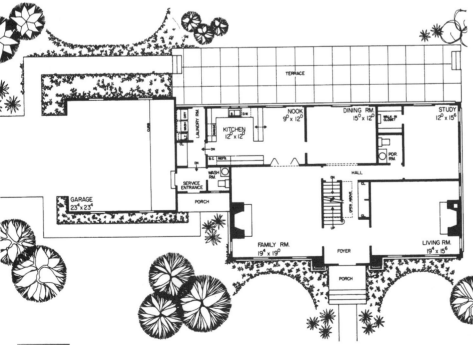

Width 61'-8"
Depth 36'-8"

■ The inside of this design is just as majestic as its exterior. The grand foyer is dramatically adorned with pillars and opens to a two-story living room with a fireplace and magnificent views, as well as multiple access to the rear verandas. An octagonal tower will make dining an experience in the formal dining room. Pillared arches lead traffic to the casual family area, highlighted by a well-designed kitchen, a sunny nook and a leisure room with a fireplace and outdoor access. The private master wing includes a separate study and an elegant master bath with dual walk-in closets, separate basins and a corner tub designed for relaxation. The second floor features three bedrooms, two with their own decks, and a gallery loft with views to the living room below.

VIEWED TO BE THE BEST™

Complete Pella Window Specifications Provided With Every Home Plan

DESIGN 2988

First Floor: 1,458 square feet
Second Floor: 1,075 square feet
Third Floor: 462 square feet
Total: 2,995 square feet

L D

■ The bell-shaped gambrel roof was a trademark of farmhouses in the 17th-Century Dutch colony of New Netherland. Front and rear covered porches encourage outdoor activities, while second-story dormers provide natural light for the bedrooms. With a large bay window, snack bar/work island, pantry and built-in desk, the country kitchen will be the center of family life. Three bedrooms, two baths and stairs leading to a third-floor exercise room and study/sewing room complete the plan.

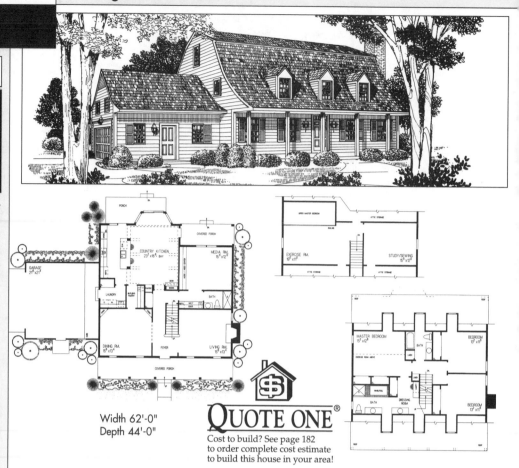

Width 62'-0"
Depth 44'-0"

QUOTE ONE®
Cost to build? See page 182 to order complete cost estimate to build this house in your area!

DESIGN 3567

First Floor: 1,778 square feet
Second Floor: 1,663 square feet
Total: 3,441 square feet

L D

■ Spring breezes and summer nights will be a joy to take in on the verandas and balcony of this Southern Colonial home. Or, if you prefer, sit back and enjoy a good book in the library, or invite a friend over for a chat in the conversation room. The first floor also includes formal dining and living rooms and a service entry with a laundry. The master bedroom sports a fireplace, two walk-in closets and a fine master bath. Three additional bedrooms occupy the second floor; one has its own bath.

Width 72'-0"
Depth 50'-0"

QUOTE ONE®
Cost to build? See page 182 to order complete cost estimate to build this house in your area!

Complete Pella Window Specifications Provided With Every Home Plan

QUOTE ONE®

Cost to build? See page 182
to order complete cost estimate
to build this house in your area!

Pella — VIEWED TO BE THE BEST™

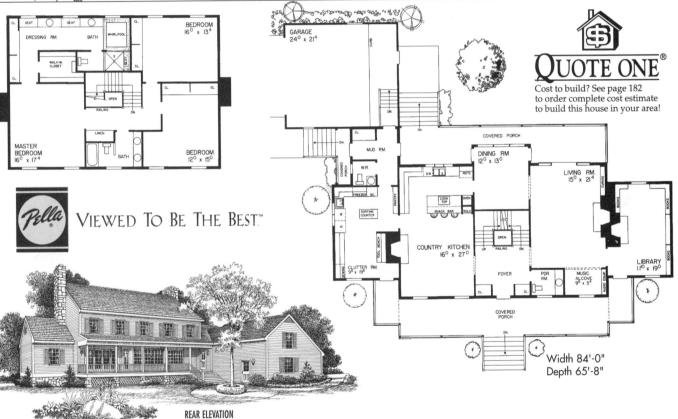

REAR ELEVATION

Width 84'-0"
Depth 65'-8"

DESIGN 2694

First Floor: 2,026 square feet
Second Floor: 1,386 square feet
Total: 3,412 square feet

L

■ This grand farmhouse is based on the retirement home of John Jay, the first chief justice of the United States. Located in Katonah, New York, it dates from around 1800, and was built on land purchased by his grandfather from Native Americans. The raised porches of this design were common in the Hudson River Valley. The first floor includes a grand living room with a fireplace and a music alcove, a library with another fireplace and built-in bookshelves, a light-filled dining room, a large country kitchen with a third fireplace and a snack bar, and a utility room with laundry facilities and a work bench. Three upstairs bedrooms include a master suite with a walk-in closet, vanity seating, a whirlpool tub and double sinks. Each of two family bedrooms contains a double closet.

Complete Pella Window Specifications Provided With Every Home Plan

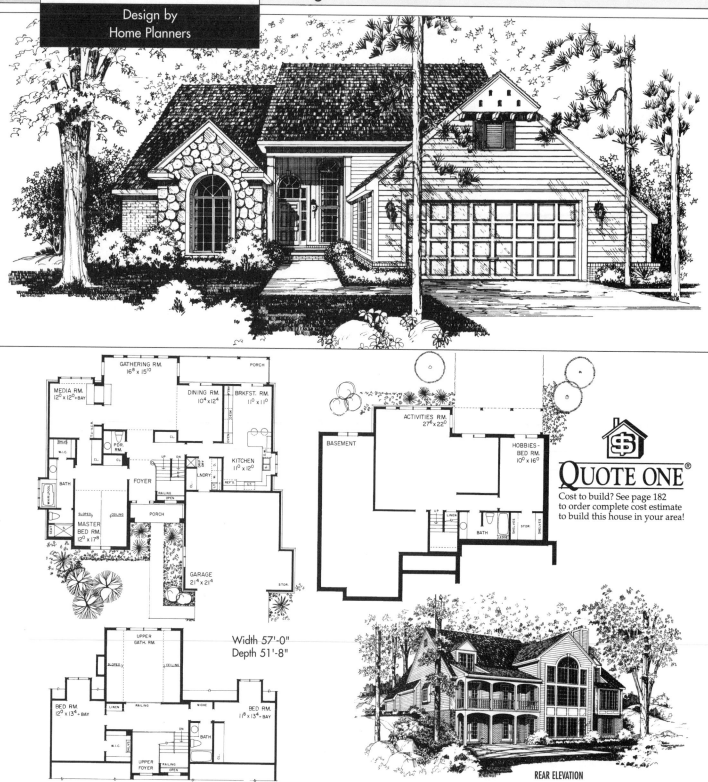

REAR ELEVATION

Width 57'-0"
Depth 51'-8"

MEDIA RM.
12⁰ x 12⁰ +BAY

GATHERING RM.
16⁸ x 15¹⁰

DINING RM.
10⁴ x 12⁴

BRKFST. RM.
11⁰ x 11⁰

KITCHEN
11⁰ x 12⁰

FOYER

LNDRY.

PORCH

BATH

MASTER BED RM.
12⁰ x 17⁸

GARAGE
21⁴ x 21⁴

ACTIVITIES RM.
27⁶ x 22⁰

BASEMENT

HOBBIES-BED RM.
10⁰ x 16⁰

BATH

UPPER GATH. RM.

BED RM.
12⁰ x 13⁴ +BAY

BED RM.
11⁸ x 13⁴ +BAY

UPPER FOYER

QUOTE ONE®
Cost to build? See page 182
to order complete cost estimate
to build this house in your area!

DESIGN 3366

Main Level: 1,638 square feet
Upper Level: 650 square feet
Lower Level: 934 square feet
Total: 3,222 square feet

L

■ There is much more to this design than meets the eye. While it may look like a 1½-story plan, bonus recreation and hobby space in the walk-out basement adds almost 1,000 square feet. The first floor holds living and dining areas as well as the deluxe master bed-room suite. Two family bedrooms share a full bath on the second floor and are connected by a balcony that overlooks the gathering room below. Notice the covered porch beyond the breakfast and dining rooms.

Complete Pella Window Specifications Provided With Every Home Plan

WINDOWSCAPING®

Design by
Larry E. Belk Designs

DESIGN 8149

First Floor: 2,263 square feet
Second Floor: 1,095 square feet
Total: 3,358 square feet

■ Two gables and a beautiful arch-top window give this farmhouse a dressy appearance. Inside, nine-foot ceilings throughout the first floor provide an open, spacious feeling. The kitchen, open to both the keeping room and the breakfast room, features a curved breakfast bar. The grand master suite is graced with two walk-in closets, separate vanities and a corner whirlpool tub. A second bedroom is conveniently situated on the first floor also. The upper level contains two bedrooms, each with a private dressing area, and a full bath. A game room and space for future expansion are also provided. Please specify crawlspace or slab foundation when ordering.

Complete Pella Window Specifications Provided With Every Home Plan

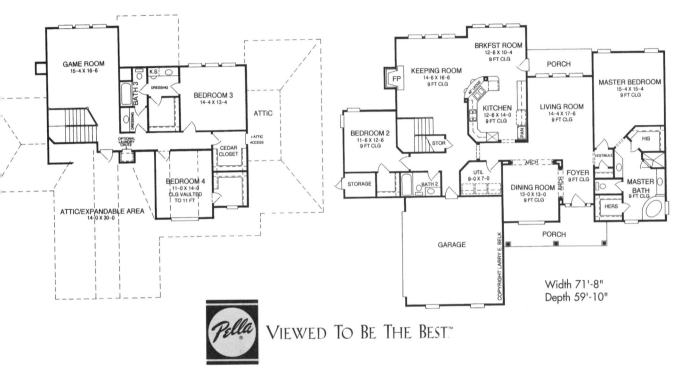

Width 71'-8"
Depth 59'-10"

VIEWED TO BE THE BEST™

DESIGN 8184

First Floor: 2,276 square feet
Second Floor: 1,049 square feet
Total: 3,325 square feet

■ Elegant angles and an abundance of space make this a most appealing design. A grand two-story foyer greets you and displays a graceful staircase. Columns define the parameters of the formal dining room and are echoed to separate the well-proportioned great room from the kitchen/breakfast room. The sumptuous master suite is replete with luxuries ranging from His and Hers walk-in closets to a pampering bath and is secluded for privacy on the first floor. Upstairs, two family bedrooms—each with walk-in closets—share a full hall bath and access to a large game room. Plenty of storage can be found in the two-car garage. Please specify crawlspace or slab foundation when ordering.

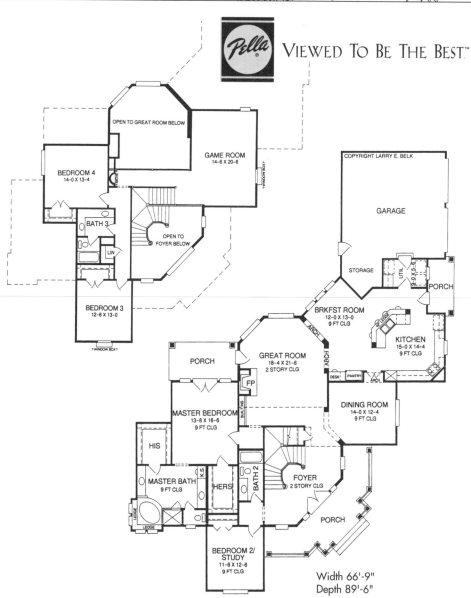

Width 66'-9"
Depth 89'-6"

Complete Pella Window Specifications Provided With Every Home Plan

WINDOWSCAPING®

Design by
The Sater Design Collection

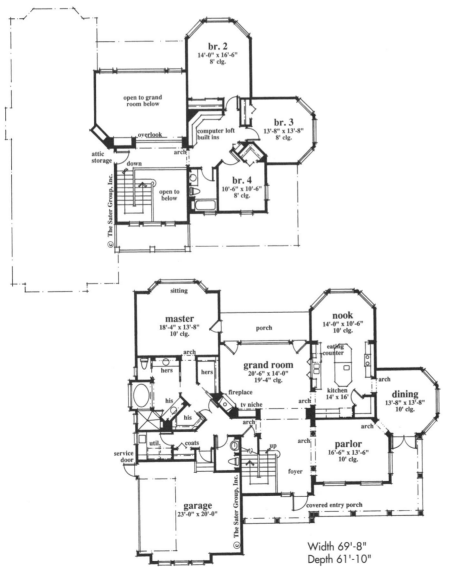

br. 2
14'-0" x 16'-6"
8' clg.

open to grand
room below

computer loft
built ins

br. 3
13'-8" x 13'-8"
8' clg.

overlook

attic
storage

arch

down

br. 4
10'-6" x 10'-6"
8' clg.

open to
below

© The Sater Group, Inc.

sitting

master
18'-4" x 13'-8"
10' clg.

porch

nook
14'-0" x 10'-6"
10' clg.

arch

hers

hers

eating
counter

grand room
20'-6" x 14'-0"
19'-4" clg.

kitchen
14' x 16'

arch

dining
13'-8" x 13'-8"
10' clg.

fireplace

his

tv niche

arch

his

arch

arch

service
door

util.

coats

up

arch

parlor
16'-6" x 13'-6"
10' clg.

foyer

arch

© The Sater Group, Inc.

garage
23'-0" x 20'-0"

covered entry porch

Width 69'-8"
Depth 61'-10"

DESIGN 6667

First Floor: 2,240 square feet
Second Floor: 943 square feet
Total: 3,183 square feet

■ This romantic farmhouse, with its open living spaces, covered porches and decorative widow's walk, is designed with gracious family living in mind. From the lovely wraparound porch, the foyer first meets the front parlor through an arched doorway. The impressive formal dining room is just beyond and will be a delight for casual meals as well as formal affairs. The grand room takes center stage with rear porch access, a corner fireplace, a built-in media center and a pass-through to the kitchen. The kitchen features a work-top island, an eating counter and a breakfast nook. The master suite is lavishly appointed with a spa-style bath, a sitting area and private access to the rear porch. Upstairs, a computer loft with built-ins serves as common area to the three family bedrooms that share a full hall bath. Please specify basement or slab foundation when ordering.

Complete Pella Window Specifications Provided With Every Home Plan

Width 63'-0"
Depth 45'-0"

DINING
13/6 X 11/0
(13'-8" CLG.)

LIVING
13/6 X 15/0
(13'-8" CLG.)

NOOK
10/0 X 13/0

12/0 X 13/8

FAMILY
15/0 X 15/8
(9' CLG.)

DEN
10/8 X 11/8
(9' CLG.)

GAMES RM.
13/6 X 18/10 +/-
(9' CLG.)

BR. 2
11/8 X 13/4

BR. 3
10/0 X 13/0

BR. 4
12/4 X 12/0

LINEN

FOYER BELOW

DN.

MASTER
16/2 X 13/0 +
(9'-9" CLG.)

STORAGE

UP

GARAGE
29/6 X 25/10 +/-

UNFINISHED STORAGE

DESIGN 7432

Main Level: 1,793 square feet
Upper Level: 1,330 square feet
Lower Level: 163 square feet
Total: 3,286 square feet

■ Palladian windows, multiple rooflines and a three-car garage give this home plenty of curb appeal. Inside, an angled staircase leads up to the second floor, while a double-door den offers a bay window for comfort. The living and dining rooms both have tray ceilings, with the living room featuring a fireplace. The efficient kitchen is full of amenities, including a corner sink with a window, a cooktop work island and a walk-in pantry. The spacious family room presents a second fireplace and double doors into a huge games room. Upstairs, three family bedrooms share a full hall bath, while the master suite is lavish with its amenities.

Complete Pella Window Specifications Provided With Every Home Plan

WINDOWSCAPING®

Design by
Alan Mascord Design Associates, Inc.

DESIGN 9550

First Floor: 1,988 square feet
Second Floor: 1,335 square feet
Total: 3,323 square feet
Bonus Room: 270 square feet

■ This traditional home has more to offer than a fine-looking exterior. Tucked behind the three-car garage is an office with access from the outside as well as the inside, making this ideal for a home-based business. The foyer leads to the bay-windowed library on the left and the formal living and dining rooms on the right. The sunny eating nook combines with a spacious kitchen featuring a walk-in pantry and an angled cook-top island. Nearby you will find the family room with built-ins flanking the fireplace. The second floor contains the sleeping area. The elaborate master suite boasts a restful sitting area and a luxurious bath with a spa and a walk-in closet. Two family bedrooms share a full bath. A large bonus room could be developed into a study or a children's media room.

Complete Pella Window Specifications Provided With Every Home Plan

VIEWED TO BE THE BEST™

Width 68'-0"
Depth 53'-6"

Design by
Donald A. Gardner Architects, Inc.

DESIGN 7602

First Floor: 2,097 square feet
Second Floor: 907 square feet
Total: 3,004 square feet
Bonus Room: 373 square feet

■ This farmhouse offers a casually elegant facade with a centered Palladian window, multipane dormers and a welcoming front porch. Formal living and dining rooms flank the foyer, with pillars framing the dining room. A luxurious master suite boasts two walk-in closets and a private master bath. A second-floor balcony and a loft overlook the spacious great room. Three family bedrooms share a full bath.

© 1994 Donald A. Gardner Architects, Inc.

© 1994 Donald A. Gardner Architects, Inc.

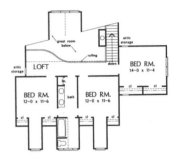

Width 70'-8"
Depth 71'-8"

DESIGN 7650

First Floor: 2,086 square feet
Second Floor: 1,077 square feet
Total: 3,163 square feet
Bonus Room: 403 square feet

■ This farmhouse, with its prominent twin gables and bays adds just the right amount of country style to modern family life. The master suite is tucked away downstairs with no rooms directly above. The family cook will love the U-shaped kitchen and adjoining bayed breakfast nook. Three large bedrooms and two full baths occupy the second floor. A curved balcony borders a versatile loft/study, which overlooks the two-story family room.

© 1996 Donald A. Gardner Architects, Inc.

© 1996 Donald A. Gardner Architects, Inc.

Width 81'-10"
Depth 51'-8"

Complete Pella Window Specifications Provided With Every Home Plan

WINDOWSCAPING®

Design by
Donald A. Gardner Architects, Inc.

© 1993 Donald A. Gardner Architects, Inc.

BONUS RM.
28-8 x 16-8

down

STORAGE
25-8 x 8-8

GARAGE
22-0 x 28-0

sto.

BRKFST.
9-8 x 7-4

PORCH

SITTING
9-8 x 4-0

KITCHEN
19-0 x 12-8

GREAT RM.
24-0 x 19-8

MASTER BED RM.
15-0 x 16-0

master bath

fireplace

balcony above

up

w d cl

UTILITY
13-8 x 8-2

cl

sto.

cl cl

pd. rm.

walk-in closet

© 1993 Donald A Gardner Architects, Inc.
attic storage

arched window above
clerestory windows

(cathedral ceiling)

great room below

bath

bath

railing

BED RM.
14-8 x 11-10

BED RM.
15-4 x 15-2

down

BED RM.
15-4 x 11-6

cl cl

cl cl

foyer below

DINING
13-0 x 17-0

LIVING/ STUDY
15-4 x 14-8

FOYER
cl 8-0 x 6-2

up

PORCH

Width 95'-4"
Depth 54'-10"

© 1993 Donald A Gardner Architects, Inc.

Pella®
VIEWED TO BE THE BEST™

DESIGN 7648

First Floor: 2,357 square feet
Second Floor: 995 square feet
Total: 3,352 square feet
Bonus Room: 545 square feet

■ From the two-story foyer with its Palladian clerestory window and stately stairway to the large great room with a cathedral ceiling and a curved balcony, impressive spaces prevail in this open farmhouse design. A colonnade opening from the great room introduces a spacious family kitchen with a center island counter and a breakfast bay. The master suite is privately located at the opposite end of the first floor. It features a bayed sitting area, an extra-large walk-in closet and a private master bath. Three family bedrooms and two full baths occupy the upper level. A bonus room and attic storage offer extra growing room.

Complete Pella Window Specifications Provided With Every Home Plan

Design by
Larry E. Belk Designs

DESIGN 8119

First Floor: 1,158 square feet
Second Floor: 1,773 square feet
Third Floor: 173 square feet
Total: 3,104 square feet

■ The facade of this home is a super prelude to an equally impressive interior. The front porch provides entry to the sleeping level. The master suite on the right features a lavish bath with a whirlpool tub and His and Hers walk-in closets, while a secondary bedroom on the left can be used as a guest room or an office. Upstairs, living areas include a family room with a sitting alcove and a living room with special ceiling treatment. The kitchen serves a breakfast room as well as a barrel-vaulted dining room. A third bedroom and two balconies further the custom nature of this home. On the third floor, an observation room with outdoor access is an extra-special touch. Please specify crawlspace or slab foundation when ordering.

Complete Pella Window Specifications Provided With Every Home Plan

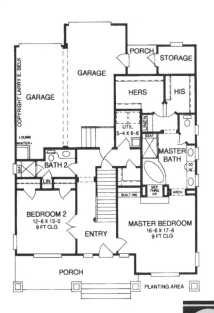

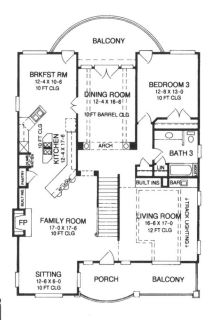

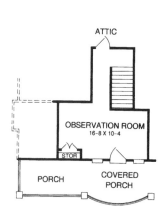

Width 39'-10"
Depth 58'-11"

Pella

VIEWED TO BE THE BEST™

WINDOWSCAPING®

Design by
The Sater Design Collection

© The Sater Group, Inc.

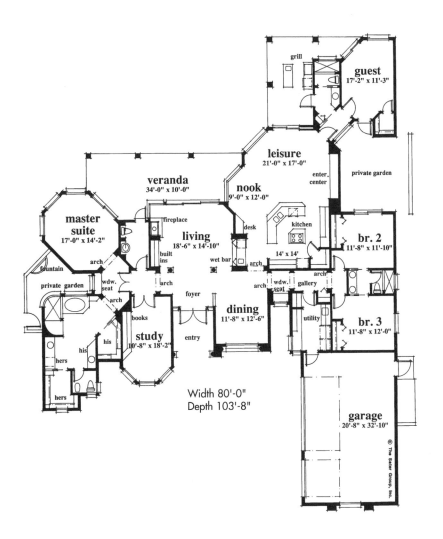

grill

guest
17'-2" x 11'-3"

leisure
21'-0" x 17'-0"

enter.
center

private garden

veranda
34'-0" x 10'-0"

nook
9'-0" x 12'-0"

fireplace

master suite
17'-0" x 14'-2"

desk

living
18'-6" x 14'-10"

kitchen

14' x 14'

br. 2
11'-8" x 11'-10"

built ins

wet bar

arch

arch

fountain

arch

wdw. seat

arch

private garden

arch

foyer

arch

arch

wdw. seat

gallery

dining
11'-8" x 12'-6"

utility

br. 3
11'-8" x 12'-0"

books

entry

his

his

his

study
10'-8" x 18'-2"

hers

hers

Width 80'-0"
Depth 103'-8"

garage
20'-8" x 32'-10"

© The Sater Group, Inc.

DESIGN 6661

Square Footage: 3,265

■ A turret study and a raised entry with half-round columns add elegance to this marvelous stucco home. Inside, columns frame the living room, which features glass doors that open to the veranda and provide spectacular views of the rear grounds. A guest suite—adjacent to the leisure room—includes a full bath, porch access and a private garden entry, making it perfect for use as an in-law suite. Secondary bedrooms share a full bath. The master suite has a foyer with a window seat overlooking a private garden and fountain area. It also features bayed windows to the backyard and veranda access. The private bath has dual closets, a garden tub and a walk-in shower with curved glass looking onto the garden space.

Complete Pella Window Specifications Provided With Every Home Plan

DESIGN 3634

Square Footage: 3,264

L

Three pediments, Doric columns and keystone arches set off the casually elegant exterior of this distinctive transitional home. Inside, a formal living room, angled for interest, warmly greets friends and provides a perfect complement to the nearby dining room. The island kitchen overlooks the covered entertainment terrace and easily serves planned and casual occasions, while the morning nook and family room invite cozy gatherings. The master suite enjoys the seclusion of its own wing, and offers a private step-down terrace and wide views of the outdoors. A dressing area leads to the master bath, which features an angled walk-in closet, a garden tub and twin lavatories. Two family bedrooms, one with a full cabana bath, complete the plan.

Width 84'-4"
Depth 75'-4"

Quote One®
Cost to build? See page 182 to order complete cost estimate to build this house in your area!

Pella — VIEWED TO BE THE BEST™

Complete Pella Window Specifications Provided With Every Home Plan

GRAND BY DESIGN:

Amenity-filled homes enhanced by natural light

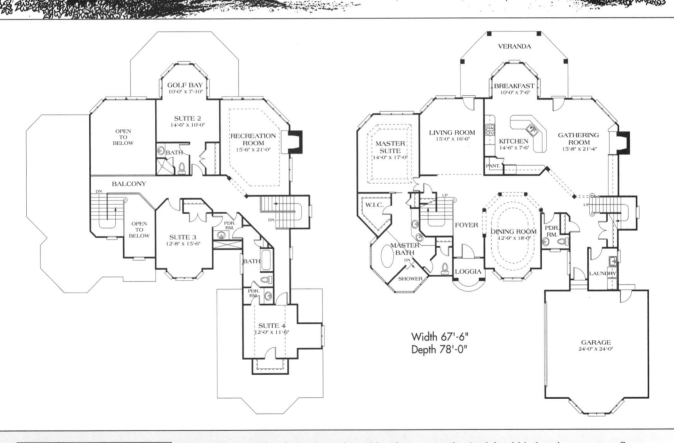

GOLF BAY
10'-0" x 7'-10"

SUITE 2
14'-6" x 10'-0"

OPEN
TO
BELOW

RECREATION
ROOM
15'-6" x 21'-0"

BATH

BALCONY

DN.

OPEN
TO
BELOW

SUITE 3
12'-8" x 15'-6"

PDR.
RM.

DN

BATH

PDR.
RM.

SUITE 4
12'-0" x 11'-6"

VERANDA

BREAKFAST
10'-0" x 7'-6"

LIVING ROOM
15'-0" x 16'-6"

KITCHEN
14'-6" x 7'-6"

GATHERING
ROOM
15'-8" x 21'-4"

MASTER
SUITE
14'-0" x 17'-0"

PANT.

W.I.C.

UP

FOYER

DINING ROOM
12'-9" x 18'-0"

PDR.
RM.

UP

MASTER
BATH

DN

SHOWER

LOGGIA

LAUNDRY

Width 67'-6"
Depth 78'-0"

GARAGE
24'-0" x 24'-0"

DESIGN A146

First Floor: 2,292 square feet
Second Floor: 1,465 square feet
Total: 3,757 square feet

■ An illusion of softness is projected by the arches, circles, bays and bows of this unique four-bedroom home—from the two-story bay window in the front to the five-sided veranda in the back. Graceful columns define the dining room with oval tray ceiling and bay window and the entrance to the gathering room with fireplace and access to the covered veranda. An island kitchen is open to a five-sided breakfast nook with windows facing the veranda. Glass block windows enclose the master bath and shower and the master bedroom features a tray ceiling. A balcony on the second floor connects three additional bedroom suites and a large recreation room with fireplace.

Complete Pella Window Specifications Provided With Every Home Plan

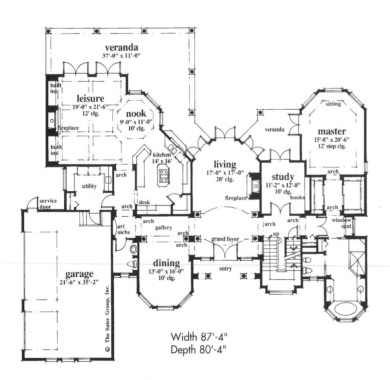

veranda
37'-0" x 11'-0"

built ins

leisure
19'-0" x 21'-6"
12' clg.

fireplace

built ins

nook
9'-0" x 11'-0"
10' clg.

kitchen
14' x 16'

utility

service door

art niche

arch

desk

gallery

garage
21'-6" x 35'-2"

© The Sater Group, Inc.

living
17'-0" x 17'-0"
20' clg.

veranda

fireplace

study
11'-2" x 12'-8"
10' clg.

books

sitting

master
15'-8" x 20'-6"
12' step clg.

arch

window seat

dining
13'-0" x 16'-0"
10' clg.

grand foyer

entry

up

Width 87'-4"
Depth 80'-4"

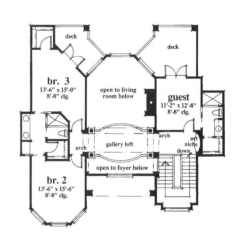

deck

deck

br. 3
13'-6" x 15'-0"
8'-8" clg.

open to living room below

guest
11'-2" x 12'-8"
8'-8" clg.

arch

gallery loft

art niche

down

arch

open to foyer below

br. 2
13'-6" x 15'-6"
8'-8" clg.

VIEWED TO BE THE BEST™

■ The interior of this design is just as majestic as its exterior. The grand foyer is dramatically adorned with pillars and opens to a two-story living room with a fireplace and magnificent views, as well as multiple access to the rear verandas. An octagonal tower will make dining an experience in the formal dining room. Pillared arches lead traffic to the casual family area, highlighted by a well-designed kitchen, a sunny nook and a leisure room with fireplace and outdoor access. The private master wing includes a separate study and an elegant master bath with dual walk-in closets, separate basins and a corner tub that will call to you after a long day. The second level features a guest suite with its own bath and deck, two family bedrooms (Bedroom 3 also has its own deck) and a gallery loft with views to the living room below. Please specify basement or slab foundation when ordering.

Complete Pella Window Specifications Provided With Every Home Plan

WINDOWSCAPING®

Design by
The Sater Design Collection

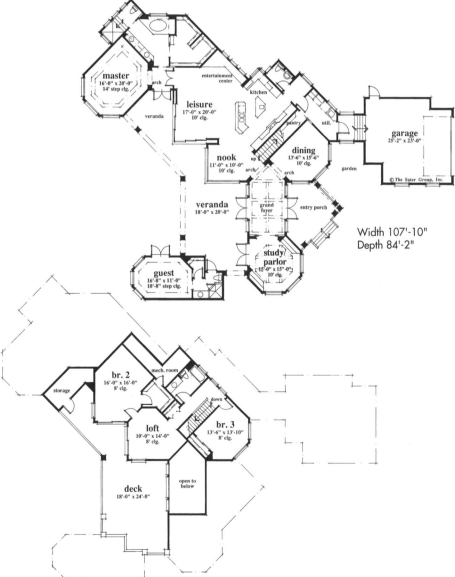

Width 107'-10"
Depth 84'-2"

© The Sater Group, Inc.

DESIGN 6668

First Floor: 2,397 square feet
Second Floor: 887 square feet
Guest Suite: 291 square feet
Total: 3,575 square feet

■ This stunning home is a gracious representation of the owner's hospitality. Enter the grand foyer, which opens straight through to the expansive veranda. A quiet study (or parlor) lies to the left of the foyer, with the formal dining room to the right. The casual area is lined with windows overlooking the veranda and centers around the oversized gourmet kitchen. Secluded at the rear of the plan, the master suite is fashioned with veranda doors, a detailed ceiling, a spa-style bath and a huge walk-in closet. On the second floor, a loft, open to the grand foyer, gives access to an upper-level deck. Two large family bedrooms share a full hall bath. Joined to the main house by the veranda, the lovely guest suite would also make a perfect cabana or maid's room.

Complete Pella Window Specifications Provided With Every Home Plan

DESIGN 6650

First Floor: 3,092 square feet
Second Floor: 656 square feet
Total: 3,748 square feet

■ Luxury is paramount in this four-bedroom traditional home. A columned entry leads to the grand foyer. The exclusive master suite is split from the two secondary bedrooms, residing to the right of the plan, and has a private entrance to the lanai. An arched entry provides access to large His and Hers closets and an extravagant master bath featuring a whirlpool tub and a separate shower. The central portion of the first floor contains the living area. The living room and adjacent dining room provide space for formal entertaining. For the best in casual living, the spacious kitchen, multi-windowed nook and leisure room are combined. The second floor contains a comfortable guest suite with a full bath and a bay-windowed study. Both enjoy private decks.

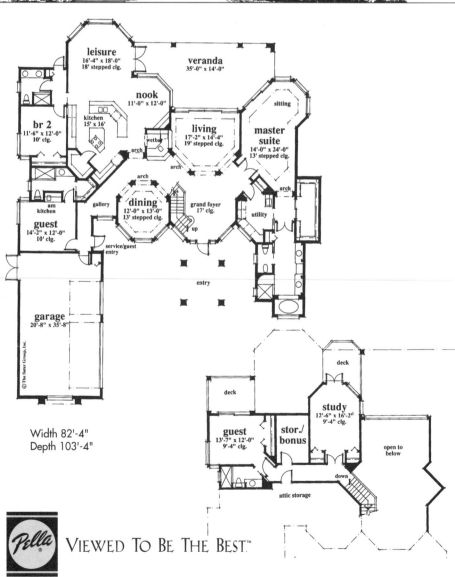

Width 82'-4"
Depth 103'-4"

Pella VIEWED TO BE THE BEST™

Complete Pella Window Specifications Provided With Every Home Plan

© The Sater Group, Inc.

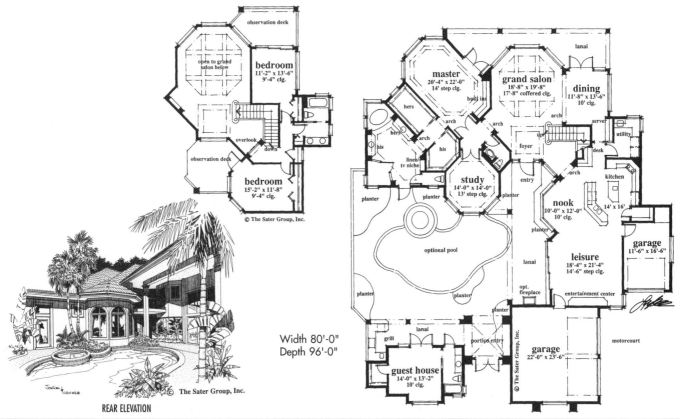

observation deck

open to grand salon below

bedroom
11'-2" x 13'-6"
9'-4" clg.

overlook

down

observation deck

bedroom
15'-2" x 11'-8"
9'-4" clg.

© The Sater Group, Inc.

REAR ELEVATION

© The Sater Group, Inc.

master
20'-4" x 22'-0"
14' step clg.

hers

grand salon
18'-8" x 19'-8"
17'-8" coffered clg.

built ins

dining
11'-8" x 13'-6"
10' clg.

hers

arch

arch

server

his

arch

his

arch

up

foyer

utility

linen
tv niche

desk

study
14'-0" x 14'-0"
13' step clg.

entry

arch

kitchen

planter

planter

planter

nook
10'-0" x 12'-0"
10' clg.

14' x 16'

planter

garage
11'-6" x 16'-6"

optional pool

lanai

leisure
18'-4" x 21'-4"
14'-6" step clg.

planter

planter

opt.
fireplace

entertainment center

planter

Width 80'-0"
Depth 96'-0"

lanai

grill

portico entry

garage
22'-0" x 23'-6"

motorcourt

guest house
14'-0" x 13'-2"
10' clg.

© The Sater Group, Inc.

DESIGN 6660

First Floor: 2,853 square feet
Second Floor: 627 square feet
Guest House: 312 square feet
Total: 3,792 square feet

■ A unique courtyard provides a happy marriage of indoor-outdoor relationships. The optional pool and outdoor living area provide optimum privacy while creating wonderful views from within the house. Inside, the foyer opens to a grand salon with a wall of glass, providing unobstructed views of the backyard. Informal areas include a leisure room with an entertainment center and glass doors that open onto a covered poolside lanai with an outdoor fireplace to enhance outdoor gatherings. The master wing is filled with amenities that include a bayed sitting area, access to the rear lanai, His and Hers closets and a corner tub. Upstairs, two bedrooms—both with private decks—share a full bath. A detached guest house has a summer kitchen and a bath with pool access.

Complete Pella Window Specifications Provided With Every Home Plan

WINDOWSCAPING®

Grand By Design

Design by
Alan Mascord Design Associates, Inc.

DESIGN 7446

First Floor: 2,006 square feet
Second Floor: 1,582 square feet
Total: 3,588 square feet
Bonus Room: 402 square feet

■ A two-story bay window framed by corner quoins creates the focal point for this wonderful home. The elegant interior of this European-inspired home starts with open, formal living and dining rooms, defined by columns and a central fireplace. The family room has built-in bookshelves and its own fire- place. Bedroom 5, which easily flexes as a den is tucked behind the garage, assuring peace and quiet. Upstairs, a spa-style tub highlights the deluxe bath that combines with the master bed- room to create a beautiful master suite. Three family bedrooms, a full bath and a bonus room complete the second floor.

Complete Pella Window Specifications Provided With Every Home Plan

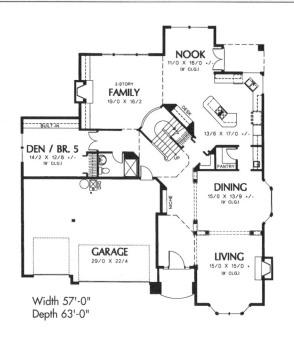

Width 57'-0"
Depth 63'-0"

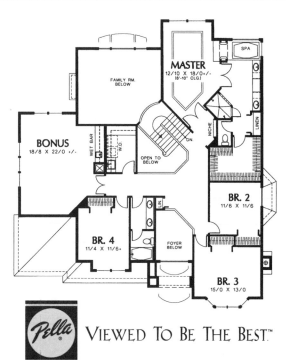

Pella VIEWED TO BE THE BEST™

WINDOWSCAPING®

Design by
Design Basics Inc.

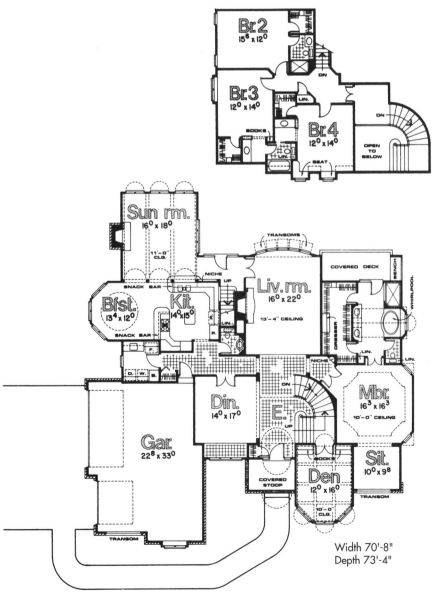

Width 70'-8"
Depth 73'-4"

Complete Pella Window Specifications Provided With Every Home Plan

DESIGN 7245

First Floor: 2,804 square feet
Second Floor: 961 square feet
Total: 3,765 square feet

■ This captivating exterior is accentuated by handsome stone columns and a dramatic cantilevered bay. Inside, formal elegance is captured in the stunning living room which features a volume ceiling, bowed windows and an impressive fireplace. For the family gourmet, the kitchen is enhanced with a butcher block island, a snack bar and a pantry. Informal gatherings will be enjoyed in the open breakfast area and the arched-entry sun room that's accented with a fireplace. On the master wing, double doors open to the master bedroom and its adjoining sitting room. The master bath boasts an arched transom window, access to a covered deck and a walk-in closet with dresser. Upstairs, at landing level is a den complete with a spider-beam ceiling, bookcases and bayed windows. The second floor houses three family bedrooms—two that share a bath, one with a private bath. A back staircase joins the family bedrooms to the rear hall and sun room.

DESIGN 9596

First Floor: 2,190 square feet
Second Floor: 1,680 square feet
Total: 3,870 square feet
Bonus Room: 697 square feet

■ Arches and bays create a pleasing facade in this four-bedroom Tudor-style home, and are just the beginning of the pleasures that this design offers. A curved foyer leads to the quiet bayed den and to an octagonal living room with a fireplace and plenty of windows for warmth and sunshine. The formal dining room features a coffered ceiling, another bay and access to a quiet side terrace. It is also conveniently located near the open island kitchen, which leads to the breakfast nook and the comfortable family room. On the upper level, Bedroom 4, with its private bath, would make a great guest suite. The master suite includes a vaulted ceiling, a walk-in closet and a sumptuous bath with a corner spa. Two family bedrooms feature walk-in closets and share a full bath. Bonus space could become a children's playroom or a family game room.

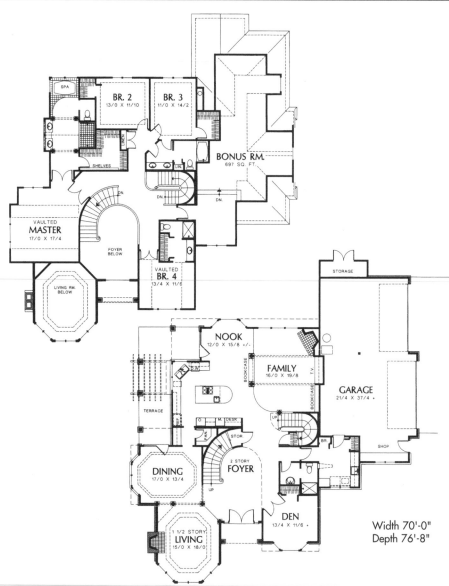

Width 70'-0"
Depth 76'-8"

Complete Pella Window Specifications Provided With Every Home Plan

WINDOWSCAPING®

Design by
Larry E. Belk Designs

COPYRIGHT LARRY E. BELK

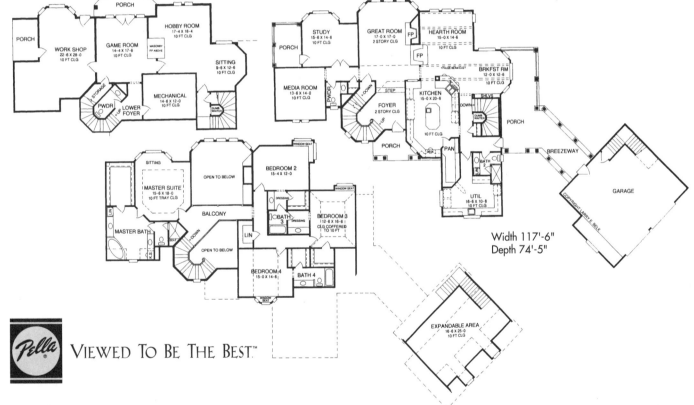

Width 117'-6"
Depth 74'-5"

VIEWED TO BE THE BEST.™

DESIGN 8147

First Floor: 2,340 square feet
Second Floor: 1,806 square feet
Total: 4,146 square feet
Optional Lower Level: 1,608 square feet

■ Full of amenities for the owner, this country estate includes a media room and a study. The two-story great room is perfect for formal entertaining. Family and friends will enjoy gathering in the large kitchen, the hearth room and the breakfast room. The luxurious master suite is located upstairs. Bedrooms 2 and 3 share a bath that includes dressing areas for both bedrooms. Bedroom 4 features a private bath. The breakfast room is adjacent to a rear stair complete with a dumbwaiter, which goes down to a walk-out basement, where you'll find an enormous workshop, a game room and a hobby room. This home may also be built with a basement or a slab foundation. Please specify your preference when ordering.

Complete Pella Window Specifications Provided With Every Home Plan

DESIGN 8034

First Floor: 2,639 square feet
Second Floor: 1,625 square feet
Total: 4,264 square feet

■ European traditional style is the hallmark of this best-selling plan. The two-story foyer is graced by a lovely staircase and a balcony overlook from upstairs. Two columns flank the entry to the great room, notable for its beautiful window wall facing the rear grounds. Two-story double bays on the rear of the home form the keeping room and the breakfast room on one side and the master bedroom and its sitting area on the other. A huge walk-in pantry and an adjacent butler's pantry connect the dining room to the kitchen. Rear stairs from the kitchen join the family gathering area with the three bedrooms and game room upstairs. With a large study downstairs and walk-in attic storage available for expansion upstairs, this home provides all the amenities needed for today's busy family.

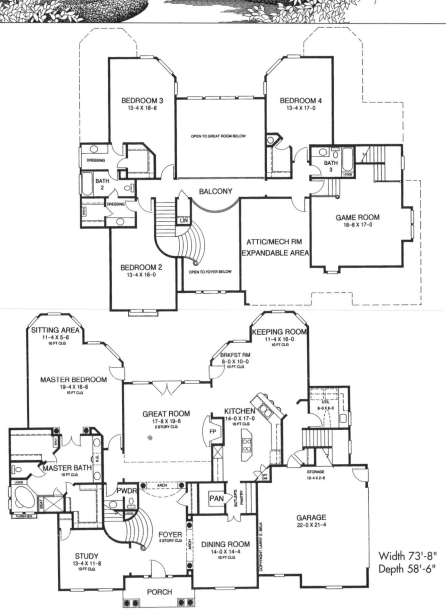

Width 73'-8"
Depth 58'-6"

Complete Pella Window Specifications Provided With Every Home Plan

WINDOWSCAPING®

Design by
Larry E. Belk Designs

BRKFST ROOM
12-6 X 10-6
10 FT CLG

PORCH

MASTER
BATH

LEDGE

K.S.

FAMILY ROOM
14-6 X 19-0
10 FT CLG

FP.

44" HIGH

LIVING ROOM
19-0 X 15-8
VAULTED TO 2 STORY

MASTER BEDROOM
16-0 X 15-4
10 FT CLG

KITCHEN
12-6 X 15-4

PANTRY
CABINET

UTIL
9-0 X 10-6

BATH 2

PWDR

DINING ROOM
11-6 X 12-6
10 FT CLG

FOYER
2 STORY CLG

STUDY/BEDRM 5
13-6 X 12-2
10 FT CLG

3 CAR GARAGE

PORCH

COPYRIGHT LARRY E. BELK

Width 67'-8"
Depth 77'-2"

STORAGE

K.S.

DRESSING

BEDROOM 3
12-6 X 16-6

BATH
4

DRESSING

BEDROOM 4
14-6 X 13-6

BATH
3

LIN

OPEN TO LIVING ROOM BELOW

BALCONY

TO ATTIC

BEDROOM 2
11-6 X 14-0

OPEN TO
FOYER BELOW

ATTIC/FUTURE
GAME ROOM

Pella® VIEWED TO BE THE BEST™

DESIGN 8103

First Floor: 2,547 square feet
Second Floor: 1,128 square feet
Total: 3,675 square feet
Bonus Room: 357 square feet

■ An impressive entrance with massive columns connected by twin arches is the focal point for this European traditional design. A two-story foyer and living room give the home an elegant, open feeling. The kitchen and breakfast room are open to a large family room—a great place for informal gatherings. The large utility room and the three-car garage are situated nearby. The master suite and the study are located on the opposite side of the home and provide a private retreat for the owner. Three bedrooms and two baths are located upstairs. Bath 4 features two dressing areas for privacy. All the bedrooms are designed with large walk-in closets. Walk-in access is available to the attic and the large area over the garage can be finished for a game room or an in-home office. Please specify crawlspace or slab foundation when ordering.

Complete Pella Window Specifications Provided With Every Home Plan

DESIGN A168

First Floor: 2,386 square feet
Second Floor: 1,872 square feet
Total: 4,258 square feet

■ A split garage is a unique feature often found only in the finest custom homes. Inside, the foyer opens through French doors to a quiet den on the left; to the right, a formal dining room framed by square columns. The family room combines with the kitchen and angled nook to create a light, spacious gathering area. Just beyond is a screened porch. A sun-filled master suite completes the first floor. Three suites—each with a walk-in closet—an office and a large recreation room occupy the second floor.

Width 64'-2"
Depth 71'-2"

DESIGN A219

First Floor: 2,590 square feet
Second Floor: 1,715 square feet
Total: 4,305 square feet

■ Walls of windows provide a front row seat to enjoy nature's bounty, and at the same time, enhance the rear elevation. Columns play an important role in defining the living and dining areas. Adjacent to the Florida room, the den easily converts to a guest suite. The first-floor master suite—featuring a large walk-in closet and spacious bath—is designed for relaxation. Three suites, two baths and a recreation room/loft filled with sunlight complete the plan. Please specify basement or crawlspace foundation when ordering.

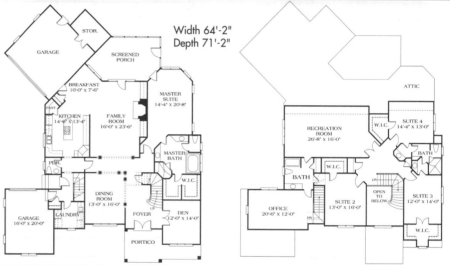

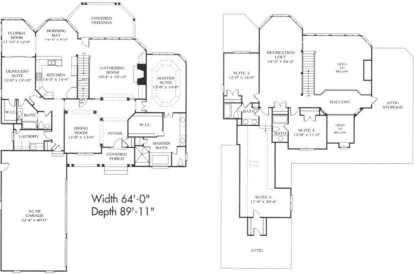

Width 64'-0"
Depth 89'-11"

Complete Pella Window Specifications Provided With Every Home Plan

WINDOWSCAPING®

Design by
Living Concepts Home Planning

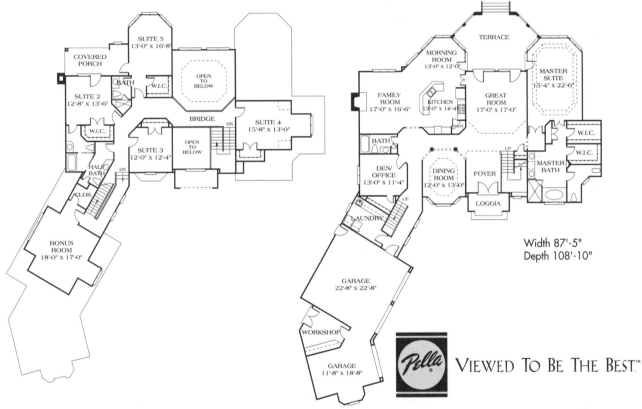

SUITE 5
13'-0" x 16'-8"

COVERED
PORCH

OPEN
TO
BELOW

BATH

W.I.C.

SUITE 2
12'-8" x 13'-6"

W.I.C.

BRIDGE

DN

SUITE 4
15'-8" x 13'-0"

HALF
BATH

SUITE 3
12'-0" x 12'-4"

OPEN
TO
BELOW

CLOS.

DN

BONUS
ROOM
18'-0" x 17'-0"

TERRACE

MORNING
ROOM
13'-0" x 12'-0"

MASTER
SUITE
15'-4" x 22'-6"

FAMILY
ROOM
17'-0" x 16'-6"

KITCHEN
13'-0" x 14'-4"

GREAT
ROOM
17'-0" x 17'-0"

PANT.

W.I.C.

BATH

W.I.C.

DEN/
OFFICE
13'-0" x 11'-4"

DINING
ROOM
12'-0" x 13'-0"

FOYER

UP

MASTER
BATH

LOGGIA

LAUNDRY

UP

Width 87'-5"
Depth 108'-10"

GARAGE
22'-8" x 22'-8"

WORKSHOP

GARAGE
11'-8" x 18'-8"

Pella

VIEWED TO BE THE BEST™

DESIGN A222

First Floor: 2,886 square feet
Second Floor: 1,561 square feet
Total: 4,447 square feet
Bonus Room: 338 square feet

■ Stone accents, corner quoins and a copper metal roof are the finishing touches on this grand French manor. An impressive two-story entry leads through the foyer to a great room with an unbroken view of the terrace and backyard. The formal dining room is nearby for easy entertaining. An open, informal area consists of a family room and a morning room, separated from the kitchen by an angled snack bar. Filling the right side of the plan, the master suite features a compartmented toilet, twin walk-in closets and access to the terrace. The second floor offers four bedrooms, two of which share a covered porch.

Complete Pella Window Specifications Provided With Every Home Plan

DESIGN 8106

First Floor: 2,903 square feet
Second Floor: 1,167 square feet
Total: 4,070 square feet

■ A series of gables and exterior materials lend themselves to creating a handsome traditional exterior. The family room sports a beam ceiling and a fireplace, as well as open planning with the kitchen and breakfast room. In the living room, double doors open to a rear covered porch. A handy utility room features its own separate entrance sheltered by a covered porch. In the master bedroom, His and Hers closets and a pampering bath invite you to relax and enjoy. An upstairs game room is located near family bedrooms and two full baths. Please specify crawlspace or slab foundation when ordering.

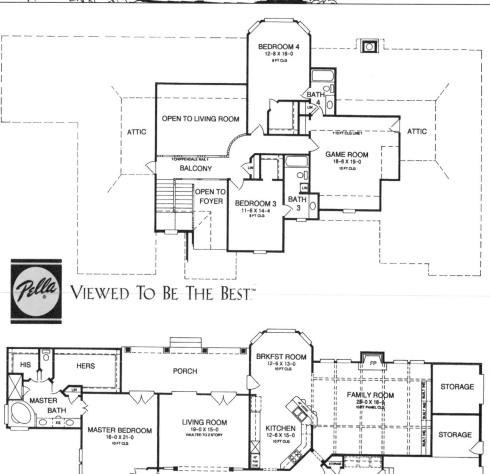

VIEWED TO BE THE BEST™

Complete Pella Window Specifications Provided With Every Home Plan

WINDOWSCAPING®

Design by
Donald A. Gardner Architects, Inc.

DESIGN 7646

First Floor: 2,330 square feet
Second Floor: 1,187 square feet
Total: 3,517 square feet

© 1997 Donald A. Gardner Architects, Inc.

© 1997 Donald A. Gardner Architects, Inc.

Width 90'-2"
Depth 47'-2"

■ This home's stunning exterior includes an arched entry and brick detailing, while its interior dazzles with space and style. The living room/study is warmed by a fireplace, as is the two-story family room. The master suite features a tray ceiling, rear porch access and a relaxing bath. Three bedrooms—each with a walk-in closet—and two full baths are located upstairs.

Design by
Design Basics Inc.

DESIGN 7246

First Floor: 2,813 square feet
Second Floor: 1,091 square feet
Total: 3,904 square feet

Width 85'-5"
Depth 74'-8"

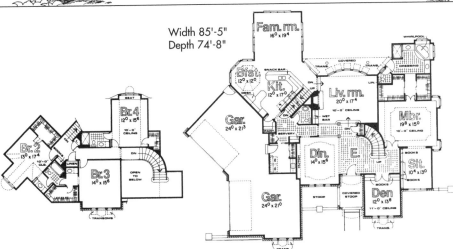

■ Open planning creates an easy flow on the interior of this stately, traditional home. To the left of the two-story foyer is a bay-windowed dining room; to the right, a study/library. The kitchen shares space with a sun-filled breakfast room that opens onto the patio/terrace. Luxury is paramount in the grand master suite with a bath that invites relaxation. The second-floor bedrooms share space with a bonus room and a recreation room that has a fireplace and an abundance of windows.

Complete Pella Window Specifications Provided With Every Home Plan

Design by
Living Concepts Home Planning

DESIGN A200

First Floor: 2,340 square feet
Second Floor: 1,164 square feet
Total: 3,504 square feet
Bonus Room: 455 square feet

■ Open planning creates an easy flow on the interior of this stately, traditional home. To the left of the two-story foyer is a bay-windowed dining room; to the right, a study/library. The kitchen shares space with a sun-filled breakfast room that opens onto the patio/terrace. Luxury is paramount in the grand master suite with a bath that invites relaxation. The second-floor bedrooms share space with a bonus room and a recreation room that has a fireplace and an abundance of windows.

Width 62'-8"
Depth 75'-6"

DESIGN A204

First Floor: 1,741 square feet
Second Floor: 1,884 square feet
Total: 3,625 square feet

■ Corner quoins, gabled rooflines and shutters give this four-bedroom home plenty of curb appeal. Inside, the floor plan is designed for entertaining. For formal occasions, there is the living/dining room combination. Casual gatherings will be welcomed in the family room, which features a fireplace and access to the rear deck via French doors. Upstairs, three bedrooms share two baths and a playroom/loft. The master suite features two walk-in closets and a luxurious bath.

Width 61'-9"
Depth 48'-10"

Complete Pella Window Specifications Provided With Every Home Plan

WINDOWSCAPING®

Design by
Design Basics Inc.

DESIGN 7268

First Floor: 2,040 square feet
Second Floor: 1,952 square feet
Total: 3,992 square feet

■ This stately brick home offers a magnificent elevation from every angle, with a particularly impressive arched portico. The entry hall is highlighted by a majestic staircase. The formal dining room includes two built-in china cabinets, and is easily reached from the living room with its fireplace and attractive window seat. Between them is a den with floor-to-ceiling cabinetry, a window seat and a spider-beam ceiling.

A gourmet kitchen with a walk-in pantry and an island cooktop/snack bar opens into a family room featuring a built-in rolltop desk, an entertainment center and a raised-hearth fireplace. Upstairs, a lavish master suite includes a sitting room with a fireplace, a two-person whirlpool bath and two walk-in closets. Two of the family bedrooms feature flip-top window seats for added storage.

Complete Pella Window Specifications Provided With Every Home Plan

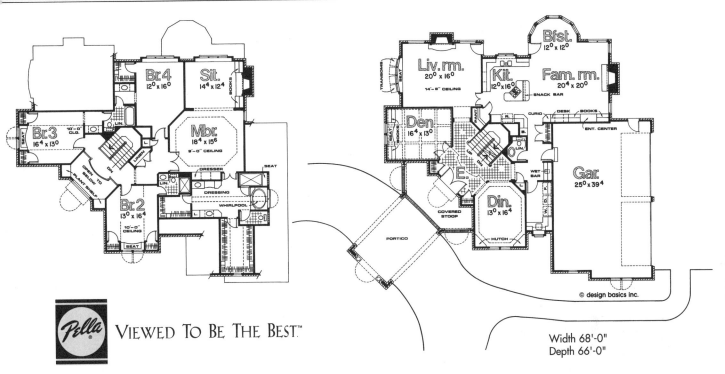

VIEWED TO BE THE BEST™

Width 68'-0"
Depth 66'-0"

WINDOWSCAPING®

Design by
Living Concepts Home Planning

Grand By Design

DESIGN A209

Square Footage: 3,797

■ Within this elegant facade, open planning offers an aura of spaciousness in the formal living areas, defined by decorative columns. A secluded den or guest suite includes a walk-in closet and French doors that lead outside. The opposite wing holds a deluxe master suite with a multi-windowed sitting room and a fireplace. Each of the family bedrooms has a walk-in closet and its own door to a shared bath.

Width 82'-6"
Depth 102'-4"

DESIGN A212

First Floor: 2,588 square feet
Second Floor: 1,375 square feet
Total: 3,963 square feet
Bonus Room: 460 square feet

■ Inside this lovely brick home, the foyer is flanked by a formal, bayed dining room and a formal, bayed living room. Directly ahead is the lake gathering room, a spacious living area with a warming fireplace and access to the veranda. A gourmet kitchen features a wet bar and an adjacent morning room, which opens onto the screened porch. The master suite is located on the first floor for privacy. Three suites inhabit the upstairs and share two full baths and a spacious bonus room.

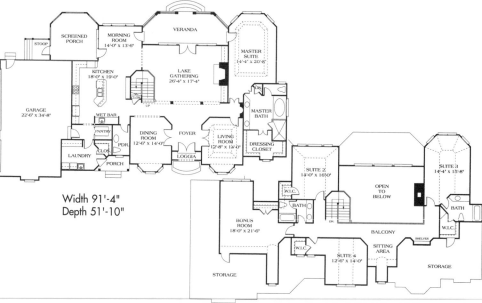

Width 91'-4"
Depth 51'-10"

Complete Pella Window Specifications Provided With Every Home Plan

WINDOWSCAPING®

Design by
Alan Mascord Design Associates, Inc.

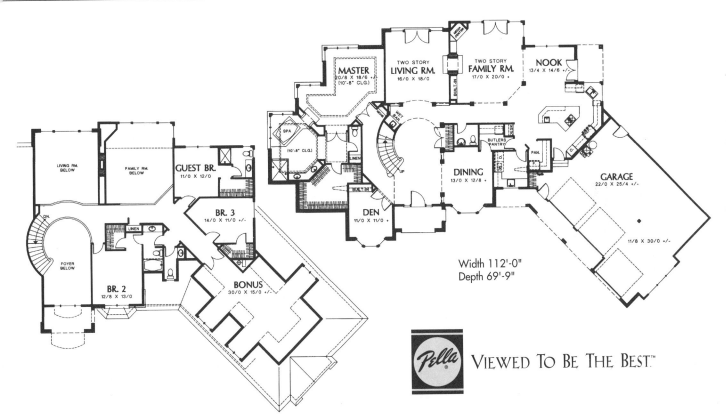

Width 112'-0"
Depth 69'-9"

Pella VIEWED TO BE THE BEST™

DESIGN 9565

First Floor: 3,098 square feet
Second Floor: 1,113 square feet
Total: 4,211 square feet
Bonus Room: 567 square feet

■ The magnificent entry of this elegant traditional home makes a grand impression. The soaring ceiling of the foyer looks over a curved staircase that leads to secondary sleeping quarters. The first-floor master suite offers an expansive retreat for the homeowner, with mitered windows and a through-fireplace shared with the spacious, spa-style bath. Formal rooms open from the foyer, while a gallery hall leads to the casual living area, with a two-story family room and French doors to the outside. The three-car garage offers wardrobe space for cloaks.

Complete Pella Window Specifications Provided With Every Home Plan

DESIGN 2980

First Floor: 1,648 square feet
Second Floor: 1,368 square feet
Third Floor: 567 square feet
Total: 3,583 square feet

■ This late Georgian adaptation is reminiscent of the Cowles house built in Farmington, Connecticut around 1786. The projecting central pavilion, Ionic columns, Palladian window and pedimented gable are among the details that set the character of this historic house. Dentils, wooden quoins and bracketed cornices complete the picture of elegance. Inside, the foyer leads to the formal living room, the library and the U-shaped kitchen. The family room opens to the sunroom and shares a snack bar and a desk with the kitchen. A through-fireplace warms the living and dining rooms, while individual fireplaces are also found in the library and the master bedroom. The master bath features a whirlpool tub, twin lavatories, a vanity and a walk-in closet. The third floor offers a private guest suite and a large area for hobbies and other activities.

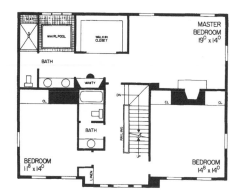

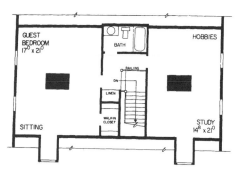

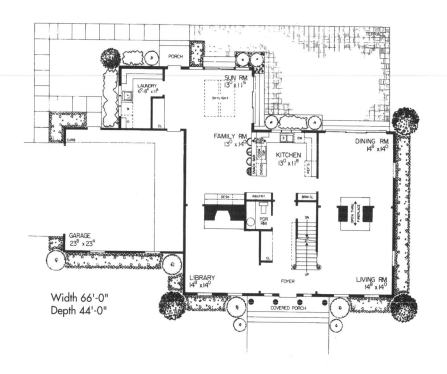

Width 66'-0"
Depth 44'-0"

Complete Pella Window Specifications Provided With Every Home Plan

WINDOWSCAPING®
Design by Home Planners

QUOTE ONE®

Cost to build? See page 182
to order complete cost estimate
to build this house in your area!

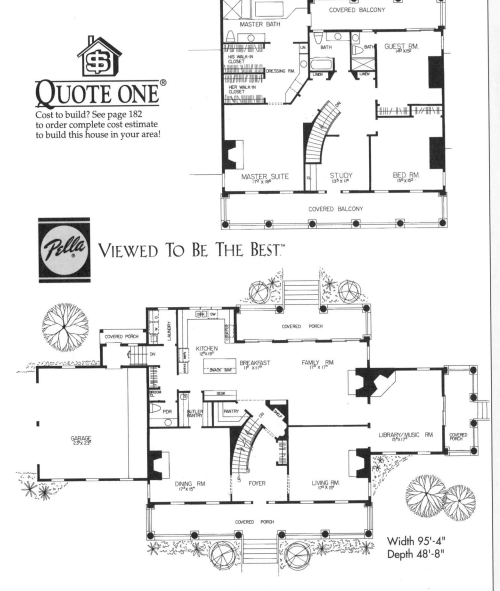

MASTER BATH

COVERED BALCONY

LIN.

BATH

BATH

GUEST RM.
14⁰ X15²

HIS WALK-IN
CLOSET

DRESSING RM.

LINEN

LINEN

HER WALK-IN
CLOSET

DN

MASTER SUITE
17² X18⁶

STUDY
13⁶ X11⁴

BED RM.
15⁶ X15²

COVERED BALCONY

Pella
VIEWED TO BE THE BEST™

COVERED PORCH

LAUNDRY

DW

KITCHEN
12² X19⁸

COVERED PORCH

DN

BREAKFAST
11⁶ X11¹⁰

FAMILY RM.
17² X17⁴

SNACK BAR

BROOM
CL.

DESK

PDR.

BUTLER
PANTRY

PANTRY

DN

GARAGE
23² X23²

DINING RM.
17² X15⁴

FOYER

LIVING RM.
17² X15⁴

LIBRARY/MUSIC RM.
15² X17²

COVERED PORCH

COVERED PORCH

Width 95'-4"
Depth 48'-8"

DESIGN 3508

First Floor: 2,098 square feet
Second Floor: 1,735 square feet
Total: 3,833 square feet

L

■ Make history with this adaptation of Louisiana's "Rosedown House," built in 1835 for Daniel Turnbull, a wealthy planter, and his wife Martha. Originally, the house had just one wing—the matching one was added when a newly purchased bed was too tall to fit into the main house. Like its predecessor, this is a lovely plantation of classic style and proportions. The foyer, featuring a graceful, curving staircase, is flanked by the dining and living rooms—each highlighted by a fireplace. The library (or music room) offers a corner fireplace and a covered porch. The family room opens to a breakfast room, kitchen and rear covered porch. Upstairs, a gracious master suite opens with double doors and encourages a romantic feeling with a fireplace. A large dressing room with two walk-in closets leads to the luxury bath. There are two more bedrooms (one with its own bath) and a study.

Complete Pella Window Specifications Provided With Every Home Plan

DESIGN 3527

First Floor: 2,000 square feet
Second Floor: 2,000 square feet
Total: 4,000 square feet
Bonus Room: 264 square feet

■ This gracious Colonial design features an abundance of lovely windows that allow natural light to enhance the second floor. A pediment tops a double portico and creates a dazzling entry for this comfortable home. Fireplaces warm the formal rooms, while casual living space features built-in seats that frame a tile-hearth fireplace. A planning desk, a walk-in pantry and a snack counter highlight the roomy, well-planned kitchen, which serves the dining room through a butler's pantry.

Complete Pella Window Specifications Provided With Every Home Plan

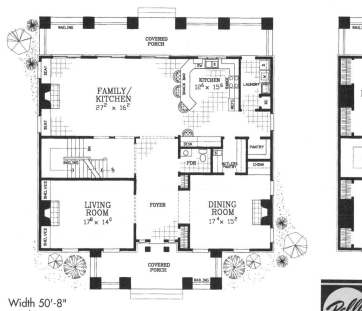

Width 50'-8"
Depth 56'-8"

VIEWED TO BE THE BEST™

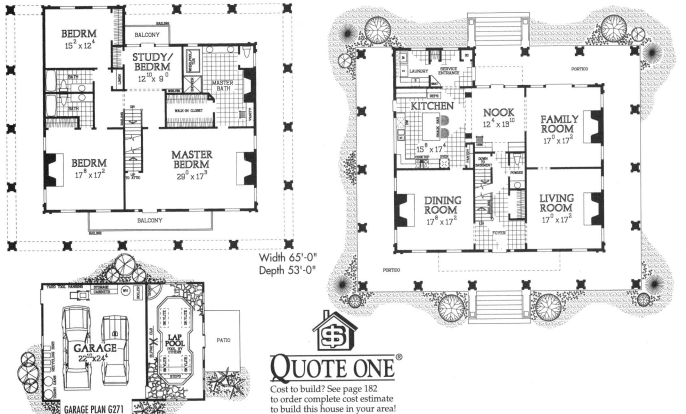

Width 65'-0"
Depth 53'-0"

BEDRM 15² x 12⁴

BALCONY

STUDY/ BEDRM 12¹⁰ x 9⁰

MASTER BATH

BATH

BATH

WALK-IN CLOSET

DN

UP TO ATTIC

BEDRM 17⁸ x 17²

MASTER BEDRM 29⁰ x 17³

BALCONY

RAILING

LAUNDRY

SERVICE ENTRANCE

PORTICO

KITCHEN 15⁸ x 17⁴

NOOK 12⁴ x 13¹⁰

FAMILY ROOM 17⁰ x 17²

DOWN TO BASEMENT

PANTRY

POWDER

DINING ROOM 17⁸ x 17²

LIVING ROOM 17⁰ x 17²

FOYER

PORTICO

PORTICO

YARD TOOL HANGING

STORAGE CABINETS

GARAGE 22¹⁰ x 24⁴

LAP POOL POOL BY OTHERS

PATIO

SKYLITE

STEPS

GARAGE PLAN G271

QUOTE ONE®
Cost to build? See page 182
to order complete cost estimate
to build this house in your area!

DESIGN 3518

First Floor: 1,877 square feet
Second Floor: 1,877 square feet
Total: 3,754 square feet

L **D**

■ The gracious hospitality and the genteel, easy lifestyle of the South are personified in this elegant Southern Colonial home. Contributing to the exterior's stucco warmth are square columns surrounding the home, shutters and a cupola. Inside, the warmth continues with six fireplaces found throughout the home: formal dining room, living room, family room—and on the second floor—family bedroom, romantic master bedroom and master bath. First-floor views of the rear grounds are enjoyed from the family room and sun-filled nook. The second floor contains two family bedrooms—each with its own bath—and a lavish master suite with a balcony and a pampering bath. A study/bedroom with a balcony completes the upstairs. Plans for a detached garage with an enclosed lap pool are included with the blueprints.

Complete Pella Window Specifications Provided With Every Home Plan

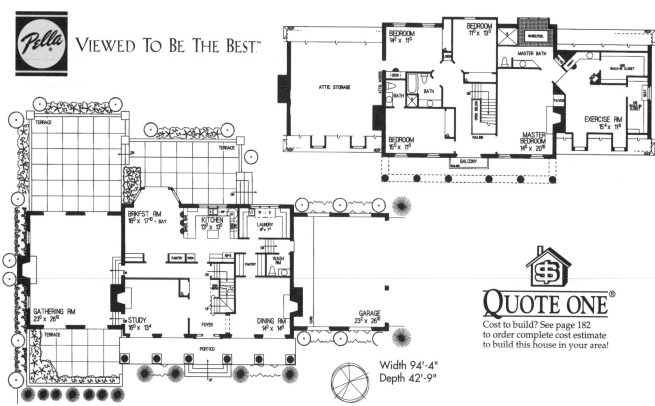

VIEWED TO BE THE BEST™

QUOTE ONE®

Cost to build? See page 182
to order complete cost estimate
to build this house in your area!

Width 94'-4"
Depth 42'-9"

DESIGN 3337

First Floor: 2,167 square feet
Second Floor: 1,992 square feet
Total: 4,159 square feet

L

■ The elegant facade of this design with its columned portico, fanlights and dormers houses an amenity-filled interior. The gathering room, study and dining room, each with a fireplace, provide plenty of room for relaxing and entertaining. A large work area contains a kitchen with a breakfast room, a snack bar, a laundry room and a pantry. The four-bedroom upstairs includes a master suite with a sumptuous bath and an exercise room.

Complete Pella Window Specifications Provided With Every Home Plan

WINDOWSCAPING®

Design by
Home Planners

DESIGN 2889

First Floor: 2,348 square feet
Second Floor: 1,872 square feet
Total: 4,220 square feet

L D

■ It's easy to imagine our spirited, patriotic forefathers meeting in a home such as this. The pediment gable with its cornice work and dentils and the beautifully proportioned columns identify this home as an elegant Georgian. Enter a large receiving hall bound by grand living and dining rooms and graced by a curving double staircase. Beyond the living room is a study with access to the rear terrace. Informal family get-togethers will be enjoyed in the spacious gathering room warmed by a central fireplace bordered by full windows. The efficient kitchen features an island cooktop and shares space with a breakfast room, a walk-in pantry and a powder room. The second floor holds three family bedrooms, two full baths and an outstanding master suite that personifies elegance and romance.

Complete Pella Window Specifications Provided With Every Home Plan

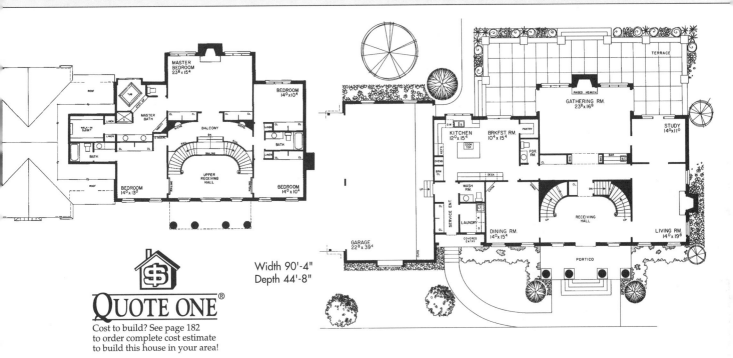

Width 90'-4"
Depth 44'-8"

QUOTE ONE®

Cost to build? See page 182 to order complete cost estimate to build this house in your area!

DESIGN 3505

First Floor: 2,899 square feet
Second Floor: 1,519 square feet
Total: 4,418 square feet
Bonus Room: 540 square feet

L

■ A sweeping veranda with tapered columns supports this Southern raised cottage's low-pitched roof and its delicately detailed cornice work. The wood railing effectively complements the lattice-work below. Horizontal siding and double-hung windows with muntins and shutters enhance the historic appeal of this 1½-story home. Inside, the spacious central foyer has a high ceiling and a dramatic, curving staircase to the second floor. Two formal areas flank the foyer and include the living room to the left and the dining room to the right. The U-shaped kitchen easily services the latter through a butler's pantry. A library and gathering room flank the kitchen. Sleeping accommodations excel with a spacious master suite. At the top of the dramatic staircase is a generous sitting area shared by three bedrooms. A bonus room further enhances this family home.

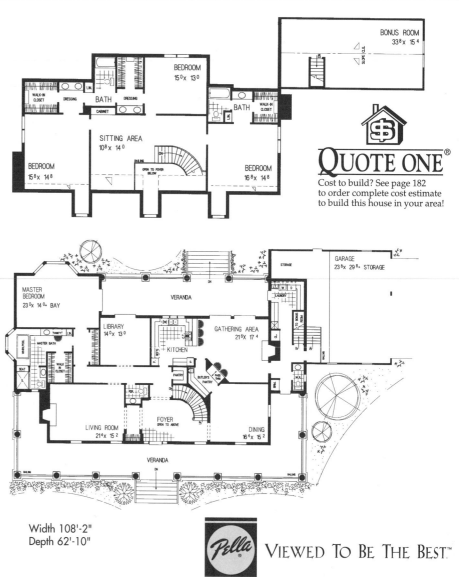

QUOTE ONE®
Cost to build? See page 182 to order complete cost estimate to build this house in your area!

Width 108'-2"
Depth 62'-10"

Pella

VIEWED TO BE THE BEST™

Complete Pella Window Specifications Provided With Every Home Plan

WINDOWSCAPING®

Design by
Donald A. Gardner Architects, Inc.

© 1996 Donald A. Gardner Architects, Inc.

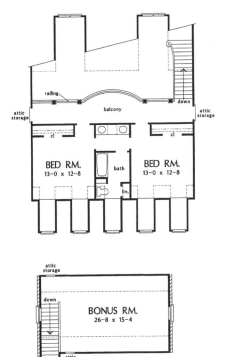

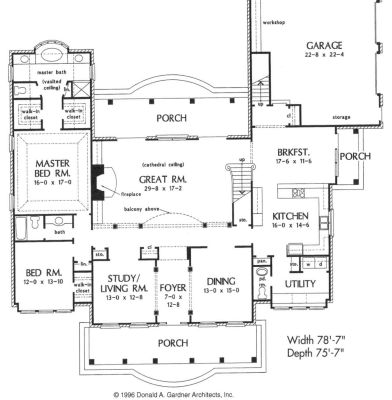

© 1996 Donald A. Gardner Architects, Inc.

DESIGN 7622

First Floor: 2,920 square feet
Second Floor: 853 square feet
Total: 3,773 square feet
Bonus Room: 458 square feet

■ This elegant country home is a delight in its symmetry, from its gabled dormers to the matching triple windows flanking the arched and columned porch. Inside, the foyer leads to a magnificent great room that overlooks a mirror-image porch at the rear. Separated from the foyer by decorative columns are the formal dining room and a living room that could also serve as a study. The U-shaped kitchen easily serves the dining room and the breakfast room and is next to a handy utility room. The master bedroom features a tray ceiling and a compartmented, vaulted bath with twin walk-in closets, separate vanities and a bumped-out oval tub. A secondary bedroom at the front of the house has its own bath, making it a perfect guest suite, while two bedrooms upstairs share a bath with twin vanities and a balcony overlooking the great room.

Complete Pella Window Specifications Provided With Every Home Plan

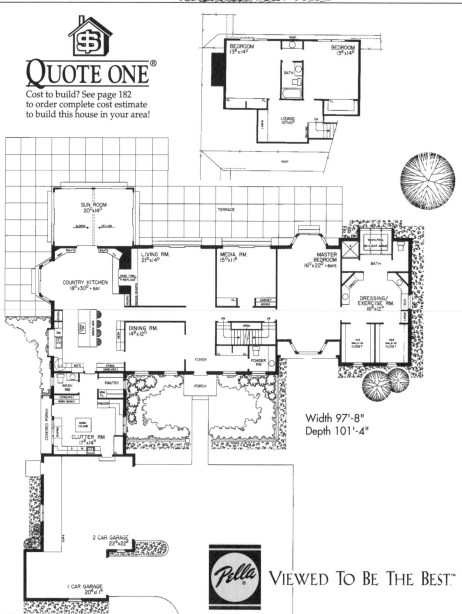

DESIGN 2921

First Floor: 3,215 square feet
Second Floor: 711 square feet
Total: 3,926 square feet
Sun Room: 296 square feet

L D

■ Organized zoning makes this traditional design a comfortable home for living. A central foyer facilitates flexible traffic patterns. Quiet areas of the house include a media room and luxurious master bedroom suite with fitness area, spacious closet space and bath, as well as a lounge or writing area. Informal living areas of the house include a sun room, large country kitchen and an efficient food preparation area with an island. Formal living areas include a living area and formal dining room. The second floor holds two bedrooms and a lounge. Service areas include a room just off the garage for laundry, sewing or hobbies.

QUOTE ONE®
Cost to build? See page 182 to order complete cost estimate to build this house in your area!

Width 97'-8"
Depth 101'-4"

Pella
VIEWED TO BE THE BEST™

Complete Pella Window Specifications Provided With Every Home Plan

WINDOWSCAPING®

Design by Home Planners

DESIGN 3360

Main Level: 2,673 square feet
Lower Level: 1,389 square feet
Total: 4,062 square feet

L

■ Expanding families and empty-nesters take a good look at this plan! Not only does it accommodate a difficult lot, but it is completely livable on the main level, with expansion capabilities on the lower level. The foyer is raised slightly and leads to a large gathering room/dining room combination at the rear of the home. A curved wet bar serves this area. The kitchen features a U-shaped counter area (one wing is a pass-through snack bar) and a casual breakfast area. A media room (or a guest room) has handy space for video equipment. Bedrooms include the lavish master suite and a secondary bedroom on the main level and a third bedroom on the lower level. A huge activities room with a summer kitchen dominates the additional space at the lower level.

Complete Pella Window Specifications Provided With Every Home Plan

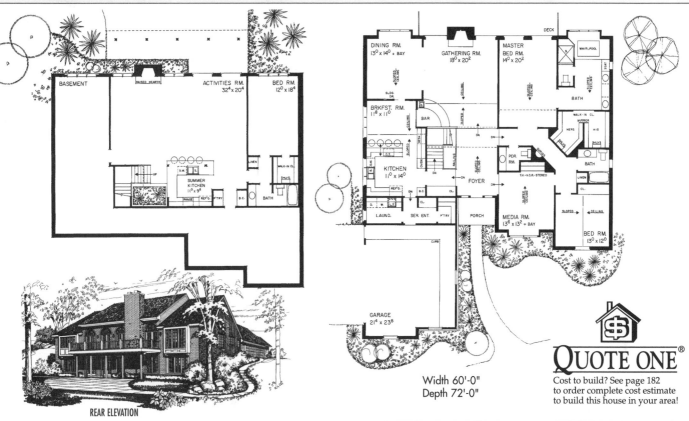

REAR ELEVATION

Width 60'-0"
Depth 72'-0"

QUOTE ONE®

Cost to build? See page 182 to order complete cost estimate to build this house in your area!

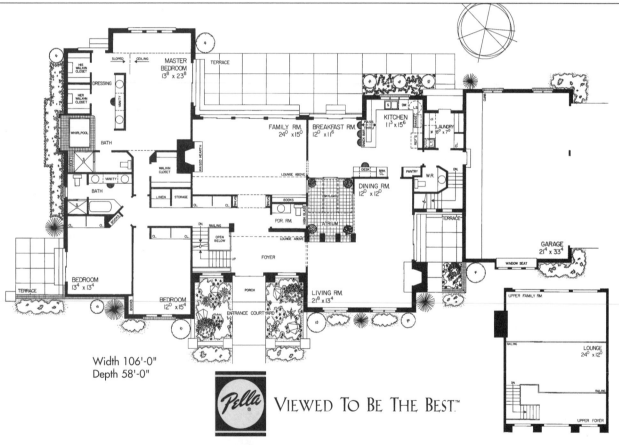

Width 106'-0"
Depth 58'-0"

Pella
VIEWED TO BE THE BEST™

DESIGN 2966

First Floor: 3,403 square feet
Lounge: 284 square feet
Total: 3,687 square feet

■ This Tudor adaptation is as dramatic inside as it is outside. From the front entrance courtyard to the rear terrace, there is much that catches the eye. The spacious foyer with its sloping ceiling looks up into the balcony-type lounge. The focal point of the living room is the delightful atrium. Both the formal living room and the informal family room feature a fireplace. Each of the full baths highlights a tub and shower, a vanity and twin lavatories. A staircase located near the three-car garage provides secondary access to the basement.

Complete Pella Window Specifications Provided With Every Home Plan

LIVABLE LUXURY:
Classically elegant designs with a new perspective

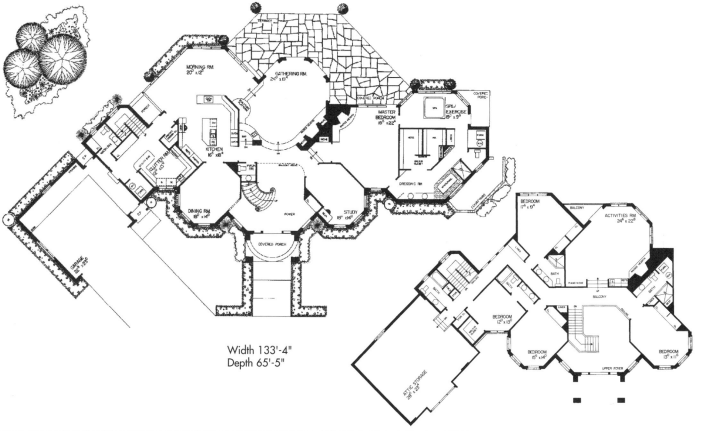

Width 133'-4"
Depth 65'-5"

DESIGN 2968

First Floor: 3,736 square feet
Second Floor: 2,264 square feet
Total: 6,000 square feet

L

■ The distinctive covered entry to this stunning manor, flanked by twin turrets, leads to a gracious foyer with impressive fanlights. The plan opens from the foyer to a formal dining room, a master study and a step-down gathering room. The spacious kitchen has numerous amenities, including an island work station and a built-in desk. The adjacent morning room and the gathering room, with a wet bar and a raised-hearth fireplace, are bathed in light and open to the terrace for outdoor entertaining. The luxurious and secluded master suite includes two walk-in closets, a dressing area and an exercise area with a spa. The second floor features four bedrooms and an oversized activities room with a fireplace and a balcony. Unfinished attic space can be completed to your specifications.

Complete Pella Window Specifications Provided With Every Home Plan

DESIGN 2940

First Floor: 4,786 square feet
Second Floor: 1,842 square feet
Total: 6,628 square feet

L D

■ Graceful window arches soften the massive chimneys and hip roof of this grand Norman manor. A two-story gathering room is two steps down from the adjacent lounge with impressive wet bar and semi-circular music alcove. The highly efficient galley-style kitchen overlooks the family room fireplace and spectacular windowed breakfast room. The master suite is a private retreat with a fireplace and a wood box tucked into the corner of its sitting room. Separate His and Hers baths and dressing rooms guarantee plenty of space and privacy. A large, built-in whirlpool tub adds the final touch. Upstairs, a second-floor balcony overlooks the gathering room below. There are also four additional bedrooms, each with a private bath.

QUOTE ONE®

Cost to build? See page 182
to order complete cost estimate
to build this house in your area!

Pella

VIEWED TO BE THE BEST.™

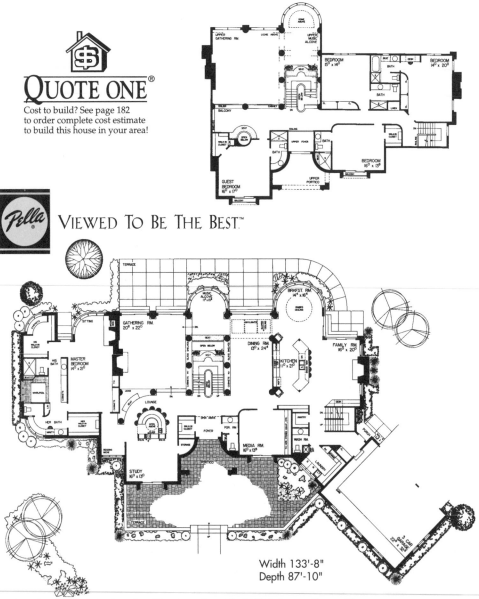

Width 133'-8"
Depth 87'-10"

Complete Pella Window Specifications Provided With Every Home Plan

WINDOWSCAPING®

Design by
Home Planners

DESIGN 3305

First Floor: 3,644 square feet
Second Floor: 2,005 square feet
Total: 5,649 square feet

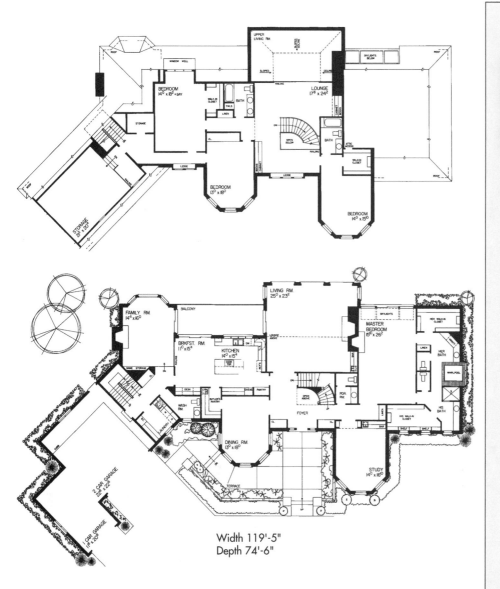

Width 119'-5"
Depth 74'-6"

■ A steeply pitched roof, a generous supply of multi-pane windows, and fanlights and glass side panels that accent the front entry enhance the grand design of this beautiful home. Highlights include a magnificent first-floor master suite that features a warming fireplace in the skylit bedroom. An opulent bath is designed with "His and Hers" relaxation in mind. A sun-filled living room overlooking the rear grounds and bay windows in the family room, dining room and study provide an abundance of natural light.

Complete Pella Window Specifications Provided With Every Home Plan

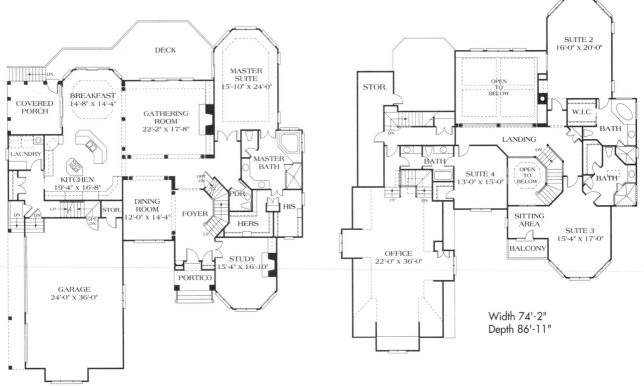

DECK

MASTER
SUITE
15'-10" X 24'-0"

COVERED
PORCH

BREAKFAST
14'-8" X 14'-4"

GATHERING
ROOM
22'-2" X 17'-8"

LAUNDRY

KITCHEN
19'-4" X 16'-8"

MASTER
BATH

DINING
ROOM
12'-0" X 14'-4"

STOR.

FOYER

HIS

HERS

PDR.

STUDY
15'-4" X 16'-10"

PORTICO

GARAGE
24'-0" X 36'-0"

SUITE 2
16'-0" X 20'-0"

STOR.

OPEN
TO
BELOW

W.I.C.

BATH

LANDING

BATH

SUITE 4
13'-0" X 15'-0"

OPEN
TO
BELOW

BATH

SITTING
AREA

SUITE 3
15'-4" X 17'-0"

OFFICE
22'-0" X 36'-0"

BALCONY

Width 74'-2"
Depth 86'-11"

DESIGN A231

First Floor: 2,893 square feet
Second Floor: 2,865 square feet
Total: 5,758 square feet

■ Stucco details, varied window treatments and elegant design give this home lots of appeal. Lavish with its luxuries inside as well as out, this plan is designed for the discriminating homeowner. A bayed study opens off the foyer and offers the warmth of a fireplace. The formal dining room and spacious gather- ing room are defined by graceful columns. The master suite is designed to pamper. With elegant angles, the efficient kitchen works well with the bay-windowed breakfast room. Three suites—each with a private bath— reside on the second floor. A spacious home office completes the plan.

Complete Pella Window Specifications Provided With Every Home Plan

WINDOWSCAPING®

Design by
Alan Mascord Design Associates, Inc.

Width 111'-0"
Depth 64'-0"

Pella VIEWED TO BE THE BEST™

DESIGN 7427

First Floor: 3,614 square feet
Second Floor: 922 square feet
Total: 4,536 square feet

■ This dormered stone-and-stucco Tudor offers its owners a special luxury that will be envied. Flanking the entry are the formal living areas—a formal dining room on the left and a formal living room with a cozy fireplace on the right. The entry leads to a sunlit gallery with views to the covered terrace. The informal family area features an immense island kitchen, a breakfast nook, a large family room with a box-bay window and a fireplace, and a full bathroom with a shower. The owner's wing includes a vaulted master suite with a bay window, a luxurious master bath with separate sinks and a spa tub, a large walk-in closet and a quiet den. Three bedrooms and two full baths are located on the second floor.

Complete Pella Window Specifications Provided With Every Home Plan

Design by
Alan Mascord Design Associates, Inc.

DESIGN 7426

First Floor: 4,205 square feet
Second Floor: 1,618 square feet
Total: 5,823 square feet
Bonus Room: 504 square feet

■ A sunlit two-story foyer offers access to every room of this exciting Mediterranean manor. Each main room is provided the added luxury of a coffered ceiling. The bayed formal dining room leads to the gourmet island kitchen through a butler's pantry. A wet bar connects the kitchen to the large family room with its built-in media center and corner fireplace. A breakfast nook offers French-door access to the side yard. The private first-floor owner's wing includes a quiet den and a large master bedroom with a lavish master bath that features two walk-in closets, a dressing area and a spa tub. Three second-floor family bedrooms are graced with their own private baths. A large media room with a built-in media center and a bonus room complete this impressive design.

Complete Pella Window Specifications Provided With Every Home Plan

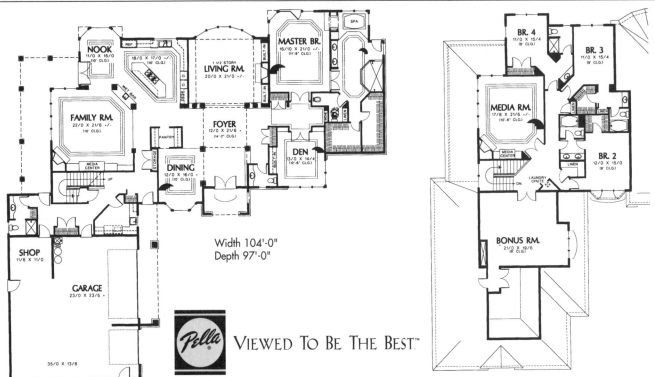

Width 104'-0"
Depth 97'-0"

VIEWED TO BE THE BEST™

WINDOWSCAPING®
Design by
Larry E. Belk Designs

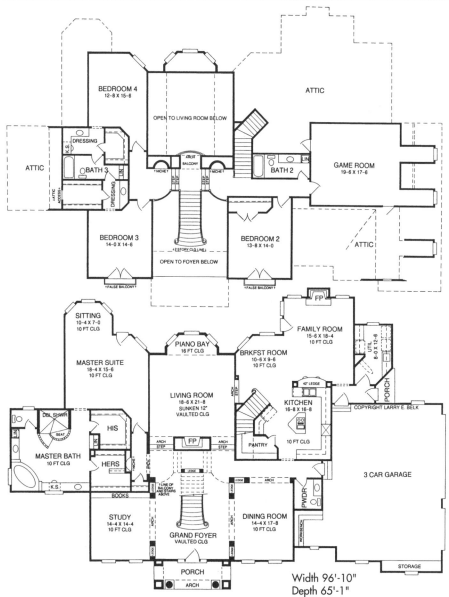

DESIGN 8185

First Floor: 3,264 square feet
Second Floor: 1,671 square feet
Total: 4,935 square feet

■ An impressive entry, multi-pane windows, and balconies combine to give this facade an elegance of which to be proud. The grand foyer showcases a stunning staircase and is flanked by a formal dining room to the right and a cozy study to the left. The elegant sunken living room is graced by a fireplace, a wondrous piano bay and a vaulted ceiling. The openness of the sunny breakfast room and the family room make casual entertaining a breeze. Located on the first floor for privacy, the master bedroom suite is lavish with its luxuries. A bayed sitting area encourages early morning repose, while the bath revels in pampering you. Upstairs, three bedrooms share two full baths and have access to a large game room over the three-car garage. Please specify crawlspace or slab foundation when ordering.

Width 96'-10"
Depth 65'-1"

Complete Pella Window Specifications Provided With Every Home Plan

DESIGN 2951

First Floor: 4,195 square feet
Second Floor: 2,094 square feet
Total: 6,289 square feet

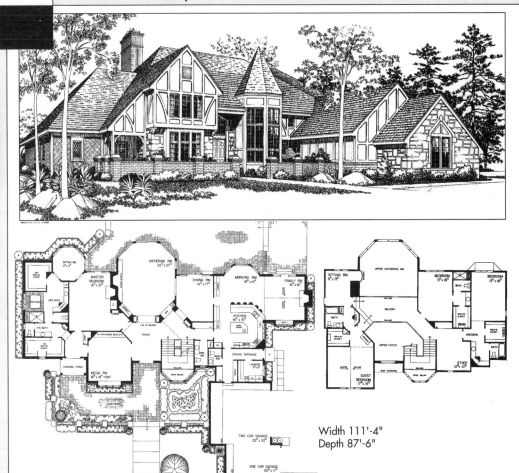

Width 111'-4"
Depth 87'-6"

■ A turret with two-story divided windows is the focal point on the exterior of this stately Tudor home. The large gathering room features a wet bar and a fireplace with a raised hearth that runs the entire length of the wall. An octagon-shaped sitting room is tucked into the corner of the impressive first-floor master suite. Three bedrooms—one a guest suite with sitting room—three baths and a study are located on the second floor.

DESIGN 2955

First Floor: 3,840 square feet
Second Floor: 3,435 square feet
Total: 7,275 square feet

■ A circular staircase provides an impressive path to the second floor. From the foyer, two steps lead down to the living room with music alcove or the library with wet bar. The second floor holds four bedrooms; two with fireplaces. The grand master suite also enjoys the warmth of a fireplace and a nursery/exercise room nearby.

Width 133'-9"
Depth 85'-6"

Complete Pella Window Specifications Provided With Every Home Plan

QUOTE ONE®
Cost to build? See page 182
to order complete cost estimate
to build this house in your area!

Pella
VIEWED TO BE THE BEST.™

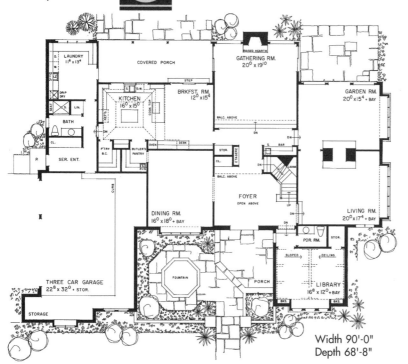

Width 90'-0"
Depth 68'-8"

DESIGN 3554

First Floor: 3,275 square feet
Second Floor: 2,363 square feet
Total: 5,638 square feet

L **D**

■ A splendid garden entry welcomes visitors to this regal
Tudor home. Past the double
doors is a two-story foyer that
leads to the various living areas
of the home. A quiet library is
secluded directly off the foyer
and includes a box-bay window,
a private powder room and a
sloped ceiling. Formal living
takes place to the right of the
foyer—an attached garden room
shares a through-fireplace with
this area. Formal dining is found
to the left of the foyer, accessed
from the kitchen via a butler's
pantry. The gathering room han-
dles casual occasions and is just
across the hall from the wet bar.
Upstairs, there is a grand master
suite with a lavish bath, a sitting
room and a private covered
porch. Three secondary bedrooms, each with a private bath,
complete the plan.

Complete Pella Window Specifications Provided With Every Home Plan

DESIGN A234

First Floor: 3,062 square feet
Second Floor: 2,698 square feet
Total: 5,760 square feet

■ An abundance of elegance is evident on this four-bedroom mansion. The beauty begins at the entry, where a grand facade entices friends and family to enter and enjoy the amenities that wait inside. The foyer is flanked by a formal dining room and a media room and leads through a rotunda and gallery to the spacious grand room. For intimate gatherings, there's the lake gathering room, complete with a corner fireplace, access to a snack bar and a private screened porch. For the gourmet of the family, there is a large kitchen, which features an angled work island and an adjacent breakfast area. Note the direct access to a covered veranda here. The sleeping zone is filled with amenities; three suites—each with walk-in closets—share two full baths, a deluxe master suite waits to pamper the homeowner and a study/play loft. The basement is complete with a gymnasium, sauna, full bath, juice bar and outdoor access.

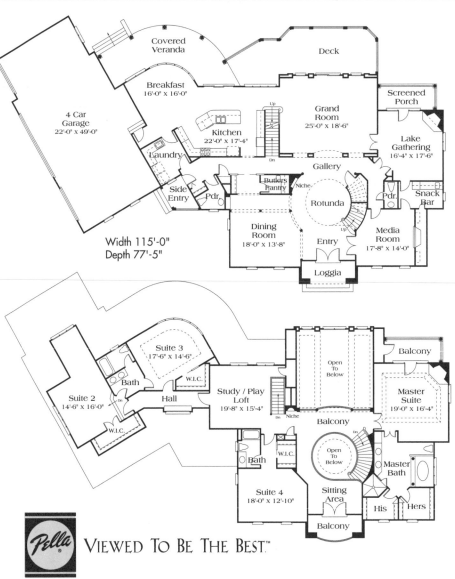

Complete Pella Window Specifications Provided With Every Home Plan

WINDOWSCAPING®
Design by
Living Concepts Home Planning

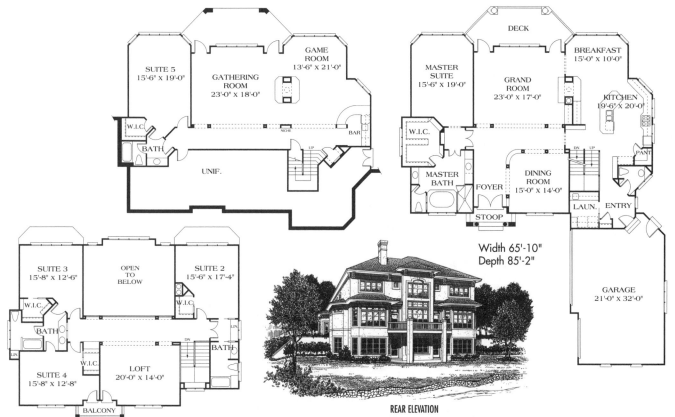

GAME ROOM
13'-6" x 21'-0"

SUITE 5
15'-6" x 19'-0"

GATHERING ROOM
23'-0" x 18'-0"

W.I.C.

BATH

NICHE

BAR

UP

UNIF.

DECK

MASTER SUITE
15'-6" x 19'-0"

GRAND ROOM
23'-0" x 17'-0"

BREAKFAST
15'-0" x 10'-0"

KITCHEN
19'-6" x 20'-0"

W.I.C.

PANT

MASTER BATH

FOYER

DINING ROOM
15'-0" x 14'-0"

DN UP

LAUN.

ENTRY

STOOP

Width 65'-10"
Depth 85'-2"

GARAGE
21'-0" x 32'-0"

SUITE 3
15'-8" x 12'-6"

OPEN TO BELOW

SUITE 2
15'-6" x 17'-4"

W.I.C.

W.I.C.

BATH

LIN

BATH

LIN

SUITE 4
15'-8" x 12'-8"

W.I.C.

LOFT
20'-0" x 14'-0"

DN

BALCONY

REAR ELEVATION

DESIGN A215

Main Level: 2,450 square feet
Upper Level: 1,675 square feet
Lower Level: 1,568 square feet
Total: 5,693 square feet

■ Designed for sloping lots, this magnificent estate home offers windows that overlook the rear grounds from three separate levels. From the first floor, the foyer opens onto a spacious dining room and grand room enriched by decorative columns and an abundance of windows. To the right is a large kitchen with an adjacent breakfast nook from which you can relax with a cup of your favorite brew and also enjoy unsurpassed views. The classic master suite claims the remainder of the first floor. Upstairs, three suites and a loft feature opportunities to survey the surrounding landscape, both front and back. The lower level provides lots of space for family and friends. A gathering room and game room share the warmth of a fireplace and access to a covered patio. An additional suite that's well suited for guests or family members who desire an extra measure of privacy completes the plan.

Complete Pella Window Specifications Provided With Every Home Plan

Design by
Donald A. Gardner Architects, Inc.

DESIGN 7660

Square Footage: 4,523

©1997 Donald A. Gardner Architects, Inc.

■ Unique window treatments create an interesting brick exterior on this one-story home. Inside, a spacious great room has a fireplace, built-ins and access to the rear porch. The kitchen has a walk-in pantry and a butler's pantry with a wet bar. Nearby, a bay-windowed breakfast room opens to a sunroom. The formal dining room has a tray ceiling and a lovely triple window. Two master baths, each with its own walk-in closet, lavatory and toilet provide individual privacy in the master retreat. Each of the two family bedrooms has a private toilet and lavatory.

© 1997 Donald A. Gardner Architects, Inc.

Width 114'-4"
Depth 82'-3"

Design by
Living Concepts
Home Planning

DESIGN A225

First Floor: 3,329 square feet
Second Floor: 1,485 square feet
Total: 4,814 square feet

■ A curving wall of glass, impressive pilasters and gently arched windows furnish a beautiful facade on this grand manor. The master wing includes a bayed lounge, an exercise room and a media room, as well as a sumptuous bath. A glass-enclosed morning room completes the gourmet kitchen, while a round study offers a retreat from the formality of the grand room or the bustle of the gathering room. Upstairs, the captain's quarters might be anything from a game room to a romantic retreat. This is truly a home to challenge your imagination!

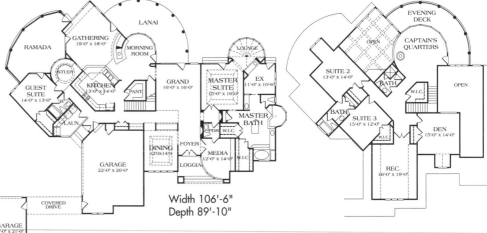

Width 106'-6"
Depth 89'-10"

Complete Pella Window Specifications Provided With Every Home Plan

WINDOWSCAPING®

Design by
The Sater Design Collection

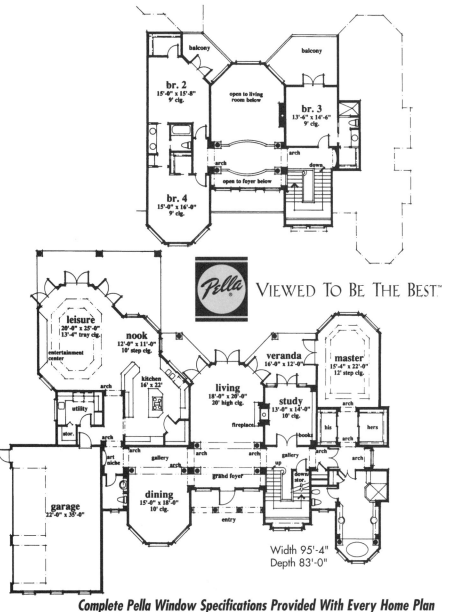

Pella® VIEWED TO BE THE BEST™

br. 2
15'-0" x 15'-8"
9' clg.

open to living room below

br. 3
13'-6" x 14'-6"
9' clg.

balcony

balcony

arch

arch

arch

open to foyer below

down

br. 4
15'-0" x 16'-0"
9' clg.

leisure
20'-0" x 25'-0"
13'-4" tray clg.

entertainment center

nook
12'-0" x 11'-0"
10' step clg.

veranda
16'-0" x 12'-0"

master
15'-4" x 22'-0"
12' step clg.

utility

kitchen
16' x 22'

living
18'-0" x 20'-0"
20' high clg.

study
13'-0" x 14'-0"
10' clg.

arch

stor.

fireplace

arch

his

hers

arch

art niche

gallery

arch

arch

arch

arch

books

gallery

arch

garage
22'-0" x 35'-0"

dining
15'-0" x 18'-0"
10' clg.

grand foyer

up

down
stor.

entry

Width 95'-4"
Depth 83'-0"

Complete Pella Window Specifications Provided With Every Home Plan

DESIGN 6651

First Floor: 3,546 square feet
Second Floor: 1,213 square feet
Total: 4,759 square feet

■ A marvelously arched entry welcomes you to this beautiful home. Inside, the two-story foyer opens onto the lavish living room, which is graced by a through-fireplace to the study and three sets of double French doors to the rear terrace. A huge octagonal leisure room at the back of the plan offers a built-in entertainment center. A large kitchen with a cooktop island easily serves both the formal dining room and the sunny breakfast nook. The master suite, located at the far right of the plan, has access to a rear veranda. Large His and Hers walk-in closets will fulfill all your storage needs and a sumptuous master bath is designed to pamper. Upstairs, three family bedrooms each have walk-in closets. Two share a full bath while the third has a private bath. A three-car garage will easily handle the family fleet. Please specify basement or slab foundation when ordering.

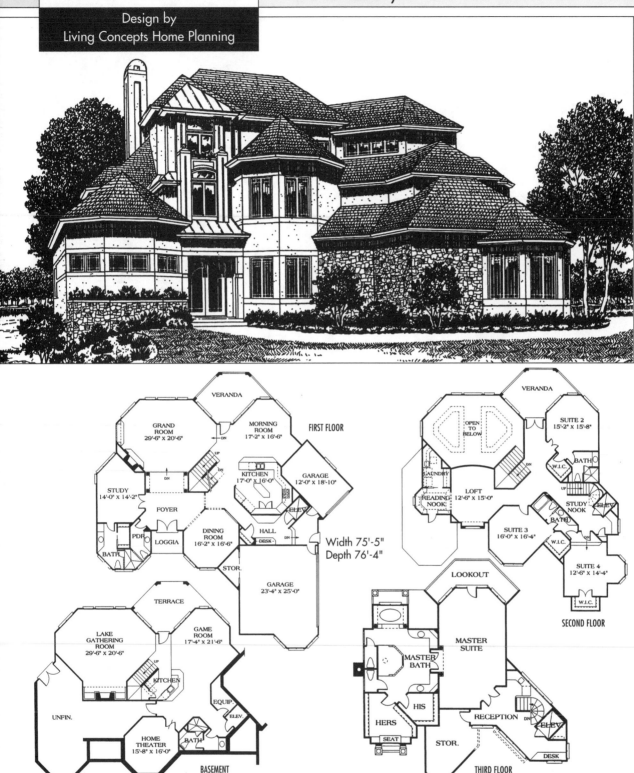

VERANDA

GRAND ROOM
29'-6" x 20'-6"

MORNING ROOM
17'-2" x 16'-6"

FIRST FLOOR

DN
UP
DN

KITCHEN
17'-0" x 16'-0"

GARAGE
12'-0" x 18'-10"

STUDY
14'-0" x 14'-2"

FOYER

ELEV.

PDR.
LOGGIA

DINING ROOM
16'-2" x 16'-6"

HALL
DESK
DN

BATH

STOR.

Width 75'-5"
Depth 76'-4"

GARAGE
23'-4" x 25'-0"

TERRACE

LAKE GATHERING ROOM
29'-6" x 20'-6"

GAME ROOM
17'-4" x 21'-6"

UP
KITCHEN

UNFIN.

EQUIP.
ELEV.

HOME THEATER
15'-8" x 16'-0"

BATH

BASEMENT

VERANDA

OPEN TO BELOW

SUITE 2
15'-2" x 15'-8"

LAUNDRY

BATH
W.I.C.

READING NOOK

LOFT
12'-6" x 15'-0"

DN
UP

STUDY NOOK

ELEV.

SUITE 3
16'-0" x 16'-4"

BATH

W.I.C.

DN

SUITE 4
12'-6" x 14'-4"

W.I.C.

SECOND FLOOR

LOOKOUT

MASTER SUITE

MASTER BATH

HIS

HERS

RECEPTION
DN
ELEV.

SEAT

STOR.

DESK

THIRD FLOOR

DESIGN A235

First Floor: 2,347 square feet
Second Floor: 1,800 square feet
Third Floor: 1,182 square feet
Basement: 1,688 square feet
Total: 7,017 square feet

■ If an opulent manor is cast for your future, this four level plan has everything. Wake up in the master suite, step out on the lookout balcony to watch the sunrise, then take the elevator to the basement for a workout with your own equipment. Breakfast awaits in the first-floor morning room, then it's off to the study to take care of the day's business. Designed for relaxation, three bedrooms on the second floor share a loft with a reading nook and access to the veranda. Later in the day, enjoy a soak in the third-floor master suite's garden tub and select something elegant to wear for the festive evening ahead. After an unforgettable dinner in the formal dining room, a viewing of a new movie release is offered in the home theater. Complete the evening with a nightcap in front of the fireplace in the lake gathering room—the end of a perfect day.

Complete Pella Window Specifications Provided With Every Home Plan

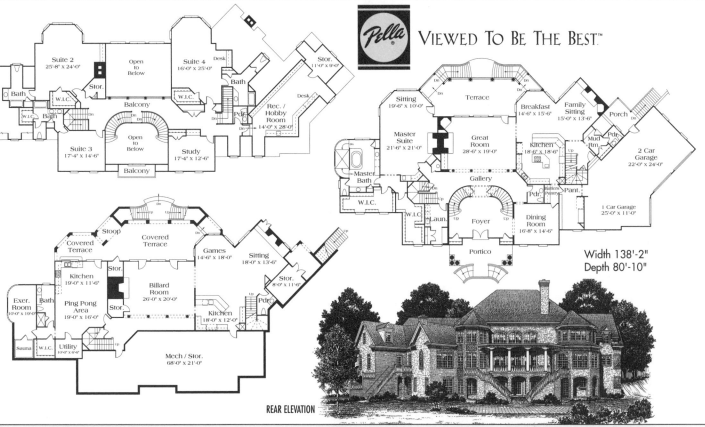

VIEWED TO BE THE BEST™

Width 138'-2"
Depth 80'-10"

REAR ELEVATION

DESIGN A237

First Floor: 4,528 square feet
Second Floor: 3,590 square feet
Basement: 2,992 square feet
Total: 11,110 square feet

■ If you're looking for a home that fits a sloping lot, yet retains a strength and character that matches our Colonial forefathers, you need look no farther. The front elevation reflects a traditional style that incorporates design elements of that earlier period. However, the floor plan and the rear elevation provide a contemporary twist. Beyond the portico, you'll enter a two-story foyer framed by twin curving staircases. Straight ahead, a spacious great room separates the private master suite to the left, and the formal dining room, kitchen, breakfast room and family/sitting room to the right. The second floor contains three suites—two with bay windows—three and a half baths, a study and a recreation room. The basement sports a billiard room, two kitchens, an exercise room, a full bath, a ping pong area and a separate games and sitting room.

Complete Pella Window Specifications Provided With Every Home Plan

DESIGN A228

First Floor: 3,129 square feet
Second Floor: 1,812 square feet
Total: 4,941 square feet

■ This classic entry announces an open interior decked with both comfort and style. The foyer leads to a gallery hall that opens to the grand room through decorative columns. This flexible space offers a warming fireplace and French doors to the rear terrace. Sunlight opens the breakfast bay to a sense of the outdoors and brightens the kitchen, which has a walk-in pantry. The right wing of the house is dedicated to a deluxe master suite with a spacious bath that features a dressing area, two walk-in closets and a garden tub. The second floor contains three suites—each with a private bath—and lots of closet space. A large recreation room completes this level.

SUITE 4
13'-8" x 20'-6"

OPEN TO BELOW

BATH

BATH

REC. ROOM
12'-0" x 28'-6"

SUITE 3
14'-6" x 17'-0"

OPEN TO BELOW

SUITE 2
14'-6" x 17'-0"

W.I.C.

BATH

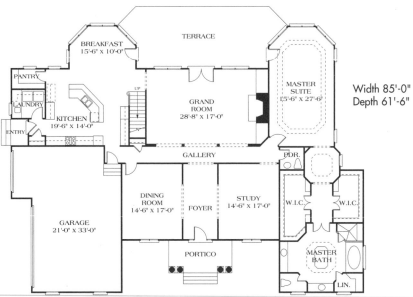

BREAKFAST
15'-6" x 10'-0"

TERRACE

PANTRY

LAUNDRY

KITCHEN
19'-6" x 14'-0"

ENTRY

GRAND ROOM
28'-8" x 17'-0"

MASTER SUITE
15'-6" x 27'-6"

Width 85'-0"
Depth 61'-6"

GALLERY

PDR.

GARAGE
21'-0" x 33'-0"

DINING ROOM
14'-6" x 17'-0"

FOYER

STUDY
14'-6" x 17'-0"

W.I.C.

W.I.C.

PORTICO

MASTER BATH

LIN.

Complete Pella Window Specifications Provided With Every Home Plan

WINDOWSCAPING®

Design by Home Planners

REAR ELEVATION

Width 104'-0"
Depth 54'-8"

Pella VIEWED TO BE THE BEST™

DESIGN 2984

First Floor: 3,116 square feet
Second Floor: 1,997 square feet
Total: 5,113 square feet

L

■ An echo of Whitehall, built in 1765 in Anne Arundel County, Maryland, resounds in this home. Its classic symmetry and columned facade herald a grand interior. There's no lack of space whether entertaining formally or just enjoying a family get-together, and all are kept cozy with fireplaces in the gathering room, study and family room. An island kitchen with attached breakfast room handily serves the nearby dining room. Four second-floor bedrooms include a large master suite with another fireplace, a whirlpool tub and His and Hers closets in the bath. Three more full baths are found on this floor.

Complete Pella Window Specifications Provided With Every Home Plan

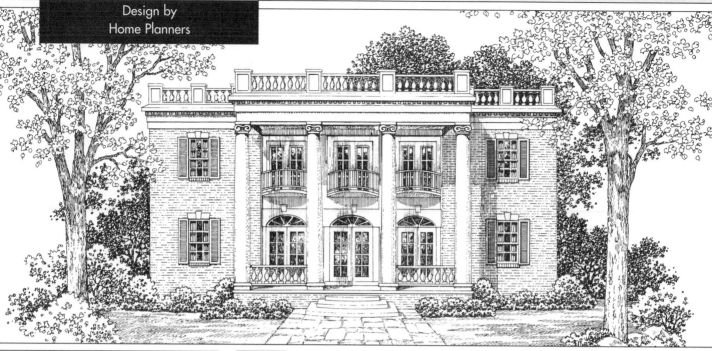

DESIGN 2993

First Floor: 2,440 square feet
Second Floor: 2,250 square feet
Total: 4,690 square feet

L D

■ 18th-Century Charleston, South Carolina, was known for the "single house," one room deep, with the narrow end facing the street. This adaptation recalls the 1750 home of Robert William Roper, with tall pillars and a handsome brick exterior crowned by a balustrade. The original has a fragment of a Civil War cannon on its roof, sent there in 1865 when the cannon was blown up to keep it from Sherman's troops. (It was deemed safer to leave it there than to try to remove it.) This version adds a family room and a garage to the floor plan. The sunken gathering room opens to the long hall through a colonnade and is flanked by the dining room and a library. Upstairs is a sumptuous master suite with a through-fireplace and three other bedrooms.

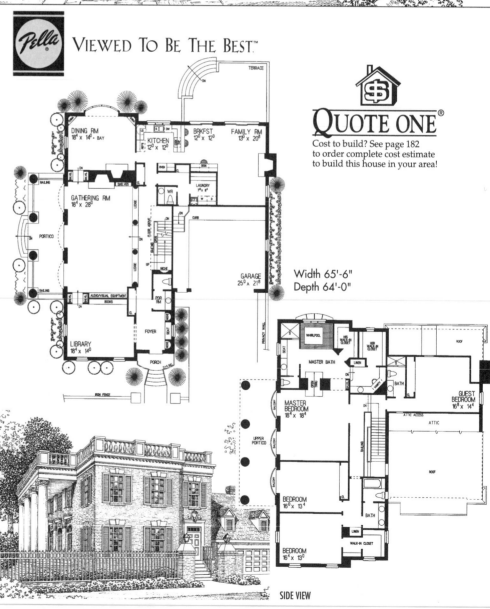

VIEWED TO BE THE BEST™

QUOTE ONE®
Cost to build? See page 182 to order complete cost estimate to build this house in your area!

Width 65'-6"
Depth 64'-0"

SIDE VIEW

Complete Pella Window Specifications Provided With Every Home Plan

WINDOWSCAPING®

Design by Home Planners

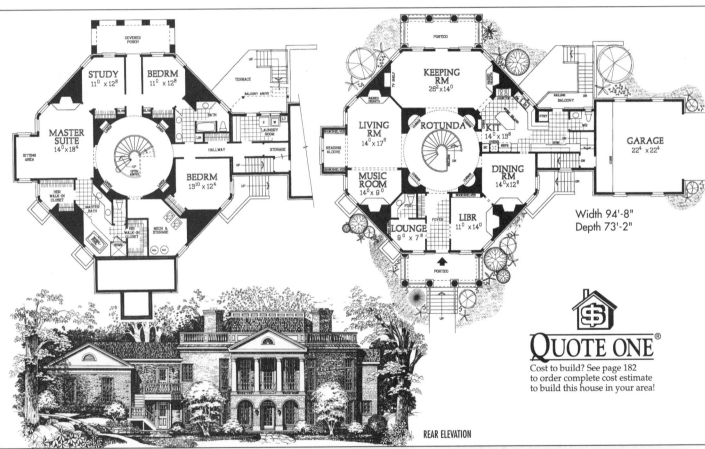

REAR ELEVATION

Width 94'-8"
Depth 73'-2"

QUOTE ONE®
Cost to build? See page 182
to order complete cost estimate
to build this house in your area!

DESIGN 3509

Main Level: 2,434 square feet
Lower Level: 2,434 square feet
Total: 4,868 square feet

■ If you're looking to do something a little different for your home-building experience, this adaptation of Jefferson's "Poplar Forest" home may be just the ticket. Named for the tulip poplars that still grow nearby, the red-brick porticoed house was started by Jefferson in 1806, and was laid out as an octagon, a shape he had experimented with in architectural sketches for years. Located near Lynchburg, Virginia, Poplar Forest was Jefferson's retreat from the hustle and bustle of politics. Inside, the rooms radiate out from a central rotunda, which is decorated with round curio niches. Fireplaces adorn all of the major living areas on the upper, entry level—music room, living room, keeping room, dining room and library. The island kitchen is roomy, with a china closet, desk and pantry. Downstairs bedrooms include a master suite with a fireplace, a study and a private luxury bath.

Complete Pella Window Specifications Provided With Every Home Plan

When You're Ready To Order . . .

Let Us Show You Our Home Blueprint Package.

Building a home? Planning a home? Our Blueprint Package has nearly everything you need to get the job done right, whether you're working on your own or with help from an architect, designer, builder or subcontractors. Each Blueprint Package is the result of many hours of work by licensed architects or professional designers.

QUALITY

Hundreds of hours of painstaking effort have gone into the development of your blueprint set. Each home has been quality-checked by professionals to insure accuracy and buildability.

VALUE

Because we sell in volume, you can buy professional-quality blueprints at a fraction of their development cost. With our plans, your dream home design costs only a few hundred dollars, not the thousands of dollars that custom architects charge.

SERVICE

Once you've chosen your favorite home plan, you'll receive fast, efficient service whether you choose to mail or fax your order to us or call us toll free at 1-800-521-6797. For customer service, call toll free 1-888-690-1116.

SATISFACTION

Over 50 years of service to satisfied home plan buyers provide us unparalleled experience and knowledge in producing quality blueprints. What this means to you is satisfaction with our product and performance.

ORDER TOLL FREE 1-800-521-6797

After you've looked over our Blueprint Package and Important Extras on the following pages, simply mail the order form on page 189 or call toll free on our Blueprint Hotline: 1-800-521-6797. We're ready and eager to serve you. For customer service, call toll free 1-888-690-1116.

Each set of blueprints is an interrelated collection of detail sheets which includes components such as floor plans, interior and exterior elevations, dimensions, cross-sections, diagrams and notations. These sheets show exactly how your house is to be built.

Among the sheets included may be:

Frontal Sheet
This artist's sketch of the exterior of the house gives you an idea of how the house will look when built and landscaped. Large ink-line floor plans show all levels of the house and provide an overview of your new home's livability, as well as a handy reference for deciding on furniture placement.

Foundation Plan
This sheet shows the foundation layout includ-

SAMPLE PACKAGE

ing support walls, excavated and unexcavated areas, if any, and foundation notes. If slab construction rather than basement, the plan shows footings and details for a monolithic slab. This page, or another in the set, may include a sample plot plan for locating your house on a building site.

Detailed Floor Plans
These plans show the layout of each floor of the house. Rooms and interior spaces are carefully dimensioned and keys are given for cross-section details provided later in the plans. The positions of electrical outlets and switches are shown.

House Cross-Sections
Large-scale views show sections or cut-aways of the foundation, interior walls, exterior walls, floors, stairways and roof details. Additional cross-sections may show important changes in floor, ceiling or roof heights or the relationship of one level to another. Extremely valuable for construction, these sections show exactly how the various parts of the house fit together.

Interior Elevations
Many of our drawings show the design and placement of kitchen and bathroom cabinets, laundry areas, fireplaces, bookcases and other built-ins. Little "extras," such as mantelpiece and wainscoting drawings, plus moulding sections, provide details that give your home that custom touch.

Exterior Elevations
These drawings show the front, rear and sides of your house and give necessary notes on exterior materials and finishes. Particular attention is given to cornice detail, brick and stone accents or other finish items that make your home unique.

Frontal Sheet

Foundation Plans

Detailed Floor Plans

Exterior Elevations

Interior Elevations

House Cross-Sections

*I*mportant Extras To Do The Job Right!

Introducing eight important planning and construction aids developed by our professionals to help you succeed in your home-building project.

MATERIALS LIST

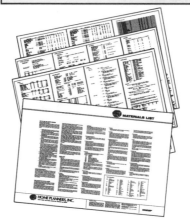

For many of the designs in our portfolio, we offer a customized materials take-off that is invaluable in planning and estimating the cost of your new home. This Materials List outlines the quantity, type and size of materials needed to build your house (with the exception of mechanical system items). Included are framing lumber, windows and doors, kitchen and bath cabinetry, rough and finish hardware, and much more. This handy list helps you or your builder cost out materials and serves as a reference sheet when you're compiling bids. A Materials List cannot be ordered before blueprints are ordered.

(Note: Because of the diversity of local building codes, our Materials List does not include mechanical materials.)

SPECIFICATION OUTLINE

This valuable 16-page document is critical to building your house correctly. Designed to be filled in by you or your builder, this book lists 166 stages or items crucial to the building process. It provides a comprehensive review of the construction process and helps in making choices of materials. When combined with the blueprints, a signed contract, and a schedule, it becomes a legal document and record for the building of your home.

QUOTE ONE®

Summary Cost Report / Materials Cost Report

A new service for estimating the cost of building select designs, the Quote One® system is available in two separate stages: The Summary Cost Report and the Materials Cost Report.

Make even more informed decisions about your home-building project with the second phase of our package, our Materials Cost Report. This tool is invaluable in planning and estimating the cost of your new home. The material and installation (labor and equipment) cost is shown for each of over 1,000 line items provided in the Materials List (Standard grade) which is included when you purchase this estimating tool. It allows you to determine building costs for your specific zip-code area and for your chosen home design. Space is allowed for additional estimates from contractors and subcontractors, such as for mechanical materials, which are not included in our packages. This invaluable tool is available for a price of $110 ($120 for a Schedule E plan) which includes a Materials List. A Materials Cost Report cannot be ordered before blueprints are ordered.

The Summary Cost Report is the first stage in the package and shows the total cost per square foot for your chosen home in your zip-code area and then breaks that cost down into various categories showing the costs for building materials, labor and installation. The total cost for the report (which includes three grades: Budget, Standard and Custom) is just $19.95 for one home, and additionals are only $14.95. These reports allow you to evaluate your building budget and compare the costs of building a variety of homes in your area.

The Quote One® program is continually updated with new plans. If you are interested in a plan that is not indicated as Quote One®, please call and ask our sales reps, they will be happy to verify the status for you. To order these invaluable reports, use the order form on page 189 or call 1-800-521-6797.

CONSTRUCTION INFORMATION

If you want to know more about techniques—and deal more confidently with subcontractors we offer these useful sheets. Each set is an excellent tool that will add to your understanding of these technical subjects.

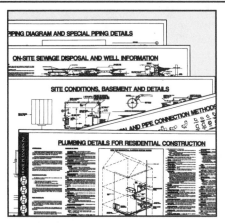

PLUMBING

The Blueprint Package includes locations for all the plumbing fixtures in your new house, including sinks, lavatories, tubs, showers, toilets, laundry trays and water heaters. However, if you want to know more about the complete plumbing system, these 24x36-inch detail sheets will prove very useful. Prepared to meet requirements of the National Plumbing Code, these six fact-filled sheets give general information on pipe schedules, fittings, sump-pump details, water-softener hookups, septic system details and much more. Color-coded sheets include a glossary of terms.

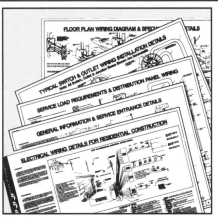

ELECTRICAL

The locations for every electrical switch, plug and outlet are shown in your Blueprint Package. However, these Electrical Details go further to take the mystery out of household electrical systems. Prepared to meet requirements of the National Electrical Code, these comprehensive 24x36-inch drawings come packed with helpful information, including wire sizing, switch-installation schematics, cable-routing details, appliance wattage, door-bell hookups, typical service panel circuitry and much more. Six sheets are bound together and color-coded for easy reference. A glossary of terms is also included.

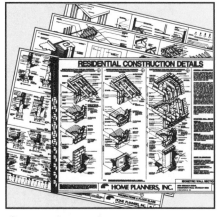

CONSTRUCTION

The Blueprint Package contains everything an experienced builder needs to construct a particular house. However, it doesn't show all the ways that houses can be built, nor does it explain alternate construction methods. To help you understand how your house will be built—and offer additional techniques—this set of drawings depicts the materials and methods used to build foundations, fireplaces, walls, floors and roofs. Where appropriate, the drawings show acceptable alternatives. These six sheets will answer questions for the advanced do-it-yourselfer or home planner.

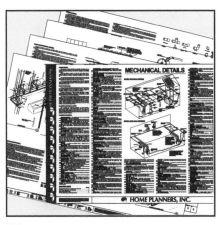

MECHANICAL

This package contains fundamental principles and useful data that will help you make informed decisions and communicate with subcontractors about heating and cooling systems. The 24x36-inch drawings contain instructions and samples that allow you to make simple load calculations and preliminary sizing and costing analysis. Covered are today's most commonly used systems from heat pumps to solar fuel systems. The package is packed full of illustrations and diagrams to help you visualize components and how they relate to one another.

Plan-A-Home®

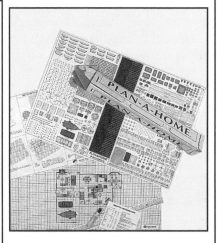

Plan-A-Home® is an easy-to-use tool that helps you design a new home, arrange furniture in a new or existing home, or plan a remodeling project. Each package contains:

- **More than 700 reusable peel-off planning symbols** on a self-stick vinyl sheet, including walls, windows, doors, all types of furniture, kitchen components, bath fixtures and many more.

- **A reusable, transparent, 1/4-inch scale planning grid** that matches the scale of actual working drawings (1/4-inch equals 1 foot). This grid provides the basis for house layouts of up to 140x92 feet.

- **Tracing paper** and a protective sheet for copying or transferring your completed plan.

- **A felt-tip pen,** with water-soluble ink that wipes away quickly.

Plan-A-Home® lets you lay out areas as large as a 7,500 square foot, six-bedroom, seven-bath house.

To Order, Call Toll Free 1-800-521-6797

To add these important extras to your Blueprint Package, simply indicate your choices on the order form on page 189 or call us Toll Free 1-800-521-6797 and we'll tell you more about these exciting products.
For customer service, call toll free 1-888-690-1116.

D *The Deck Blueprint Package*

Many of the homes in this book can be enhanced with a professionally designed Home Planners' Deck Plan. Those home plans highlighted with a **D** have a matching or corresponding deck plan available which includes a Deck Plan Frontal Sheet, Deck Framing and Floor Plans, Deck Elevations and a Deck Materials List. A Standard Deck Details Package, also available, provides all the how-to information necessary for building *any* deck. Our Complete Deck Building Package contains 1 set of Custom Deck Plans of your choice, plus 1 set of Standard Deck Building Details all for one low price. Our plans and details are carefully prepared in an easy-to-understand format that will guide you through every stage of your deck-building project. This page contains a sampling of 12 of the 25 different Deck layouts to match your favorite house. See page 186 for prices and ordering information.

SPLIT-LEVEL SUN DECK
Deck Plan D100

BI-LEVEL DECK WITH COVERED DINING
Deck Plan D101

WRAP-AROUND FAMILY DECK
Deck Plan D104

DECK FOR DINING AND VIEWS
Deck Plan D107

TREND SETTER DECK
Deck Plan D110

TURN-OF-THE-CENTURY DECK
Deck Plan D111

WEEKEND ENTERTAINER DECK
Deck Plan D112

CENTER-VIEW DECK
Deck Plan D114

KITCHEN-EXTENDER DECK
Deck Plan D115

SPLIT-LEVEL ACTIVITY DECK
Deck Plan D117

TRI-LEVEL DECK WITH GRILL
Deck Plan D119

CONTEMPORARY LEISURE DECK
Deck Plan D120

⬛ *The Landscape Blueprint Package*

For the homes marked with an ⬛ in this book, Home Planners has created a front-yard landscape plan that matches or is complementary in design to the house plan. These comprehensive blueprint packages include a Frontal Sheet, Plan View, Regionalized Plant & Materials List, a sheet on Planting and Maintaining Your Landscape, Zone Maps and Plant Size and Description Guide. These plans will help you achieve professional results, adding value and enjoyment to your property for years to come. Each set of blueprints is a full 18" x 24" in size with clear, complete instructions and easy-to-read type. Six of the forty front yard Landscape Plans to match your favorite house are shown below.

Regional Order Map

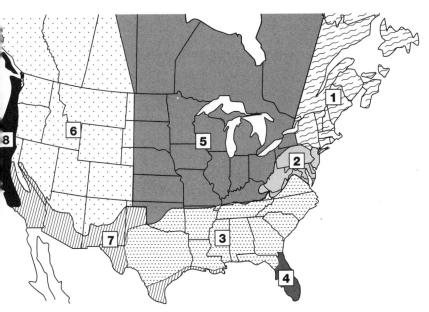

Most of the Landscape Plans shown on these pages are available with a Plant & Materials List adapted by horticultural experts to 8 different regions of the country. Please specify Geographic Region when ordering your plan. See page 186 for prices, ordering information and regional availability.

Region	1	Northeast
Region	2	Mid-Atlantic
Region	3	Deep South
Region	4	Florida & Gulf Coast
Region	5	Midwest
Region	6	Rocky Mountains
Region	7	Southern California & Desert Southwest
Region	8	Northern California & Pacific Northwest

CAPE COD COTTAGE
Landscape Plan L202

GAMBREL-ROOF COLONIAL
Landscape Plan L203

CENTER-HALL COLONIAL
Landscape Plan L204

CLASSIC NEW ENGLAND COLONIAL
Landscape Plan L205

COUNTRY-STYLE FARMHOUSE
Landscape Plan L207

TRADITIONAL SPLIT-LEVEL
Landscape Plan L228

Price Schedule & Plans Index

House Blueprint Price Schedule
(Prices guaranteed through December 31, 1999)

Tier	1-set Study Package	4-set Building Package	8-set Building Package	1-set Reproducible Sepias	Home Customizer® Package
A	$390	$435	$495	$595	$645
B	$430	$475	$535	$655	$705
C	$470	$515	$575	$715	$765
D	$510	$555	$615	$775	$825
E	$630	$675	$735	$835	$885
F	$730	$775	$835	$935	$985
G	$830	$885	$835	$1035	$1085

Prices for 4- or 8-set Building Packages honored only at time of original order.

Additional Identical Blueprints (standard or reverse) in same order ..$50 per set
Reverse Blueprints (mirror image) with 4- or 8-set order ....$50 per order
Specification Outlines ....$10 each
Materials Lists (available only for those designers listed below):
- ▲ Home Planners Designs...$50
- † Design Basics Designs...$75
- ◆ Donald Gardner Designs..$50
- ● Larry Belk Designs..$50
- ✷ Alan Mascord Designs...$50

Materials Lists for "E-G" price plans are an additional $10.

Deck Plans Price Schedule

CUSTOM DECK PLANS

Price Group	Q	R	S
1 Set Custom Plans	$25	$30	$35

Additional identical sets $10 each
Reverse sets (mirror image) $10 each

STANDARD DECK DETAILS
1 Set Generic Construction Details ....$14.95 each

COMPLETE DECK BUILDING PACKAGE

Price Group	Q	R	S
1 Set Custom Plans, plus 1 Set Standard Deck Details	$35	$40	$45

Landscape Plans Price Schedule

Price Group	X	Y	Z
1 set	$35	$45	$55
3 sets	$50	$60	$70
6 sets	$65	$75	$85

Additional Identical Sets....................................$10 each
Reverse Sets (mirror image)..............................$10 each

Index

To use the Index below, refer to the design number listed in numerical order (a helpful page reference is also given). Note the price index letter and refer to the House Blueprint Price Schedule above for the cost of one, four or eight sets of blueprints or the cost of a reproducible sepia. Additional prices are shown for identical and reverse blueprint sets, as well as a very useful Materials List for some of the plans. Also note in the Index below those plans that have matching or complementary Deck Plans or Landscape Plans. Refer to the schedules above for prices of these plans. All Home Planners' plans can be customized with Home Planners' Home Customizer® Package. These plans are indicated below with this symbol: 🏠. See page 189 for information. Some plans are also part of our Quote One® estimating service and are indicated by this symbol: 🏠. See page 182 for more information.

To Order: Fill in and send the order form on page 189—or call toll free 1-800-521-6797 or 520-297-8200.

DESIGN	PRICE	PAGE	CUSTOMIZABLE	QUOTE ONE®	DECK	DECK PRICE	LANDSCAPE	LANDSCAPE PRICE	REGIONS
▲2522	C	117	🏠						
▲2694	C	119	🏠	🏠			L209	Y	1-6,8
▲2889	D	155	🏠	🏠	D107	S	L215	Z	1-6,8
▲2921	D	158	🏠	🏠	D104	S	L212	Z	1-8
▲2940	E	162	🏠	🏠	D114	R	L230	Z	1-8
▲2951	E	168	🏠						
▲2955	D	168	🏠						
▲2966	D	160	🏠						
▲2968	E	161	🏠				L227	Z	1-8
▲2980	C	150	🏠						
▲2984	E	177	🏠				L214	Z	1-3,5,6,8
▲2988	B	118	🏠	🏠	D120	R	L201	Y	1-3,5,6,8
▲2989	D	116	🏠	🏠			L215	Z	1-6,8
▲2993	D	178	🏠	🏠	D115	Q	L214	Z	1-3,5,6,8
▲3305	E	163	🏠						
▲3337	D	154	🏠	🏠			L214	Z	1-3,5,6,8
▲3360	D	159	🏠	🏠			L207	Z	1-6,8
▲3366	D	120	🏠	🏠			L220	Y	1-3,5,6,8
▲3505	E	156	🏠	🏠			L204	Y	1-3,5,6,8
▲3508	C	151	🏠	🏠			L206	Z	1-6,8
▲3509	E	179	🏠	🏠					
▲3513	D	115	🏠	🏠	D111	S	L214	Z	1-3,5,6,8
▲3518	E	153		🏠	D110	R	L202	X	1-3,5,6,8
▲3527	E	152							
▲3554	E	169	🏠	🏠	D124	S	L219	Z	1-3,5,6,8
▲3567	D	118	🏠	🏠	D106	S	L217	Y	1-8
▲3612	C	89	🏠	🏠			L206	Z	1-6,8
▲3622	C	62	🏠	🏠			L224	Y	1-3,5,6,8
▲3631	C	90	🏠	🏠			L214	Z	1-3,5,6,8
▲3634	D	130	🏠	🏠			L224	Y	1-3,5,6,8
▲3638	C	91	🏠	🏠			L215	Z	1-6,8
▲3664	C	63	🏠	🏠			L287	Z	1-8
▲3687	B	44	🏠	🏠	D110	R	L282	X	1-8
▲3805	B	45	🏠	🏠	D110	R	L224	Y	1-3,5,6,8
4559	D	43							
6650	E	134							
6651	E	173							
6652	E	81							
6656	E	132							
6660	E	135							
6661	E	129							
6663	D	90							

Plans G207 and R100-R125 additional sets are $15 each.

Before You Order . . .

Before filling out the coupon at right or calling us on our Toll-Free Blueprint Hotline, you may want to learn more about our services and products. Here's some information you will find helpful.

Quick Turnaround

We process and ship every blueprint order from our office within two business days. Because of this quick turnaround, we won't send a formal notice acknowledging receipt of your order. Note: Remodeling plans may require more turnaround time that two business days.

Our Exchange Policy

Since blueprints are printed in response to your order, we cannot honor requests for refunds. However, we will exchange your entire first order for an equal number of blueprints at a price of $50 for the first set and $10 for each additional set; $70 total exchange fee for 4 sets; $100 total exchange fee for 8 sets . . . *plus* the difference in cost if exchanging for a design in a higher price bracket or *less* the difference in cost if exchanging for a design in lower price bracket. One exchange is allowed within a year of purchase date. **(Sepias are not exchangeable.)** All sets from the first order must be returned before the exchange can take place. Please add $18 for postage and handling via Regular Service; $30 via Priority Service; $40 via Express Service. Returns and exchanges are subject to a 20% restocking fee, shipping and handling charges are not refundable.

About Reverse Blueprints

If you want to build in reverse of the plan as shown, we will reverse any number of blueprints (mirror image) from a 4- or 8-set package for an additional fee of $50. Although lettering and dimensions will appear backward, reverses will be a useful aid if you decide to flop the plan.

Revising, Modifying and Customizing Plans

The wide variety of designs available in this publication allows you to select ideas and concepts for a home to fit your building site and match your family's needs, wants and budget. Like many homeowners who buy these plans, you and your builder, architect or engineer may want to make changes to them. Some minor changes may be made by your builder, but we recommend that most changes be made by a licensed architect or engineer. If you need to make alterations to a design that is customizable, you need only order our Home Customizer® Package to get you started. As set forth below, we cannot assume any responsibility for blueprints which have been changed, whether by you, your builder or by professionals selected by you or referred to you by us, because such individuals are outside our supervision and control.

Architectural and Engineering Seals

Some cities and states are now requiring that a licensed architect or engineer review and "seal" a blueprint, or officially approve it, prior to construction due to concerns over energy costs, safety and other factors. Prior to application for a building permit or the start of actual construction, we strongly advise that you consult your local building official who can tell you if such a review is required.

About the Designers

The architects and designers whose work appears in this publication are among America's leading residential designers. Each plan was designed to meet the requirements of a nationally recognized model building code in effect at the time and place the plan was drawn. Because national building codes change from time to time, plans may not comply with any such code at the time they are sold to a customer. In addition, building officials may not accept these plans as final construction documents of record as the plans may need to be modified and additional drawings and details added to suit local conditions and requirements. We strongly advise that purchasers consult a licensed architect or engineer, and their local building official, before starting any construction related to these plans.

Local Building Codes and Zoning Requirements

At the time of creation, our plans are drawn to specifications published by the Building Officials and Code Administrators (BOCA) International, Inc.; the Southern Building Code Congress (SBCCI) International, Inc.; the International Conference of Building Officials; or the Council of American Building Officials (CABO). Our plans are designed to meet or exceed national building standards. Because of the great differences in geography and climate throughout the United States and Canada, each state, county and municipality has its own building codes, zone requirements, ordinances and building regulations. Your plan may need to be modified to comply with local requirements regarding snow loads, energy codes, soil and seismic conditions and a wide range of other matters. In addition, you may need to obtain permits or inspections from local governments before and in the course of construction. Prior to using blueprints ordered from us, we strongly advise that you consult a licensed architect or engineer—and speak with your local building official—before applying for any permit or beginning construction. We authorize the use of our blueprints on the express condition that you strictly comply with all local building codes, zoning requirements and other applicable laws, regulations, ordinances and requirements. **Notice:** Plans for homes to be built in Nevada must be re-drawn by a Nevada-registered professional. Consult your building official for more information on this subject.

Foundation and Exterior Wall Changes

Most of our plans are drawn with either a full or partial basement foundation. Depending on your specific climate or regional building practices, you may wish to change this basement to a slab or crawlspace. Most professional contractors and builders can easily adapt your plans to alternate foundation types. Likewise, most can easily change 2x4 wall construction to 2x6, or vice versa.

Disclaimer

We and the designers we work with have put substantial care and effort into the creation of our blueprints. However, because we cannot provide on-site consultation, supervision and control over actual construction, and because of the great variance in local building requirements, building practices and soil, seismic, weather and other conditions, WE CANNOT MAKE ANY WARRANTY, EXPRESS OR IMPLIED, WITH RESPECT TO THE CONTENT OR USE OF OUR BLUEPRINTS, INCLUDING BUT NOT LIMITED TO ANY WARRANTY OF MERCHANTABILITY OR OF FITNESS FOR A PARTICULAR PURPOSE.

Terms and Conditions

These designs are protected under the terms of United States Copyright Law and may not be copied or reproduced in any way, by any means, unless you have purchased Sepias or Reproducibles which clearly indicate your right to copy or reproduce. We authorize the use of your chosen design as an aid in the construction of one single family home only. You may not use this design to build a second or multiple dwellings without purchasing another blueprint or blueprints or paying additional design fees.

How Many Blueprints Do You Need?

A single set of blueprints is sufficient to study a home in greater detail. However, if you are planning to obtain cost estimates from a contractor or subcontractors—or if you are planning to build immediately—you will need more sets. Because additional sets are cheaper when ordered in quantity with the original order, make sure you order enough blueprints to satisfy all requirements. The following checklist will help you determine how many you need:

____ Owner

____ Builder (generally requires at least three sets; one as a legal document, one to use during inspections, and at least one to give to subcontractors)

____ Local Building Department (often requires two sets)

____ Mortgage Lender (usually one set for a conventional loan; three sets for FHA or VA loans)

____ TOTAL NUMBER OF SETS

Toll Free 1-800-521-6797

Regular Office Hours:
8:00 a.m. to 8:00 p.m. Eastern Time, Monday through Friday
Our staff will gladly answer any questions during regular office hours. Our answering service can place orders after hours or on weekends.

If we receive your order by 4:00 p.m. Eastern Time, Monday through Friday, we'll process it and ship within two business days. When ordering by phone, please have your charge card ready. We'll also ask you for the Order Form Key Number at the bottom of the coupon.
Note: Remodeling plans may require more turnaround time than two business days.

By FAX: Copy the Order Form on the next page and send it on our FAX line: 1-800-224-6699 or 1-520-544-3086.

Canadian Customers
Order Toll-Free 1-800-561-4169

For faster service and plans that are modified for building in Canada, customers may now call in orders directly to our Canadian supplier of plans and charge the purchase to a charge card. Or, you may complete the order form at right, adding 40% to all prices and mail in Canadian funds to:

The Plan Centre 60 Baffin Place
Unit 5
Waterloo, Ontario N2V 1Z7

OR: Copy the Order Form and send it via our Canadian FAX line: 1-800-719-3291.

The Home Customizer®

"This house is perfect...if only the family room were two feet wider." Sound familiar? In response to the numerous requests for this type of modification, Home Planners has developed **The Home Customizer® Package**. This exclusive package offers our top-of-the-line materials to make it easy for anyone, anywhere to customize any Home Planners design to fit their needs. Check the index on pages 186-187 for those plans which are customizable.

Some of the changes you can make to any of our plans include:

- exterior elevation changes
- kitchen and bath modifications
- roof, wall and foundation changes
- room additions and more!

The Home Customizer® Package includes everything you'll need to make the necessary changes to your favorite Home Planners design. The package includes:

- instruction book with examples
- architectural scale and clear work film
- erasable red marker and removable correction tape
- 1/4"-scale furniture cutouts
- 1 set reproducible, erasable Sepias
- 1 set study blueprints for communicating changes to your design professional
- a copyright release letter so you can make copies as you need them
- referral letter with the name, address and telephone number of the professional in your region who is trained in modifying Home Planners designs efficiently and inexpensively.

The price of the **Home Customizer® Package** ranges from $645 to $1085, depending on the price schedule of the design you have chosen. **The Home Customizer® Package** will not only save you 25% to 75% of the cost of drawing the plans from scratch with a custom architect or engineer, it will also give you the flexibility to have your changes and modifications made by our referral network or by the professional of your choice. Now it's even easier and more affordable to have the custom home you've always wanted.

ORDER TOLL FREE!

For information about any of our services or to order call 1-800-521-6797 or 520-297-8200. Plus browse our website: www.homeplanners.com

BLUEPRINTS ARE NOT REFUNDABLE EXCHANGES ONLY

For Customer Service, call toll free 1-888-690-1116.

ORDER FORM

HOME PLANNERS, LLC
Wholly owned by Hanley-Wood, Inc.
3275 WEST INA ROAD, SUITE 110
TUCSON, ARIZONA 85741

THE BASIC BLUEPRINT PACKAGE
Rush me the following (please refer to the Plans Index and Price Schedule in this section):

_____ Set(s) of blueprints for plan number(s) _____. $_____
_____ Set(s) of sepias for plan number(s) _____. $_____
_____ Home Customizer® Package for plan(s)_____. $_____
_____ Additional identical blueprints (standard or reverse) in same order @ $50 per set. $_____
_____ Reverse blueprints @ $50 fee per order. $_____

IMPORTANT EXTRAS
Rush me the following:

_____ Materials List: $50 (Must be purchased with Blueprint set.) $75 Design Basics. Add $10 for a Schedule E-G plan Materials List.$_____
_____ **Quote One®** Summary Cost Report @ $19.95 for 1, $14.95 for each additional, for plans _____ $_____
Building location: City _____ Zip Code _____
_____ **Quote One®** Materials Cost Report @ $110 Schedule A-D; $120 Schedule E for plan_____ $_____
(Must be purchased with Blueprints set.)
Building location: City _____ Zip Code _____
_____ Specification Outlines @ $10 each. $_____
_____ Detail Sets @ $14.95 each; any two for $22.95; any three for $29.95; all four for $39.95 (save $19.85). $_____
❑ Plumbing ❑ Electrical ❑ Construction ❑ Mechanical
(These helpful details provide general construction advice and are not specific to any single plan.)
_____ Plan-A-Home® @ $29.95 each. $_____

DECK BLUEPRINTS
_____ Set(s) of Deck Plan _____. $_____
_____ Additional identical blueprints in same order @ $10 per set. $_____
_____ Reverse blueprints @ $10 per set. $_____
_____ Set of Standard Deck Details @ $14.95 per set. $_____
_____ Set of Complete Building Package (Best Buy!)
Includes Custom Deck Plan _____.
(See Index and Price Schedule)
Plus Standard Deck Details $_____

LANDSCAPE BLUEPRINTS
_____ Set(s) of Landscape Plan _____. $_____
_____ Additional identical blueprints in same order @ $10 per set. $_____
_____ Reverse blueprints @ $10 per set. $_____

Please indicate the appropriate region of the country for Plant & Material List. (See Map on page 185): Region _____

POSTAGE AND HANDLING		1-3 sets	4+ sets
Signature is required for all deliveries.			
DELIVERY No CODs (Requires street address - No P.O. Boxes)			
•Regular Service (Allow 7-10 business days delivery)		❑ $15.00	❑ $18.00
•Priority (Allow 4-5 business days delivery)		❑ $20.00	❑ $30.00
•Express (Allow 3 business days delivery)		❑ $30.00	❑ $40.00
CERTIFIED MAIL		❑ $20.00	❑ $30.00
If no street address available. (Allow 7-10 days delivery)			
OVERSEAS DELIVERY Note: All delivery times are from date Blueprint Package is shipped.		fax, phone or mail for quote	

POSTAGE (From box above) $_____
SUB-TOTAL $_____
SALES TAX (AZ, MI, & WA residents, please add appropriate state and local sales tax.) $_____
TOTAL (Sub-total and tax) $_____

YOUR ADDRESS (please print)

Name _____

Street _____

City _____ State _____ Zip _____

Daytime telephone number (_____) _____

FOR CREDIT CARD ORDERS ONLY
Please fill in the information below:
Credit card number _____
Exp. Date: Month/Year _____
Check one ❑ Visa ❑ MasterCard ❑ Discover Card ❑ American Express

Signature _____

Please check appropriate box: ❑ Licensed Builder-Contractor
❑ Homeowner

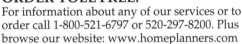

☎ ORDER TOLL FREE!
1-800-521-6797 or 520-297-8200

Order Form Key

TB61

189

Helpful Books & Software

Home Planners wants your building experience to be as pleasant and trouble-free as possible. That's why we've expanded our library of Do-It-Yourself titles to help you along. In addition to our beautiful plans books, we've added books to guide you through specific projects as well as the construction process. In fact, these are titles that will be as useful after your dream home is built as they are right now.

ONE-STORY	TWO-STORY	VACATION	MULTI-LEVEL	COUNTRY	MOVE-UP	NARROW-LOT	SMALL HOUSE

1 448 designs for all lifestyles. 860 to 5,400 square feet. 384 pages $9.95

2 460 designs for one-and-a-half and two stories. 1,245 to 7,275 square feet. 384 pages $9.95

3 345 designs for recreation, retirement and leisure. 312 pages $8.95

4 214 designs for split-levels, bi-levels, multi-levels and walkouts. 224 pages $8.95

5 200 country designs from classic to contemporary by 7 winning designers. 224 pages $8.95

6 200 stylish designs for today's growing families from 9 hot designers. 224 pages $8.95

7 200 unique homes less than 60' wide from 7 designers. Up to 3,000 square feet. 224 pages $8.95

8 200 beautiful designs chosen for versatility and affordability. 224 pages $8.95

BUDGET-SMART	EXPANDABLES	ENCYCLOPEDIA	AFFORDABLE	ENCYCLOPEDIA 2	VICTORIAN	ESTATE	LUXURY

9 200 efficient plans from 7 top designers, that you can really afford to build! 224 pages $8.95

10 200 flexible plans that expand with your needs from 7 top designers. 240 pages $8.95

11 500 exceptional plans for all styles and budgets—the best book of its kind! 352 pages $9.95

12 Completely revised and updated, featuring 300 designs for modest budgets. 256 pages $9.95

13 500 Completely new plans. Spacious and stylish designs for every budget and taste. 352 pages $9.95

14 160 striking Victorian and Farmhouse designs from three leading designers. 192 pages $12.95

15 Dream big! Twenty-one designers showcase their biggest and best plans. 208 pages. $15.95

16 154 fine luxury plans-loaded with luscious amenities! 192 pages $14.95

COTTAGES	BEST SELLERS	SPECIAL COLLECTION	COUNTRY HOUSES	CLASSIC	CONTEMPORARY	EASY-LIVING	SOUTHERN

  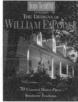     

17 25 fresh new designs that are as warm as a tropical breeze. A blend of the best aspects of many coastal styles. 64 pages $19.95

18 Our 50th Anniversary book with 200 of our very best designs in full color! 224 pages $12.95

19 70 Romantic house plans that capture the classic tradition of home design. 160 pages $17.95

20 208 Unique home plans that combine traditional style and modern livability. 224 pages $9.95

21 Timeless, elegant designs that always feel like home. Gorgeous plans that are as flexible and up-to-date as their occupants. 240 pages. $9.95

22 The most complete and imaginative collection of contemporary designs available anywhere. 240 pages. $9.95

23 200 Efficient and sophisticated plans that are small in size, but big on livability. 224 pages $8.95

24 207 homes rich in Southern styling and comfort. 240 pages $8.95

			Design Software		Outdoor Projects		
SUNBELT	WESTERN	ENERGY GUIDE	BOOK & CD ROM	3D DESIGN SUITE	OUTDOOR	GARAGES & MORE	DECKS

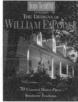      

25 215 Designs that capture the spirit of the Southwest. 208 pages $10.95

26 215 designs that capture the spirit and diversity of the Western lifestyle. 208 pages $9.95

27 The most comprehensive energy efficiency and conservation guide available. 280 pages $35.00

28 Both the Home Planners Gold book and matching Windows™ CD ROM with 3D floorplans. $24.95

29 Home design made easy! View designs in 3D, take a virtual reality tour, add decorating details and more. $59.95

30 42 unique outdoor projects. Gazebos, strombellas, bridges, sheds, playsets and more! 96 pages $7.95

31 101 Multi-use garages and outdoor structures to enhance any home. 96 pages $7.95

32 25 outstanding single-, double- and multi-level decks you can build. 112 pages $7.95

Landscape Designs

EASY CARE · **FRONT & BACK** · **BACKYARDS** · **BEDS & BORDERS** · **BATHROOMS** · **KITCHENS** · **HOUSE CONTRACTING** · **WINDOWS & DOORS**

33 41 special landscapes designed for beauty and low maintenance. 160 pages $14.95

34 The first book of do-it-yourself landscapes. 40 front, 15 backyards. 208 pages $14.95

35 40 designs focused solely on creating your own specially themed backyard oasis. 160 pages $14.95

36 Practical advice and maintenance techniques for a wide variety of yard projects. 160 pages. $14.95

37 An innovative guide to organizing, remodeling and decorating your bathroom. 96 pages $9.95

38 An imaginative guide to designing the perfect kitchen. Chock full of bright ideas to make your job easier. 176 pages $14.95

39 Everything you need to know to act as your own general contractor...and save up to 25% off building costs. 134 pages $14.95

40 Installation techniques and tips that make your project easier and more professional looking. 80 pages $7.95

      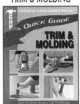

ROOFING · **FRAMING** · **VISUAL HANDBOOK** · **BASIC WIRING** · **PATIOS & WALKS** · **TILE** · **TRIM & MOLDING**

41 Information on the latest tools, materials and techniques for roof installation or repair. 80 pages $7.95

42 For those who want to take a more-hands on approach to their dream. 319 pages $19.95

43 A plain-talk guide to the construction process; financing to final walk-through, this book covers it all. 498 pages $19.95

44 A straight forward guide to one of the most misunderstood systems in the home. 160 pages $12.95

45 Clear step-by-step instructions take you from the basic design stages to the finished project. 80 pages $7.95

46 Every kind of tile for every kind of application. Includes tips on use installation and repair. 176 pages $12.95

47 Step-by-step instructions for installing baseboards, window and door casings and more. 80 pages $7.95

Additional Books Order Form

To order your books, just check the box of the book numbered below and complete the coupon. We will process your order and ship it from our office within 48 hours. Send coupon and check (in U.S. funds).

YES! Please send me the books I've indicated:

☐ 1:VO $9.95
☐ 2:VT $9.95
☐ 3:VH $8.95
☐ 4:VS $8.95
☐ 5:FH $8.95
☐ 6:MU $8.95
☐ 7:NL $8.95
☐ 8:SM $8.95
☐ 9:BS $8.95
☐ 10:EX $8.95
☐ 11:EN $9.95
☐ 12:AF $9.95
☐ 13:E2 . . . . $9.95
☐ 14:VDH $12.95
☐ 15:EDH $15.95
☐ 16:LD2 . . . . $14.95
☐ 17:CTG $19.95
☐ 18:HPG $12.95
☐ 19:WEP $17.95
☐ 20:CN $9.95
☐ 21:CS $9.95
☐ 22:CM $9.95
☐ 23:EL $8.95
☐ 24:SH $8.95

☐ 25:SW $10.95
☐ 26:WH $9.95
☐ 27:RES $35.00
☐ 28:HPGC $24.95
☐ 29:PLANSUITE . . $59.95
☐ 30:YG $7.95
☐ 31:GG $7.95
☐ 32:DP $7.95
☐ 33:ECL $14.95
☐ 34:HL $14.95
☐ 35:BYL $14.95
☐ 36:BB $14.95
☐ 37:CDB $9.95
☐ 38:CKI $14.95
☐ 39:SBC $14.95
☐ 40:CGD $7.95
☐ 41:CGR $7.95
☐ 42:SRF $19.95
☐ 43:RVH $19.95
☐ 44:CBW $12.95
☐ 45:CGW $7.95
☐ 46:CWT $12.95
☐ 47:CGT $7.95

Canadian Customers
Order Toll-Free 1-800-561-4169

Additional Books Sub-Total $_____
ADD Postage and Handling $ 4.00
Sales Tax: (AZ, MI & WA residents, please add appropriate state and local sales tax.) $_____
YOUR TOTAL (Sub-Total, Postage/Handling, Tax) $_____

YOUR ADDRESS (Please print)

Name _____
Street _____
City _____ State _____ Zip _____
Phone (_____) _____—_____

YOUR PAYMENT
Check one: ☐ Check ☐ Visa ☐ MasterCard ☐ Discover Card ☐ American Express
Required credit card information:
Credit Card Number _____
Expiration Date (Month/Year) _____/_____
Signature Required _____

Home Planners, LLC
Wholly owned by Hanley-Wood, Inc.
3275 W. Ina Road, Suite 110, Dept. BK, Tucson, AZ 85741

TB61

Design 3622, see page 62

Free with your blueprint order!

As a way of showing our appreciation, Home Planners will provide a complete window specification featuring Pella materials for every set of blueprints ordered from this book. Our experienced sales representatives are standing by, ready to help you with your plan selection. For additional ordering information, refer to page 191.

 **ORDER TOLL FREE**
1-800-521-6797 or 520-297-8200

Or, if you prefer, fax to **1-800-224-6699 or 520-297-8200**